# The Miracle and Magnificence of America

How the Hand, the Word, the Wisdom, and the Blessing of God worked in the lives of individuals, events, and institutions to shape America into the greatest nation in the history of humanity.

Trevor Grant Thomas

Readers should be aware that Internet websites mentioned as references or sources for further information may have changed or no longer be available since this book was published.

Published by Michelle Thomas

ISBN paperback: 978-0-9911291-2-6
ISBN ePub: 978-0-9911291-3-3

Retail price: $19.99

Editing by Roger Fitzpatrick, Jane Kesler, Constance Parks, and Michelle Thomas

Cover design by Sean Allen Creative

Consultation by Kevin Light, Lighten Media Group

To purchase this book for trade distribution, go to Amazon.com. To contact the publisher, go to TrevorGrantThomas.com.

201607V1

This book is dedicated to all of those who love the United States of America—especially to my wife Michelle, my four amazing children, Caleb, Jesse, Caroline, and Noah, and my parents, Edsel and Carolyn Thomas.

# Table of Contents

# ACKNOWLEDGMENTS

First and foremost, I want to thank God who created me, saved me, and gave me every good thing I have. Thank you, Heavenly Father, for life, and life abundant! Thank you for the amazing gift that is the United States of America. Thank you for allowing me to be born into the greatest nation the world has ever known! I praise You for all You are and all You do. Help me always to be what You created me to be.

Thank you to my dear wife Michelle. As my chief editor, Michelle has had her hand and her mind involved in almost everything I've ever written, and this is certainly the case with *The Miracle and Magnificence of America*. In addition to editing this book, Michelle handled all the work of formatting and publishing it. Above all, thank you, Michelle, for being an amazing wife and mother. There is no more important work in the universe! After my salvation, you are the greatest thing ever to happen in my life.

Thank you to Roger Fitzpatrick, Jane Kesler, and Constance (Connie) Parks, who also served as editors for *The Miracle and Magnificence of America*. Thank you for your patient work and your valuable wisdom and knowledge. Thank you to Julie Townley, who pointed me toward an amazing resource for research.

Thank you to Kelly Gardner for your knowledge and wisdom on copyright issues. Thank you to Sean Allen who designed the cover, and to Kevin Light for your guidance with publishing and marketing. Thank you, also, to all of my students and colleagues at Johnson High School who provided me with feedback on the cover design.

# The Miracle and Magnificence of America

# CHAPTER 1

# The Discovery

In 1986, when I was a junior in high school, the Sunday comics contained a cartoon that showed a boy in a classroom standing on a Bible while staring at a map of a flat earth. Explaining this scene to the rest of the class in a very sarcastic and derogatory manner, the teacher in the cartoon said the boy's behavior was due to the fact that his mother "was a fundamentalist." Certainly the cartoonist's aim was to deride "fundamentalists."

It often escapes those who share a worldview with this forgotten cartoonist that, if it were not for such fundamentalists, the greatest nation in the history of humanity would never have existed. In fact, before America was even a thought in a single suffering European's mind, fundamentalists were making their presence known in the New World.

One of the most skilled mariners of his day, Christopher Columbus not only knew that the earth was a sphere, but was also extremely capable in all of the known science required to navigate an ocean. In addition, Columbus was a devoted Christian who was known to be a man of prayer and a serious student of God's Word.

Born in late 1451 to Domenico Colombo, a poor to middle-class wool weaver, and Susanna Fontanarossa, at a young age Cristoforo (Italian for "Christ-bearer") Colombo showed intelligence, drive, and a distinct impression of God at work in his life.

As Columbus would explain later in his life:

> I have had commerce and conversation with
> knowledgeable people of the clergy and the laity,
> Latins and Greeks, Jews and Moors, and with
> many others of different religions. Our Lord has
> favored my occupation and has given me an
> intelligent mind. He has endowed me with a
> great talent for seamanship; sufficient ability in
> astrology, geometry, and arithmetic; and the
> mental and physical dexterity required to draw
> spherical maps . . . with everything in its proper
> place.
>
> During this time I have studied all kinds of texts:
> cosmography, histories, chronicles, philosophy,
> and other disciplines. Through these writings, the
> hand of Our Lord opened my mind to the
> possibility of sailing to the Indies and gave me
> the will to attempt the voyage. . . . Who could
> doubt that this flash of understanding was the
> work of the Holy Spirit . . . ?[1]

With access to the personal papers of Columbus, noted sixteenth
century missionary, theologian, historian, and Dominican friar
Bishop Bartolomé de Las Casas was able to describe in great detail
the "Divine Providence" present in Columbus's life. In order to
achieve "one of the mightiest and divine exploits" in the history of
the world, Las Casas noted that when the time had come, the
"divine and supreme Master" entrusted the "illustrious and great"
Christopher Columbus with "virtue, mind, zeal, labours,
knowledge, and wisdom."

Las Casas also revealed the significance of Columbus's name:

> He was therefore named Cristóbal, i.e. Christum ferens, which means bringer or bearer of Christ, and so he often signed his name; for in truth he was the first to open the gates of this Ocean sea by which he brought out Saviour, Jesus Christ, to these remote lands and realms, until then unknown…His surname was Colón, which means repopulator, a name befitting one thanks to whose labour so many souls, through the preaching of the Gospel.[2]

With prophetic accuracy, Las Casas wrote of the "Christian and happy republic" that Columbus aimed to bring to the previously unknown "remote lands and realms." In his *History of the Indies*, Las Casas described Columbus as,

> a gentle man of great force and spirit, of lofty thoughts and naturally inclined to undertake worthy deeds and signal enterprises; patient and longsuffering, a forgiver of injustices who wished no more than that those who offended him should recognize their errors, and that the delinquents be reconciled to him.[3]

With significant detail, Las Casas was able to describe the physical appearance of Columbus:

> As for his outward person and bodily disposition, he was tall more than average; his face long and of a noble bearing; his nose aquiline; his eyes blue; his complexion white, and somewhat fiery red; his beard and hair fair in his youth, though they soon turned white through hardships borne;

13

he was quick-witted and gay in his speech and,
as the aforesaid Portuguese history says,
eloquent and high-sounding in his business; he
was moderately grave; affable towards strangers;
sweet and good-humoured with those of his
house...of a discreet conversation and thus able
to draw love from all who saw him. Finally, his
person and venerable mien revealed a person of
great state and authority and worthy of all
reverence.[4]

Most importantly, Las Casas also described the faith of the
"Christ-bearer:"

In matters of Christian religion no doubt he
was a Catholic and of great devotion; ...He
fasted with the utmost strictness when ordained
by the Church; he confessed often and took
Communion; he prayed at all canonical hours as
do Churchmen and friars; most averse to
blasphemies and oaths...he seemed to be very
grateful to God for the benefits received at the
Divine Hand, and so it was almost a proverb
with him, which he quoted every hour, that God
had shown him great favour, as to David...He
was a most jealous keeper of the honour of God;
eager to convert the peoples and to see the seed
and faith of Jesus Christ spread everywhere...
and in this devotion and the confidence which he
had that God would help him in the discovery of
this World which he promised, he begged Queen
Isabel to make a vow that she should spend all
the wealth gained by the Crown as a result of the
discovery in winning back the land and holy
house of Jerusalem, which the Queen did,
as hereafter will be said.[5]

Contrary to what many modern historians reveal, Columbus was not heading out across the vast Atlantic Ocean merely searching for gold and spices. Though there was a desire for gold, as Las Casas reveals, among other things, Columbus had a desire to fund a crusade to rid the Holy Land of its Muslim invaders. On December 26, 1492, in his personal journal, Columbus recalled that he urged King Ferdinand and Queen Isabella, the Spanish sovereigns, "to spend all the profits of this my enterprise on the conquest of Jerusalem."[6]

Because of events such as the Great Plague, during the fifteenth century there was widespread belief that the end of time was near. Many Christians of this time also believed that before Christ would return, Jerusalem had to be in the hands of Christians. As the result of his study of Scripture, along with his study of the works of first century Jewish historian Flavius Josephus and noted theologian and philosopher Saint Augustine, Columbus believed the same. Thus Columbus literally saw himself as an agent of the apocalypse. Also, as the result of reading of the travels of Marco Polo—where it was revealed that the Chinese monarchs expressed an interest in Christianity—and because he believed that sailing west he would land in Asia, Columbus wanted to convert the Chinese.

When it came to his quest for the "New World," Columbus's faith was instrumental in most everything that he did—from his initial efforts to obtain funding from European monarchs to his later expeditions into the Americas. Not everything he did was Christ-like, but as Columbus notes in his own journal,

> It was the Lord who put into my mind (I could feel His hand upon me) the fact that it would be possible to sail from here to the Indies...There is no question that the inspiration was from the Holy Spirit, because he comforted me with rays of marvelous illumination from the Holy Scriptures...[7]

Columbus saw himself as a man on a mission—and not just any mission, but a holy mission. He was, after all, the "Christ-bearer." Venturing into literally unknown waters, such an inspiration was necessary for the mission to be a success. In spite of being confident in his calling, Columbus almost certainly knew that trying times were before him. As any seasoned Christian knows, accomplishing great things for the Kingdom of God is never easy. The enemy simply won't sit by and allow us easily to bring light into his darkness.

Columbus's "talent for seamanship" served him well. He began his career at sea in the Portuguese merchant marine. He sailed the Mediterranean, multiple parts of Africa, including the Gulf of Guinea, to Ireland, and even to Iceland. In 1476, when most of the nations and city-states of the Mediterranean were at war, he nearly lost his life in a sea battle off of the coast of Portugal. Late in his life he would boast, "I have gone to every place that has heretofore been navigated." Though, in typical Columbus style, he would also admit, "He [our Lord] has bestowed the marine arts upon me in abundance."[8]

In 1479 Columbus married Filipa Moniz Perestrelo, the daughter of the Porto Santo governor and Portuguese nobleman, Bartolomeu Perestrelo. Around 1480, the couple's first and only child, son Diego Columbus, was born. Filipa died in 1485, and Columbus was left alone to raise his son.

It is not known exactly when Columbus first conceived his plan to cross the Atlantic. It is known that by 1484 Columbus was in the exclusive business of mapmaking with his brother Bartolomeo. This experience, combined with his significant time at sea, made him as knowledgeable of the Atlantic as nearly anyone in the world. By 1484 Columbus began seeking funding for his ambitious expedition.

For eight years Columbus traveled throughout Europe seeking a sponsor. Given Columbus's heritage, his first efforts were with the King of Portugal, John II. In addition to being his homeland, Portugal was, at that time, sending out the most successful explorers of the Atlantic. John II turned over Columbus's proposal to a royal commission of scholars for consideration.

Lacking faith in Columbus's mathematics and geography, and finding him to be vain and greedy, the royal commission summarily rejected his proposal. Undeterred, Columbus sent his brother Bartolomeo to Henry VII of England. The English were also unimpressed. In 1485 Columbus made a fortuitous move to Castile. In 1469 the marriage of the Castilian Queen Isabella, and the King of Aragon, Ferdinand II, created what would later be known as Spain. Convinced that God had reserved the Spaniards for the honor of sending the light of the Gospel into new lands, Columbus would spend the next seven-and-a-half years attempting to convince King Ferdinand and Queen Isabella to support his quest.

However, Spain's attention was focused on conducting a holy war against the Moors. Thus, the Spaniards were rather deliberate—taking over four years—in reaching the same conclusion as the Portuguese: Columbus's plan "rested on weak foundations."[9] The door was not completely closed though, as Columbus was invited to resubmit his proposal after the Moors were defeated. The Spanish even put Columbus on a small retainer to help him survive.

The waiting was trying for Columbus. He almost certainly began to doubt any holy calling upon his life and his quest. He sought direction and comfort from Father Juan Perez, the Prior of the monastery where Columbus had left his son Diego several years earlier when he had no means to care for him (a common practice during this time).

Perez was close to Queen Isabella, as he had at an earlier time been her confessor. He convinced Columbus to approach the queen again with his plans and obtained the explorer an audience with her. Perez also wrote a letter to her highness telling her that he was convinced that God's hand was upon Columbus. Moreover, by late 1491 the Spanish war against the Moors was about to end, with Spain being victorious. The Spaniards were jubilant, and the king and queen were in the mood for adventure, especially one that would advance the kingdom of God.

Columbus's lofty demands for his personal gain nearly did him in. Among other things, upon success he requested the unprecedented rank of Admiral of the Ocean Sea in return for leading the mission. Nevertheless, the Queen ultimately agreed to his proposal. The next several months were spent gathering a crew and obtaining and outfitting the vessels that would make the historic journey.

Columbus's experience as a mapmaker gave him access to the latest geographic information. One of the newest world maps at this time was by Toscanelli of Florence. (Though, by 1492 the world map by Martellus was available.) Toscanelli was one of the most distinguished mathematicians of his time and his credentials as a geographer were exemplary. It is generally accepted that Columbus sought Toscanelli's counsel before setting out on his westward expedition. On August 3, 1492, with three ships—the *Niña*, *Pinta*, and *Santa María*—Columbus and his crew set out on their journey for the New World.

Heading out into the vast Atlantic Ocean without a really good idea of how long it will be before you reach land requires not only faith, but great boldness. Of course, as time passes on, boldness can turn into frustration, and frustration can breed fear and anger. With hope waning and mutiny brewing, two months after departing Spain, Columbus told the Pinzón brothers (owners of the *Pinta* and the *Niña*) that if land were not sighted in three days, they would turn about and head home.

On October 12, 1492, with less than four hours remaining on the deadline, a cry of "Tierra! Tierra!" ("Land! Land!") rang out from the *Pinta*. Columbus was the first to set foot on dry land, followed by the Pinzón brothers carrying a huge white banner adorned with a large green cross and the crowned initials of Ferdinand and Isabella on either side of it. Columbus christened the island *San Salvador*, which meant "Holy Savior."

Columbus and his crew later erected a large wooden cross, as they did on every island at which they stopped, to be, in his words, "a token of Jesus Christ our Lord, and in honor of the Christian faith."[10] Sadly, Columbus often failed miserably to live out his Christian faith. As Peter Marshall and David Manuel note, Columbus succumbed to "the three things the world prizes most: money…position…and power."[11]

Yet, in his journal Columbus noted his reasons for seeking "undiscovered worlds:" to "bring the Gospel of Jesus Christ to the heathens" and to "bring the Word of God to unknown coastlands."[12] In these efforts, Columbus was eager to note the presence and power of God. In March of 1493, upon returning to Europe after his initial voyage to the Americas, Columbus wrote,

> Of this voyage, I observe…that it has miraculously been shown, as may be understood by this writing, by the many signal miracles that He has shown on the voyage, and for me, who for so great a time was in the court of Your Highnesses with the opposition and against the opinion of so many high personages of your household, who were all against me, alleging this undertaking to be folly, which I hope in Our Lord will be to the greater glory of Christianity, which to some extent already has happened.[13]

In spite of all of his shortcomings, at his core, Columbus was a man of faith. Time and again he would prove himself devoted to the Great Commission of his Lord and Savior—to spread the Good News of Jesus Christ to all the nations of the earth. In spite of frequent failures and repeated rejections, the faith, devotion, and hard work of one man would change the destiny of the world. The efforts of Columbus would lay the groundwork for even more miraculous events that would culminate in the most magnificent nation the world has ever known.

# CHAPTER 2

# Laying the Foundation: The Faithful Friars, Dominicans, and Jesuits

The miracle of America was still distant, but the seeds were being planted. Carried out mostly by Spaniards and driven mostly by greed, exploration and exploitation of the New World continued in the sixteenth century. To a great extent, the conquering conquistadors were proving themselves to be as godless as the Native cannibals, including those who practiced human sacrifice. However, accompanying the conquistadors were Franciscan, Dominican, and Augustinian friars. For the most part, these were deeply devoted Christians who had a great desire to be a light for Christ in lands that were steeped in spiritual darkness. They were vital to the evangelization of the New World. These first friars built churches, orphanages, and schools to serve the Natives. Through their efforts, tens of thousands of Natives would come to know Christ.

Though the evangelical efforts in the New World coincided with the Protestant Reformation, for well over a century, the evangelism that took place was almost exclusively Catholic. This was also the case in what would become the United States. As author Leonard Woolsey Bacon declares in *A History of American Christianity*, "For a hundred years the colonization and evangelization of

America were, in the narrowest sense of that large word, Catholic, not Protestant."[1]

As Bacon also notes, it was the Catholicism of the sixteenth century, not that of the corrupt fifteenth century, that was brought to the New World. Moreover as Bacon points out,

> It was in Spain itself, in which the corruption of the church had been foulest, but from which all symptoms of 'heretical [depravity]' were purged away with the fiercest zeal as fast as they appeared—in Spain under the reign of Ferdinand and Isabella the Catholic—that the demand for a Catholic reformation made itself earliest and most effectually felt... The earlier pages of American church history will not be intelligently read unless it is well understood that the Christianity first to be transplanted to the soil of the New World was the Christianity of Spain.[2]

The Caribbean—being the first territory that the Spanish dominated—was the first target for evangelization. The results were disappointing. European diseases and mistreatment of the Natives by some of the Spanish meant a tragic loss of life for the Natives and a tragic loss of spiritual opportunity for the evangelists. A "royal instruction" in 1503 laid down more structured guidelines for evangelizing.[3] Soon, schools, churches, and hospitals were being built.

In an attempt to curb the greed of Spanish colonists, greed that resulted in terrible mistreatment and enslavement of the Natives, a Dominican Friar named Antonio de Montesinos delivered a powerful and scathing sermon. Delivered on the fourth Sunday in Advent of 1511, in a small church on Española, this sermon exhorted the conquering Spaniards to eschew their tyrannical and cruel practices:

In order to make this known to you, I have come
up here, for I am the voice of Christ crying in the
wilderness of this island, and therefore you had
better listen to me, not with indifference but with
all your heart and with all your senses. For this
voice will be the strangest you have ever heard,
the harshest and the hardest, the most terrifying
that you ever thought that you would hear. . . .
This voice says that you are in mortal sin and
live and die in it because of the cruelty and
tyranny that you use against these innocent
peoples. Tell me, by what right or justice do you
hold these Indians in such cruel and horrible
slavery? By what authority do you wage such
detestable wars on these peoples, who lived
mildly and peacefully in their own lands, in
which you have destroyed countless numbers of
them with unheard-of murders and ruin. . . . Are
they not men? Do they not have rational souls?
Are you not bound to love them as you love
yourselves? Don't you understand this? Don't
you feel this? . . . Be sure that in your present
state you can no more be saved than the Moors
or Turks, who do not have and do not want the
faith of Jesus Christ.[4]

The message was not well received. However, significant debate
was sparked, and men like Bartolomé de Las Casas led the way in
the commitment to spread the Gospel through peaceful means.
Around 1530, Las Casas began writing *De Unico Vocationis Modo
Omnium Infidelium ad Veram Religonem (The Only Way of
Attracting All Unbelievers to the True Religion)*, a Latin treatise
noted as "one of the most important missionary tracts in the history
of the church."[5] The treatise was a blueprint for Las Casas'
peaceful missionary methods. The efforts of Las Casas and other
committed Catholic missionaries led to the papal bull *Sublimis
Deus* delivered by Pope Paul III in 1537. The bull pronounced the
Natives rational beings with souls worthy of Christian

evangelization. The bull also condemned and prohibited slavery and declared that the Natives had rights to liberty and property.

Note that, we see Christians at the forefront of denouncing slavery and pronouncing the right of individuals to liberty and property. Also note the importance placed on the right to ownership of private property. Even four centuries ago, Christians understood well that a man cannot be truly free unless he has economic independence.

Around the same time, the man described as "the most influential Spanish theologian of the sixteenth century,"[6] Dominican Francisco de Vitoria, also produced important work in defense of the rights of the New World Natives. A teacher of theology, Vitoria helped train many young Dominicans for missionary work in the New World. Beginning in 1524, he was elected to the principle chair of theology at the University of Salamanca. His lectures declared that the Natives had a right to own property and taught against unlawful conquest of the Natives, although he believed that the savage practices of some Natives, such as cannibalism and human sacrifice, justified conquest. Vitoria's work also helped advance "just war" theory. He has been described as "the father of international law."

In 1516, the Spanish began to explore the eastern coast of modern Mexico. Such exploration opened up the next great period in the Spanish conquest of the New World. The conquest of Mexico also began a great step forward in missionary efforts in the New World. These efforts led to great field experience which helped to develop a process of evangelization that, with modifications, would be used throughout Spanish America in the colonial period.[7] Puerto Rico, Cuba, Panama, Colombia, Venezuela, Honduras, Peru, Mexico, Florida, and so on were all soon targets of Spanish conquest and missionary efforts.

By the 1520s, the Franciscans and Dominicans started arriving in the New Spain. By the early 1530s, the Augustinians arrived. As author Robert Ricard noted, the "Spiritual Conquest of Mexico" had begun.[8] Though there were significant differences in the missionary tactics of the Franciscans, Dominicans, and

Augustinians, their goals and their challenges were very similar: the evangelization of the New Spain.

The various and widespread Native populations of Central America, each with its own language, presented the friars with a daunting missionary challenge. Also, some of the missionary methods left open the opportunity for abuse, which usually meant suffering on the part of the Natives. Furthermore, Mexican missionaries often found themselves in positions of power. Most had never had such experience, and thus, charges of "religious imperialism" were sometimes leveled.

However, churches, schools, hospitals, and orphanages were built. The Jesuits built several exceptional schools in the New Spain, including twenty-five colleges, eleven seminaries, and six houses for priests.[9] Not only did these men of faith create the first educational opportunities in the Americas, there is also evidence that, because of their efforts, by 1583 all of the larger towns in the archdiocese of Mexico had a hospital.[10]

While the Spaniards were exploring Mexico, the first efforts at Christianity in the United States began with Ponce de Leon foolishly searching for the Fountain of Youth. Ponce de Leon used the threat of death and slavery in a tragic attempt to force the Catholic faith upon the Natives of Florida. However, de Leon's invasion was met, as it deserved, by a violent volley of arrows from Calusa (a tribe native to Florida's southwest coast) braves. Wounded by a poison arrow, and failing to gain a religious or a territorial foothold, de Leon was driven back to Cuba where he died of his wounds.[11]

Nearly a half-century would pass before successful Christian missions would be established in Florida. In 1565, the foundations of the oldest city in the U.S., St. Augustine, were laid. Dominicans, Jesuits, and Franciscans were soon populating the mission fields of Florida. By 1635, there were nearly 30,000 Native American Christians in the region around St. Augustine.

By the fourth decade of the sixteenth century, Spanish missions had expanded into South America. These efforts proved much more difficult than those in Central America. Spanish conquest into South America in the decades prior to the efforts of the missionaries made the efforts of sincere Christians very difficult. By the mid-sixteenth century, Spanish friars were living among the Natives of South America. Again, it was not long until hospitals, schools, and churches were being built. However, many priests turned out to be far too susceptible to the same material temptations that led astray other Spanish settlers in South America.

The Portuguese, through the efforts of the Jesuits, introduced Christianity to Brazil. In 1549, Tomé de Sousa brought 1,000 settlers, including six Jesuits, to the Brazilian coast. For several decades, the Jesuits were the only Catholic missionaries in Brazil. They remained the dominant missionary force in Brazil for nearly two centuries. The Jesuits were staunch defenders of the Natives against colonial efforts to enslave them.

From New Spain, the Jesuits spread the Gospel north and northwest, while the Franciscans went east and northeast. Soon the Jesuits were evangelizing the west and southwest of the United States. By the early seventeenth century, Friar Alonso de Benavides reported that 80,000 Natives had been baptized, while over 20 missions in what is today's American Southwest served 90 Native American communities.

Without fear of death (which many would experience), these brave missionaries would later enter what is now New Mexico and lower California. The famed and universally loved Junípero Serra, a former professor of philosophy turned Franciscan Friar, established a total of nine missions, including those at San Diego, San Carlos, and San Francisco.

Serra was an intellectual and an accomplished orator. He worked tirelessly, and his zealous efforts to bring the lost to Christ made him a legend in his own time. There were instances when he walked hundreds of miles in a single expedition. By the time of his death in 1784, the nine missions he founded had converted several thousand Native Americans to Christianity.

For over a century, the Spanish had the exclusive opportunity of evangelizing North, Central, and South America. However, because the missionary efforts of the faithful Franciscans, Dominicans, and Augustinians almost always came on the heels of greedy conquest, and though the stamp of Spanish Catholic missionary efforts in Central and South America can still be seen today, for the most part, the Christianity that shaped and molded the United States of America was not directly the result of these efforts. As Catholic Church historians conclude,

> It was glorious work, and the recital of it impresses us by the vastness and success of the toil. Yet, as we look around to-day, we can find nothing of it that remains. Names of saints in melodious Spanish stand out from maps in all that section where the Spanish monk trod, toiled, and died. A few thousand Christian Indians, descendants of those converted and civilized, still survive in New Mexico and Arizona, and that is all.[12]

French Catholics ultimately fared somewhat better.

> Instead of a greedy scramble after other men's property in gold and silver, the business basis of the French enterprises was to consist in a widely organized and laboriously prosecuted traffic in furs. Instead of a series of desultory and savage campaigns of conquest, the ferocity of which was aggravated by the show of zeal for the kingdom of righteousness and peace, was a large-minded and far-sighted scheme of empire, under which remote and hostile tribes were to be combined by ties of mutual interest and common advantage. And the missions, instead of following servilely in the track of bloody conquest to assume the tutelage of subjugated and enslaved races, were to share with the soldier

and the trader the perilous adventures of
exploration, and not so much to be supported and
defended as to be themselves the support and
protection of the settlements, through the
influence of Christian love and self-sacrifice
over the savage heart. Such elements of moral
dignity, as well as of imperial grandeur, marked
the plans for the French occupation of North
America.[13]

Until the King of Spain, Charles III, ordered their expulsion in
1767, the French Jesuits also had a presence in America's West.
However, the Jesuits' efforts on the East Coast, though difficult,
would go more undeterred. These zealous, brilliant, and disciplined
"soldiers of God" were deeply committed to the mission field. As
was the case with Columbus, such a commitment was necessary,
for along with the many other harsh experiences that came with an
unfamiliar and untamed wilderness land, several Jesuits ended up
as martyrs.

Not only were these brave souls martyred, but many were
subjected to unspeakable tortures prior to death. The Iroquois were
especially cruel. In spite of the dangers presented by the Iroquois,
the Jesuits continued to minister to the Iroquois and other Native
American nations. The city of Montreal was set up as a base for
missions.

In 1608, the "Father of New France," Samuel de Champlain, set up
the first French settlement in North America in Quebec. With a
particular concern for establishing "the Christian faith in the wilds
of America," it was Champlain who was the most effective
Frenchman at missionary efforts in North America. According to
Champlain, the Natives were living "like brute beasts, without
faith, without law, without religion, without God."[14]

Befriending the Huron, in 1615 Champlain secured the service of
four Franciscan friars of the Recollect Order. One of these friars
was Joseph Le Caron. With an escort of Hurons, Le Caron headed
westward to Lake Huron's Georgian Bay. There, he built a chapel,

and the Native Americans were introduced to the worship of Christ. From there, the Gospel of Jesus was spread north to the Algonquins of Ottawa, east to the Abenakis of Maine and Nova Scotia, and south to the Iroquois. Through the efforts of these friars, the Chippewas, Illinois, and other Native tribes of the Great Lakes region were also introduced to Christianity.

The Jesuits were required to keep meticulous journals of their exploits and efforts in New France. These journals were compiled into a publication called *Relations*. In order to inspire interest in the mission field of New France, *Relations* was distributed throughout France. One young reader was so inspired that he would become what many consider the most famous French-American explorer, Father Jacques Marquette.

For 12 years Marquette dedicated himself to study in the Jesuit colleges of France. In 1666, he was assigned to Quebec. Marquette had a tremendous ability for learning languages, which would serve him well in New France. Marquette learned six different Native American languages and would become an expert in the Huron language. He established the first European settlement in Michigan, and along with his friend Louis Joliet, was the first to explore and map the northern part of the Mississippi River. All during the exploration, Marquette was focused on spreading the Gospel among the people he encountered.

French expansion was fast, vast, and sure. In a few short decades, Quebec had a hospital, a nunnery, and a seminary for educating priests. Quebec was also a significant financial hub for the French, as it was the center for fur trading. However, though the French missionaries were not as plagued by greed and conquest as were the Spanish, the final efforts of the French Catholics in North America fared little better than the Spanish.

A century and a half of French Catholic colonization and evangelization is summed up as follows:

> In Maine, a thousand Catholic Indians still
> remain, to remind one of the time when, as it is

boldly claimed, the whole Indian population of that province were either converted or under Jesuit training. 1.) In like manner, a scanty score of thousands of Catholic Indians on various reservations in the remote West represent the time when, at the end of the French domination, 'all the North American Indians were more or less extensively converted' to Catholic Christianity, 'all had the gospel preached to them.' 2.) The splendid fruits of the missions among the Iroquois, from soil watered by the blood of martyrs, were wasted to nothing in savage intertribal wars. Among the Choctaws and Chickasaws of the South and Southwest, among whom the gospel was by and by to win some of its fairest trophies, the French missionaries achieved no great success. 3.) The French colonies from Canada, planted so prosperously along the Western rivers, dispersed, leaving behind them some straggling families.[15]

Though these Catholic missionary efforts would be nearly extinguished, through the efforts of the faithful Spanish and French, the light of the truth of Jesus Christ was penetrating the future United States of America from both coasts. Seeds of light were planted, the blood of martyrs moistened the soil, and the proper foundation was being laid for the greatest nation the world has ever known.

# CHAPTER 3

# The English Migration, Part 1: A Fool's Errand

Sir Walter Raleigh's first attempts at settling the New World were disastrous. Much of this was the result of refusing to put God and His will first. "The God of Martin Luther and Father Jogues did not appear to be much in fashion in Elizabethan England."[1]

The English, who were now trying to gain a foothold on the New World, were succumbing to the same greed that had earlier blinded the Spaniards. Starvation, disease, hostile Natives, and other hardships, including a whole colony lost (the Lost Colony of Roanoke), led to dampened enthusiasm for New World expeditions.

Nearly 20 years would pass after Raleigh's initial ventures before enough English interest could again be sparked for more New World adventure. In 1602, one of Raleigh's captains, Bartholomew Gosnold, sailed to what is now Maine with 32 men.

Fearing the Natives, disease, and the coming winter, they returned to England less than four months after leaving it. Undeterred, Gosnold obtained an exclusive charter from King James I to form The Virginia Company with the purpose of establishing permanent settlements in North America. King James—sponsor of the King James Bible—in the preamble of the Company's charter, which he wrote, exhorted the explorers to evangelize Natives with whom they came in contact. With the king's support, Gosnold and his fellow adventurers on December 16, 1606, again sailed for North America.

Despite recruiting sermons that contained messages of evangelical outreach, and despite the call for, "...propagating of Christian religion to such people as yet live in darkness and miserable ignorance of the true knowledge and worship of God, and may in time bring the infidels and savages, living in these parts, to human civility and to a settled and quiet government,"[2] the lust for gold was, again, what drove the men of this expedition.

Evidence of this fact was that this first expedition sent by The Virginia Company contained exclusively men, 144 of them, nor were these men heads of households going to prepare a homestead. Also, among these 144 was only one minister. Just like the conquistadors, according to Marshall and Manuel, these 144 men "were interested in one thing: getting their gold chamber pots and returning to England as soon as possible."[3]

On May 14, 1607, headed by a seven-man council, which included John Smith, these 144 men settled Jamestown. Because of their misguided efforts, the settlement was a disaster from the beginning.

These men battled the elements, disease (including malaria), Native Americans, starvation, and one another. The lone minister on the adventure, Robert Hunt, did his best to keep the others focused on God, but sermons went mostly unheeded. By February of 1608 only 38 of the 144 remained alive.

News of what was happening in Virginia began to get back to England. To counteract this news, The Virginia Company increased its propaganda campaign, and they were successful for a while, so investors continued to invest and settlers continued to settle. Incredibly, the death rate in Virginia that second year was even higher than the first. Ninety percent of the people who embarked for the New World would die.[4]

**John Smith's map of Virginia. First published at Oxford, England in 1612.**

The death rate did not abate with time. Marshall and Manuel add, "For example, of the 1,200 people who went out to Virginia in 1619, only 200 were left alive by 1620. Why this horrible continuing death rate? There is no logical explanation, except one: year after year they steadfastly refused to trust God—or indeed to include Him in any of their deliberations."[5]

This is not the story we usually get when we are taught about the first English settlement in the New World. Most of us are familiar with the romanticized story of Captain John Smith, his capture by the Algonquins, and his dramatic rescue by Pocahontas. However, the spiritual battle that raged at Jamestown is almost never taught—especially in our public schools and universities.

In the middle of this spiritual battle was John Rolfe. Rolfe was a hardworking Christian who arrived with the third wave of settlers in 1610. Rolfe's very arrival in Jamestown was something of a miracle. He was one of 150 passengers aboard the *Sea Venture*, the flagship of a fleet of nine ships that set out for Jamestown in 1609.

Nearing North America, the ship was caught in a hurricane in what today is described as the Bermuda Triangle and shipwrecked off the coast of Bermuda. Miraculously, every passenger made it to shore. So legendary were these events that they became the basis for Shakespeare's play, *The Tempest*.[6]

The passengers of the *Sea Venture* were marooned at Bermuda for nearly ten months. During this time Rolfe would suffer great loss. Both his wife and infant daughter, named Bermuda, would die along with a handful of others. No other human beings inhabited the Bermuda archipelago at this time, and the Sea Venture's passengers would soon discover that Bermuda was not the "Isle of Devils" that previous shipwrecked survivors had designated it.

With its mild and healthy climate, strategic location, abundant wildlife, and ubiquitous fruits, Bermuda turned out to be quite a prize for the British Kingdom. The islands were so pleasant that some of the men of the wrecked *Sea Venture* refused to participate in the salvaging of the ship in order to build two smaller vessels and continue on to Jamestown. A survivor, William Strachey, in a voluminous and detailed letter to England, wrote of conspiracy, mutiny, and rebellion. At least one man was executed, and two men were left marooned on Bermuda when the remainder of the party departed for Jamestown.[7]

Rolfe was eager to arrive at Jamestown as he believed that there was a Christian destiny for the settlement, and he hoped to "advance the Honor of God, and to propagate his Gospel." He believed there was

> no small hope by piety, clemency, courtesy and
> civil demeanor to convert and bring to the
> knowledge and true worship of Jesus Christ
> 1000s of poor wretched and misbelieving people:
> on whose faces a good Christian cannot look,
> without sorrow, pity and commiseration; seeing
> they bear the Image of our heavenly Creator, and
> we and they come from one and the same mold. .
> [8]

Rolfe would play a significant role in turning the Virginia Colony from a death-trap into a thriving profitable venture. In 1612 John Rolfe began growing a new strain of tobacco which was sweeter than the tobacco that was native to Virginia. He had brought the difficult-to-obtain Spanish seeds with him to Virginia and named the product "Orinico tobacco."[9]

This new crop was not only significant in the lives of the Jamestown colonists, but the introduction of Rolfe's tobacco into America proved to be a very important act in the economic history of our nation. By 1614, the first export of Virginia tobacco was sold in London. Although King James disapproved—his royal highness was not a fan of tobacco—Londoners loved its taste and demand increased.

Within five years, tobacco was the chief export of the Virginia colony. In 1617, ten tons were shipped to England. In 1618, that amount doubled. By 1639, Jamestown had exported 1.5 million pounds of tobacco, and thousands of acres of land were being used to grow nothing but tobacco.[10] The Virginians were literally beginning to wear out the soil. Soon, tobacco farms were spreading well beyond Jamestown, and for the first time, America was prospering.

John Rolfe is famous for more than tobacco. While Rolfe was perfecting his tobacco crop, the young Native American princess Pocahontas was being held captive by the Jamestown settlers. Reports vary as to whether Pocahontas was taken in retaliation for the local Native American tribe capturing and holding several settlers, or, more sinisterly, taken by the starving settlers to be held for ransom.

Whatever the case, while in captivity, Pocahontas received Bible lessons daily from a young Anglican theologian named Alexander Whitaker. Soon she would convert to Christianity and change her name to Rebecca. Rolfe was smitten by Pocahontas. In April of 1614, with the permission of Pocahontas' father, Chief Powhatan, Rolfe and Pocahontas would marry. This marriage led to an eight-year period of peace with the Native Americans and allowed the settlers to focus on their new-found cash crop.

By the 1620s, Virginia had the look of prosperity. Each man of the colony was given at least 100 acres which he was to plant and work. A representative system of rule was also put into place. Two representatives (burgesses) were to be chosen (elected) from each of the 10 major plantations. The Virginia House of Burgesses was the first system of elected representatives set up in America. The first meeting of this legislature took place in the Jamestown church and was opened with prayer by the Reverend Richard Burke.[11]

However, instead of focusing on God and being a "city upon a hill," Virginians were consumed with profit and prosperity. Evidence of this is in the fact that by 1622, there were only three ministers to serve the more than 1,200 settlers scattered across 10 plantations. Also, though the tobacco boom brought hope and financial blessing to the young colonies, it also gave birth to a plague that would in coming years nearly tear a young nation apart—slavery.

The next settlers to cross the Atlantic were not seeking only wealth and prosperity but were led by the Spirit of God to a new home. They believed that America was their spiritual destiny. The Pilgrims, and the Puritans who followed them, are the people most responsible for the foundation of America as a Christian nation. These passionate and pious Protestants knew better than to undertake anything without God.

# CHAPTER 4

# The English Migration, Part 2

From the late 1500s through the early 1600s, the Church of England was controlled by the British Monarch. It was Protestant in its doctrine, but it mostly followed Catholic practices in its worship. Some British Christians had strong objections to the Catholic rituals. Two "fanatical" groups in particular were at odds with the leadership and the direction of the Church of England. The larger group was dedicated to "purifying the Church from within." However, these "Puritans" still submitted to canonical authority. The group that the bishops considered more dangerous believed that the Church of England was corrupted beyond repair. Dubbed "Separatists," (we know them as the "Pilgrims") this group rejected the notion that any one person, even King or Queen, should hold the title "Head of the Church." They believed that Jesus Christ alone was worthy of such a title.

This led to significant persecution by the Church of England. The Pilgrims were threatened, fined, thrown in prison, and even executed. According to the Baptist Press, "In an effort to curb the growth of [Pilgrims], a law was passed in April 1593 requiring everyone over the age of 16 to attend the church of their local parish, which comprised all who lived within a certain geographic boundary."[1] One month without complying with the law meant imprisonment. Upon release from prison, if another three months passed without obedience to the attendance laws, one was given the choice of exile or death. Of course, most chose exile and the Pilgrims fled to Holland.

Life in Europe became increasingly difficult for the Pilgrims. In spite of what they were hearing concerning the death and destruction at Jamestown, more and more, God's plan seemed to point to America as their home. The pastor of young William Bradford's congregation at the time was John Robinson. During this time, Pastor Robinson revealed that he believed God was calling them to a New Jerusalem—in America. Robinson wrote,

> Now as the people of God in old time were
> called out of Babylon civil, the place of their
> bodily bondage, and were to come to Jerusalem,
> and there to build the Lord's temple…so are the
> people of God now to go out of Babylon spiritual
> to Jerusalem…and build themselves as lively
> stones into a spiritual house, or temple, for the
> Lord to dwell in…for we are the sons and
> daughters of Abraham by faith.[2]

Limited space on the ship necessitated that only a fraction of Robinson's flock of more than 600 Separatists could go. Robinson would remain behind to continue to shepherd the main body. As the Pilgrims were gathered aboard the *Mayflower*, just prior to their departure for America, John Carver read a letter penned by Pastor Robinson. Near the end of the letter, Robinson admonished and advised his flock concerning government in the New World:

> Lastly, whereas you are become a body politic,
> using amongst yourselves civil government, and
> are not furnished with any persons of special
> eminency above the rest, to be chosen by you
> into office of government; let your wisdom and
> godliness appear, not only in choosing such
> persons as do entirely love and will promote the
> common good, but also in yielding unto them all
> due honor and obedience in their lawful
> administrations, not beholding in them the
> ordinariness of their persons, but God's
> ordinance for your good; not being like the
> foolish multitude who more honor the gay coat
> than either the virtuous mind of the man, or
> glorious ordinance of the Lord. But you know

better things, and that the image of the Lord's power and authority which the magistrate beareth, is honorable, in how means persons soever. And this duty you both may the more willingly and ought the more conscionably to perform, because you are at least for the present to have only them for your ordinary governors, which yourselves shall make choice of for that work.[3]

**A replica model of the Mayflower. Created by Norbert Schnitzler.**

Though he longed for it, Pastor Robinson would never see America. On March 1, 1625, just over five years after the *Mayflower* landed on the coast of what is now Massachusetts, Pastor Robinson died of a sudden illness.

Aboard the *Mayflower* were 102 passengers, less than half of whom were of Robinson's flock. After a grueling two-month voyage, on November 11, 1620, they dropped anchor in Cape Cod, and heeding the advice and wisdom of their pastor, the Pilgrims drafted a compact that would embody the same principles of government upon which the American republic would rest. It read,

> In the name of God, amen. We whose names are under-written...Having undertaken, for the glory of God and advancement of the Christian Faith and honor of our King and country, a voyage to plant the first colony in the northern parts of Virginia, do by these presents solemnly and mutually in the presence of God and one of another, covenant and combine ourselves together into a civil body politic...constitute and frame such just and equal laws, ordinances, acts, constitutions and offices from time to time, as shall be thought most meet and convenient for the general good of the colony...the 11th of November...Anno Domini 1620.[4]

John Carver, who had chartered the *Mayflower*, was chosen as the first governor of the colony. His was the first signature on the *Mayflower Compact*, which is considered by many to be the world's first written constitution. William Bradford would soon replace Carver as governor and would serve in that capacity for 31 years. On December 21, 1620, the Pilgrims settled at what would become known as Plymouth.

Though their efforts were "for the glory of God," the Pilgrims were not immune to the many hardships of an untamed America. Before long, many started dying. William Bradford's wife Dorothy was among the casualties as she fell overboard and drowned. (Initially, while dwellings were being built, the Pilgrims lived mostly aboard the *Mayflower*.) Due in part to a brutal winter, dozens would die in those first few months, including 13 of 18 wives. In spite of hardships, the Pilgrims were undeterred and drew ever closer to God.

The months turned into years and saw the Pilgrims develop good relations with the local Natives including Massasoit, a wise and welcoming chief of the local tribes, Samoset, and especially Tisquantum, or Squanto.

In the middle of March 1621, just as the Pilgrims were coming out of the devastatingly harsh winter, a guard alerted his comrades with the cry of "Indian coming!" Wearing only a loincloth as he walked into the Pilgrims' camp, Samoset astonished the English onlookers with a hearty "Welcome!" Then speaking surprisingly clear English, he followed his friendly greeting with a request, "Have you got any beer?"

The Pilgrims informed their friendly guest that they were out of beer, and offered him brandy instead. After a hearty snack of brandy, biscuit, butter, cheese, pudding, and roast duck, Samoset was ready to answer questions. In spite of their difficult and deadly plight, Samoset's words gave the Pilgrims great cause to thank God.

Having learned his English from the various fisherman who had fished the shores of Maine, Samoset revealed that the area currently occupied by the Pilgrims had been the territory of the Patuxet. The Patuxets were a large, hostile tribe of Native Americans who had viciously murdered every white man who landed on their shores. However, four years prior to the Pilgrims' arriving in America, a mysterious plague killed every member of the Patuxet tribe. Convinced that the widespread death and devastation was the work of a great supernatural spirit, neighboring tribes had avoided that area occupied by the Patuxet ever since.[5]

On March 22, 1621, Samoset returned to the Pilgrims with Squanto, who spoke even better English. Squanto's life is an amazing tale of God's provision that very closely resembles the account of Joseph from Genesis, chapter 37. In 1605, working for the recently formed East India Company and searching for a northwest passage to India, Captain George Weymouth explored the New England coast. While exploring the coast of Maine, Weymouth captured five Patuxet Natives, one of whom was Squanto.

The Natives were taken to England where they spent nine years and were taught English. While in England, Squanto met Captain John Smith, who promised to return him to the Patuxets. In 1614, Smith kept his promise and returned to the New England area of America with the Natives. However, in order to survey and explore, Smith departed what he called New Plymouth. Soon after Smith's departure, Captain Thomas Hunt, who had sailed with Smith on another ship, lured 20 Patuxets aboard his ship and slapped chains on them. They were transported to Spain where most were sold into slavery and shipped to North Africa. However, some, including Squanto, were purchased and set free by friars. These friars introduced Squanto and his fellow Natives to Christianity. Squanto and his new-found faith would play a vital role in American history.

Squanto remained in Europe for several years. In 1619, having joined an exploratory expedition along the New England coast, Squanto left Europe in order to return to his homeland.

In 1620, six months prior to the Pilgrims' arrival, Squanto arrived back in New England and soon returned to the shores of his home. Upon arriving at his village, he was shocked to discover that no one was there to greet him. Virtually every member of the Patuxets had died, perhaps from smallpox brought by the European ships. Broken and dismayed, Squanto aimlessly wandered the woods where he had grown up.

He ended up in the camp of the Wampanoag people, who were led by Massasoit. Taking pity on him, Massasoit welcomed Squanto and gave him a new home. However, without a tribe or a family, Squanto's existence seemed without purpose. He remained a broken man until he got word of a peaceful but pitiful band of Europeans who were riddled with disease and starvation on the shores near his homeland.

Soon after Samoset introduced Squanto to the Pilgrims, a meeting with Massasoit was arranged. Massasoit, Samoset, Squanto, and dozens of Wampanoag warriors traveled to Plymouth to meet the Pilgrims. With Samoset serving as the interpreter for Massasoit, the meeting was extremely fruitful. A peace treaty and a treaty of mutual aid were struck with Massasoit that would last for decades.

Massasoit and his party returned home, but Squanto remained with the Pilgrims. Being a man without a tribe, personally witnessing the desperation of the Pilgrims, and already having adopted their faith, Squanto took pity upon his new-found English friends and wanted to help them succeed in their New World. He taught them how to fish for eels and alewives, plant corn and pumpkins, refine maple syrup, trap beavers, hunt deer, and other skills essential to their survival.

Squanto was instrumental in the survival of the Pilgrims—so much so that, according to William Bradford, the Pilgrims considered Squanto "a special instrument sent of God for their good, beyond their expectation." Massasoit also was an amazing example of God's providential care for the Pilgrims. Like Powhatan had been at Jamestown, Massasoit was probably the only other Native American chief on the northeast coast of America who would have welcomed the white man as a friend.[6]

In early April of 1621, with supplies running dangerously low, the Captain of the *Mayflower*, Christopher Jones, decided he could remain in America no longer. On April 5, 1621, the *Mayflower* returned to England. As the ship disappeared over the horizon, almost certainly a nervous uneasiness came upon more than a few Pilgrims who remained in the New World. Their last ties to their former home were gone. They, perhaps, felt more alone than at any point of their amazing journey.

The summer of 1621 was beautiful and, thanks in no small measure to the help of Squanto, bountiful. Governor Bradford declared a day of public Thanksgiving to be held in October. Massasoit was invited. Surprising the Pilgrims, he showed up a day early with 90 of his tribe. To feed such a crowd, the Pilgrims would have to go deep into their food supply. However, Massasoit did not show up empty handed. He had instructed his braves to hunt for the occasion, and they came with several dressed dear and fat turkeys. The Thanksgiving turned into a three-day celebration filled with feasting and games.

**The First Thanksgiving, by Jean-Léon Gérôme.**

A few weeks after the first Thanksgiving and about a year after the Pilgrims arrived in the New World, the *Fortune* sailed into Plymouth on its way to Virginia. The main cargo was an additional 35 colonists and a charter granted from the New England Company. There was tremendous celebration over the new charter; however, unlike the Native Americans, the new colonists arrived virtually empty handed. They had no extra clothing, food, or tools. The Pilgrims would have to adjust their winter food rationing plan severely.

The winter of 1621-1622 was as difficult as feared. The Pilgrims entered what has been described as their "starving time." Some reports reveal that at times, food rations for each person were a mere five kernels of corn per day.[7] Miraculously, that winter not one Pilgrim died of starvation.

There was no Thanksgiving celebration in 1622. When the spring planting season of 1623 rolled around, the Pilgrims realized that to fend off further hunger and rationing, a corn harvest at least twice as large as last season was necessary. However, a lackluster work ethic prevailed among them. This was mainly because the contract entered into with their merchant sponsors in London required everything the Pilgrims produced was to go into a common store and be shared. As Rush Limbaugh has often pointed out on his radio broadcast that celebrates Thanksgiving Day, the Pilgrims were languishing under socialism.[8]

The leaders of the colony then decreed that for the additional planting, individual plots of land would be split, and the yield could be used at the planters' discretion. Thus, as the concept of private property was introduced, the Pilgrims seemed infused and invigorated with new hope and purpose. As Marshall and Manuel point out, "The yield that year was so abundant that the Pilgrims ended up with a surplus of corn, which they were able to use in trading that winter with northern Indians, who had not had a good growing season."[9]

On November 29, 1623, two years after the first Thanksgiving, Governor William Bradford made an official proclamation for a second day of Thanksgiving. In it Governor Bradford thanked God for their abundant harvest, bountiful game, protection from "the ravages of savages...and disease," and for the "freedom to worship God according to the dictates of our own conscience."[10] Well over a hundred Natives attended, bringing plenty of turkey and venison along with them.

The Pilgrims had the proper perspective. As Bradford would note with discernment, "As one small candle may light a thousand, so the light [of Jesus] kindled here has shown unto many, yea in some sort to our whole nation...We have noted these things so that you might see their worth and not negligently lose what your fathers have obtained with so much hardship."[11]

Just a handful of years later, another group of devout believers would set out for America's shores in search of a new home. Unlike the Separatists (Pilgrims), the Puritans did not want to break away from the Church of England. (The Puritans were very critical of the Separatists for such action.) The Puritans sought reform; however, for the most part, the Church saw no need for reform.

In general, the Puritans were more affluent than the Pilgrims. To head out for a new home, they had much more to leave behind. The decision was not as easy for them as for the Pilgrims. Furthermore, for a period of time, the Church tolerated the Puritans much more than it tolerated the Pilgrims. In order for the Puritans to get to the place they needed to be (America)—and as hindsight reveals, exactly the place where God wanted them to be—their level of suffering needed to increase.

While James I was King (1603-1625), the persecution of the Puritans was tolerable. Moreover, the Archbishop of Canterbury was sympathetic to the Puritan cause. This all changed when Charles I (1625-1649) ascended to the throne. The Puritans then began to be singled out for harassment. The King and the bishops were now making any real Church reform impossible.

Thus, for any real reform to take place—for, in spite of everything, the Puritans still desired reform—a significant distance (literally) between the Puritans and England was necessary. Therefore, America became the destiny for the Puritans as well.

On June 11, 1630, aboard the *Arbella*, John Winthrop, one of the leaders of America's first Puritans, wrote and delivered *A Model of Christian Charity*. This work was no mere stump speech given to occupy the time of restless settlers. It was a 6,000-plus-word thesis which, for much of American history, was required reading among those in the United States who considered themselves educated. What's more, it became a model for future constitutional covenants of the Colonies. It read:

> We are a Company, professing ourselves fellow
> members of Christ, (and thus) we ought to
> account ourselves knit together by this bond of
> love…For the work we have in mind, it is by a
> mutual consent through a special overruling
> providence, and a more than an ordinary
> approbation of the Churches of Christ to seek out
> a place of Cohabitation and Consortship under a

due form of Government both civil and
ecclesiastical…

Thus stands the cause between God and us. We
are entered into covenant with Him for this work.
We have taken out a commission. The Lord hath
given us leave to draw our own articles. We have
professed to enterprise these and those accounts,
upon these and those ends. We have hereupon
besought Him of favor and blessing…

We shall find that the God of Israel is among us,
when ten of us shall be able to resist a thousand
of our enemies, when He shall make us a praise
and glory, that men of succeeding plantations
shall say, "The Lord make it like that of New
England."

For we must consider that we shall be as a City
upon a Hill, the eyes of all people are upon us; so
that if we shall deal falsely with our God in this
work we have undertaken and so cause Him to
withdraw His present help from us, we shall be
made a story and a by-word through the world.[12]

Winthrop's powerful and wise words would resonate throughout
America for centuries. It was this message which first gave rise to
the notion of American Exceptionalism, and the idea of America's
Manifest Destiny.

The Puritans were not the sin-obsessed, witch-hunting, killjoys in
tall black hats that many modern pseudo-historians (especially
those in Hollywood) have made them out to be. They were
determined to build a free society around a Christianity that
worked.

In June of 1630, 10 years after the Pilgrims founded the Plymouth
Colony, Winthrop and 700 other Puritans landed in Massachusetts
Bay, marking the beginning of the Great Migration, which over a
16-year period saw more than 20,000 Puritans leave Europe for

New England. Under the leadership of their ministers, the Puritans established a representative government with annual elections. By 1641, they had a "Body of Liberties" (essentially a Bill of Rights), which was penned by the Rev. Nathaniel Ward. This document was the first legal code established by the colonists. It, too, contained over 6,000 words. It consisted of 98 declarations that governed everything from private property to capital crimes.[13]

In 1636 the Rev. Thomas Hooker, along with other Puritan ministers, founded Connecticut. They also established an elective form of government. In 1638, after hearing a sermon by Hooker, Roger Ludlow wrote the *Fundamental Orders of Connecticut*. This was the first constitution written in America. It served as a model of government for other colonies and, eventually, a union of colonies. It also served as a model for the U.S. Constitution.

The opening reads,

> FORASMUCH as it has pleased the Almighty God by the wise disposition of his divine providence so to order and dispose of things that we the inhabitants and residents of Windsor, Hartford and Wethersfield are now cohabiting and dwelling in and upon the river of Connecticut and the lands thereunto adjoining; and well knowing where a people are gathered together the word of God requires that to maintain the peace and union of such a people there should be an orderly and decent government established according to God, to order and dispose of the affairs of the people at all seasons as occasion shall require; do therefore associate and conjoin ourselves to be as one public state or commonwealth; and do, for ourselves and our successors and such as shall be adjoined to us at any time hereafter, enter into combination and confederation together, to maintain and preserve the liberty and purity of the gospel of our Lord Jesus which we now

profess, as also the discipline of the churches, which according to the truth of the said gospel is now practiced among us; as also in our civil affairs to be guided and governed according to such laws, rules, orders and decrees as shall be made, ordered and decreed, as follows...[14]

However, as historian David Barton notes,

While Connecticut produced America's first written constitution, it definitely had not produced America's first written document of governance, for such written documents had been the norm for every colony founded by Bible-minded Christians... This practice of providing written documents had been the practice of American ministers before the Rev. Hooker's constitution of 1638 and continued long after.[15]

As noted by the renowned Alexis de Tocqueville in his seminal book *Democracy in America* (more on this powerful work later), Puritanism was as much a political theory as it was a religious doctrine.[16] The general principles of Puritanism, which, as Tocqueville points out, correspond "in many points with the most absolute democratic and republican theories,"[17] laid the groundwork for future American constitutions.

The New England area of America became steeped in Puritanism, and with a lengthy period of healthy immigration from the British middle classes (as Tocqueville notes, "it was from the heart of the middle classes that the majority of the emigrants came"[18]), prosperity soon followed. Tocqueville concluded that one of the "main causes of their prosperity" was that the government of the Puritans allowed for "greater personal and political independence than the colonies of other nations."[19]

Establishing a political framework that would lead to the "Miracle of America," the governments established by the Puritans did not derive their powers from the British, or any other secular source. Instead, "We see them at all times exercising the rights of sovereignty, appointing magistrates, declaring peace or war, establishing law and order, enacting laws as if they owed allegiance to God alone."[20] This devoted allegiance to God was the foundation for the liberty and prosperity that would set America apart from the rest of the world.

# CHAPTER 5

# The Foundation of Education in America

The Puritans were devoted to education. In order to make sure that children were brought up in the Puritan way, the Massachusetts Bay Colony understood the importance of a sound education. Schools were quickly established. In 1635, the Rev. John Cotton founded the Boston Latin School, a grammar school to provide education for those who were not able to receive it at home. Instruction in classical languages, such as Latin and Greek, was emphasized. The legendary Ezekiel Cheever—known as "the chief representative of the colonial schoolmaster"—taught there for 70 years.

SUPPOSED FIRST OR SECOND SCHOOL HOUSE.
IN WHICH EZEKIEL CHEEVER PROBABLY BEGAN TO TEACH

Boston Latin School produced many famous Americans, including Samuel Adams, John Hancock, James Bowdoin, Benjamin

Franklin, William Hooper, Robert Treat Paine, Josiah Quincy, Robert Charles Winthrop (eighteenth Speaker of the U.S. House and descendant of John Winthrop, founder of the Massachusetts Bay Colony), and Cotton Mather. Five of these men would sign the Declaration of Independence.[1]

Richard Gummere, in his book *The American Colonial Mind and the Classical Tradition*, notes that, by the time a pupil reached his seventh year at the Boston Latin School, he "was reading Cicero's orations, Justinian, the Latin and Greek Testaments, Isocrates, Homer, Hesiod, Virgil, Horace, Juvenal, and dialogues from the topics in Godwin's Roman Antiquities, as well as turning the Psalms into Latin verse."[2]

In Massachusetts in 1642, the General Court passed legislation that required each town to see that children were taught, especially "to read and understand the principles of religion and the capital laws of this country..." In 1647, the Massachusetts Bay Colony enacted the Old Deluder Satan Act. It declared,

It being one chief project of that old deluder, Satan, to keep men from the knowledge of the Scriptures, as in former times by keeping them in an unknown tongue, so in these latter times by persuading from the use of tongues, that so that at least the true sense and meaning of the original might be clouded and corrupted with false glosses of saint-seeming deceivers; and to the end that learning may not be buried in the grave of our forefathers, in church and commonwealth, the Lord assisting our endeavors.

It is therefore ordered that every township in this jurisdiction, after the Lord hath increased them to fifty households shall forthwith appoint one within their town to teach all such children as shall resort to him to write and read, whose wages shall be paid either by the parents or masters of such children, or by the inhabitants in general, by way of supply, as the major part of those that order the prudentials of the town shall appoint; provided those that send their children be not oppressed by paying much more than they can have them taught for in other towns.

And it is further ordered, that when any town shall increase to the number of one hundred families or householders, they shall set up a grammar school, the master thereof being able to instruct youth so far as they may be fitted for the university, provided that if any town neglect the performance hereof above one year that every such town shall pay 5 pounds to the next school till they shall perform this order.[3]

Many consider the Massachusetts education laws of 1642 and 1647 revolutionary. Memoria Press notes,

Although the 'shot heard 'round the world' is generally considered to refer to the first gun shots fired in the War for Independence, there was another event in early America that made history: the Massachusetts Education Laws of 1642 and 1647. In many respects, these were as revolutionary as the war itself. The product of the concern for education in Puritan New England, these laws constitute the first time in history that an organized state had mandated universal education. The Puritans had the creation of a godly society as their chief end, and this, they thought, was best accomplished by educated citizens. But what is interesting about the Puritans is the kind of education they sought.

When the Massachusetts General Court passed
the School Laws, they did it with the purpose in
mind to further knowledge of the Bible by
promoting literacy. The law not only required
that every town of 50 homes or more have an
elementary school teacher, but that every town of
100 or more have a grammar school. The
grammar schools of the time emphasized Latin
and, secondarily, Greek and Hebrew. They were
designed to prepare students for college and,
ultimately, for the ministry, the law, and
sometimes medicine. They strove to prepare
them to read all the classical authors in their
original tongues.[4]

According to author Stephen McDowell,

As time went on private schools flourished more
than common schools (especially as the Puritan
influence in common schools decreased). The
Christian community saw the private schools
were more reliable. 'By 1720 Boston had far
more private schools than public ones, and by
the close of the American Revolution many
towns had no common schools at all.'... There
were no public schools in the Southern colonies
until 1730 and only five by 1776.[5]

According to author and educator Samuel Blumenfield,

"Of the 117 men who signed the Declaration of
Independence, the Articles of Confederation and
the Constitution, one out of three had had only a
few months of formal schooling, and only one in
four had gone to college. They were educated by
parents, church schools, tutors, academies,
apprenticeship, and by themselves."[6]

Nevertheless, McDowell notes,

> Almost every child in [colonial] America was
> educated. At the time of the Revolution, the
> literacy level was virtually 100% (even on the
> frontier it was greater than 70%). John Adams
> said that to find someone who couldn't read was
> as rare as a comet. The colonists had a Christian
> philosophy of education—they felt that everyone
> should be educated, because everyone needed to
> know the truth for themselves.[7]

If a private tutor was necessary, the tutor was almost always a
minister. Furthermore, in almost every case in colonial America,
those who went to college were instructed by ministers. Thus,
whether private or public, and whether elementary, secondary,
college, or university, early American schools were thoroughly
Christian.

American colonials were just as serious about higher education as
they were about teaching children to read and write. In 1636, in
order to train clergy, the Puritans founded The College at New
Towne. The school began with nine students, and classes were first
held in 1638. In 1639 the school was renamed Harvard College
after clergyman John Harvard, who had willed the school a large
sum of money along with his library of about 400 books.

Harvard's "Rules and Precepts," adopted in 1646 state:

> Let every Student be plainly instructed, and
> earnestly pressed to consider well, the main end
> of his life and studies is, to know God and Jesus
> Christ which is eternal life (John 17:3) and
> therefore to lay Christ in the bottom, as the only
> foundation of all sound Knowledge and

Learning. And seeing the Lord only giveth wisdom, Let everyone seriously set himself by prayer in secret to seek it of him (Prov. 2:3). Every one shall so exercise himself in reading the Scriptures twice a day, that he shall be ready to give such an account of his proficiency therein, both in Theoretical observations of Language and Logic, and in practical and spiritual truths, as his Tutor shall require, according to his ability; seeing the entrance of the word giveth light, it giveth understanding to the simple (Psalm 119:130).[8]

According to *Puritanism in America,*

The early Harvard curriculum featured heavy emphasis on languages. Students continued their reading of Greek each year, and in their first year began the study of Hebrew. These languages were given extensive attention. Rather less was devoted to Aramaic and Syriac, both being studied for one year. The curriculum also included lectures, always in Latin, in mathematics and astronomy, logic, physics, politics, rhetoric, history and geography, and the nature of plants. Much time was devoted to philosophy, to Aristotelian metaphysics and ethics.[9]

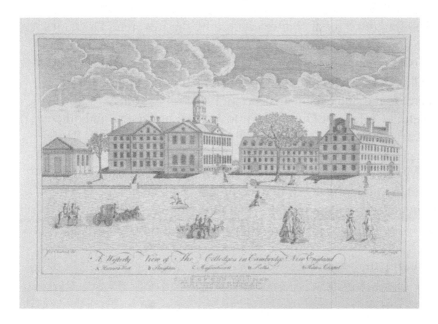

**A 1767 Engraving of Harvard College by Paul Revere.**

Additionally, "Each Saturday Harvard students focused on catechetical divinity, with William Ames *Medulla or Marrow of Sacred Theology* the text. Students were expected to know the Bible well and to be able to analyze it logically--to derive syllogisms from Biblical texts."[10] Near the end of the seventeenth century, in an address to the student body, quoting "that one true golden saying of Aristotle," the president of Harvard (and noted Puritan minster), Increase Mather, reminded the students, "Find a friend in Plato, a friend in Socrates, but above all find a friend in Truth."[11]

Harvard is the oldest institution of higher learning in the U.S., and it educated significant numbers of our nation's founders. Eight Harvard graduates—John Hancock, Samuel Adams, John Adams, William Ellery, William Williams, William Hooper, Elbridge Gerry, and Robert Treat Paine—would sign the Declaration of Independence. Likewise, eight Harvard graduates have served as President of the United States: John Adams, John Quincy Adams, Theodore Roosevelt, Franklin Roosevelt, John F. Kennedy, George W. Bush, Rutherford Hayes, and of course, Barack Obama.

In 1693, under a royal charter secured by the Reverend Dr. James Blair, The College of William and Mary, named after the reigning English monarch, was founded in Virginia. It was established by the Church of England as an Anglican institution in order to "make, found and establish a certain Place of Universal Study, a perpetual College of Divinity, Philosophy, Languages, and other good arts and sciences."[12] According to its charter of 1691, The College of William and Mary was started in order "that the Church of Virginia may be furnished with a seminary of ministers of the gospel, and that the youth may be piously educated in good letters and manners, and that the Christian religion may be propagated among the Western Indians to the glory of Almighty God."[13]

According to the school's website,

> The list of patriots who studied at William & Mary is long and distinguished and includes three American Presidents, Thomas Jefferson, James Monroe, and John Tyler, sixteen members of the Continental Congress, four signers of the Declaration of Independence, four justices of the Supreme Court of the United States, including John Marshall, and many members of Congress, cabinet members, and diplomats. Additionally, George Washington received his surveyor's license from the College and after his Presidency served as the College's Chancellor.[14]

Also, the first law school in the U.S. was established at William & Mary.

In 1701, ten Congregationalist ministers, all graduates of Harvard, led by James Pierpont, founded the Collegiate School. Not long thereafter, the president of Harvard, Increase Mather, became frustrated with what he deemed the increasingly liberal and ecclesiastically lax Harvard clergy. Thus, Cotton Mather was sent to secure financial help for Collegiate School.

In Wales, Mather approached an extremely successful businessman, Elihu Yale, who had made a fortune in trade. Yale donated a substantial sum and a large number of books. For his generosity, the school was renamed Yale College. Yale was established in 1701 "for the liberal and religious education of suitable youth…to propagate in this wilderness, the blessed reformed Protestant religion."[15]

Incoming students were instructed that,

> All scholars shall live religious, godly and blameless lives according to the rules of God's Word, diligently reading the Holy Scriptures, the fountain of light and truth; and constantly attend upon all the duties of religion, both in public and secret. That the President, or in his absence One of the Tutors Shall constantly Pray in the College-Hall every morning and Evening: and Shall read a Chapter or Suitable Portion of the Holy Scriptures, unless there be Some other Theological Discourse or Religious Exercise: and Every Member of the College whether Graduates or Undergraduates, whether Residing in the College or in the Town of New-Haven Shall Seasonably Attend…[16]

According to *The Christian College: A History of Protestant Higher Education in America* (Grand Rapids, MI: Eerdmans, 1984, p. 38), for the founders of Yale, the primary goal was that, "Every student shall consider the main end of his study to wit, to know God in Jesus Christ and answerable, to lead a Godly, sober life."[17]

A Front VIEW of YALE-COLLEGE, and the COLLEGE CHAPEL, New-Haven.

In 1746, as a product of the Great Awakening (which will be the focus of a later chapter) in order to train ministers, seven Presbyterians—Ebenezer Pemberton, Jonathan Dickinson, Aaron Burr Sr., John Pierson, who were ministers; William Smith, a lawyer; Peter Van Brugh Livingston, a merchant; and William Peartree Smith—founded The College of New Jersey. In 1756 the college moved from Newark to Princeton, New Jersey. Today it is known as Princeton University.

Among the early presidents of Princeton were men such as Jonathan Edwards, Samuel Davies, and the Rev. John Witherspoon. Edwards and Davies helped launch the Great Awakening. Davies was a huge early proponent of civil and religious liberties in the Colonies. Davies dedicated a significant part of his ministry to American slaves. He not only preached to them the gospel of Christ—due to his efforts, hundreds were converted—but he also taught them to read.[18]

Born in Scotland, Witherspoon was a staunch Protestant and an advocate of republicanism. In 1768 he became the sixth president of Princeton. He instituted significant financial and instructional reforms and turned around the fledgling college. Witherspoon, who was very influential as a minister and a teacher, numbered among his students James Madison, Aaron Burr, Philip Freneau, William Bradford, and Hugh Henry Brackenridge. Later, Rev. Witherspoon played a prominent role in the American Revolution.

His native Scotland branded Witherspoon a "rebel" and "traitor," who "inflamed the colonists with his preaching and his pen." Witherspoon was also accused of transforming Princeton into what was disparagingly called a "seminary of sedition." Moreover, a high-ranking British officer labeled Witherspoon a "political firebrand" who "poisons the minds of his young students and through them, the Continent."[19]

Witherspoon, who was elected to the first Continental Congress, was noted for his service to the young United States. While serving in Congress, his patriotism and judgment won the respect of his colleagues. Witherspoon received assignment to many congressional committees, some of them among the most important.[20] He served on more than a hundred committees, and he was frequently involved in debates. Witherspoon signed the Declaration of Independence, helped draft the Articles of Confederation, and was a strong advocate for the adoption of the U.S. Constitution.

The College of New York, or King's College (later Columbia University) was founded in 1754 by the Anglican Church. Some of the first and most prominent students and trustees of King's College were John Jay, the first chief justice of the United States; Alexander Hamilton, the first secretary of the treasury; Gouverneur Morris, the author of the final draft of the U.S. Constitution; and Robert R. Livingston, a member of the five-man committee that drafted the Declaration of Independence.[21]

In 1764 in Rhode Island, the fire of The Great Awakening inspired the Philadelphia Association of Baptist Churches to found Rhode Island College, later Brown University. The Reverend James

Manning, a Baptist minister and a graduate of Princeton, was the college's first president. In 1786 Manning served as a delegate for Rhode Island to the Continental Congress.

With the Congregationalists (Puritans), Presbyterians, Episcopalians, and Baptists already founding colleges in Colonial America, the Dutch Reformed Church was moved to do the same. Queen's College (Rutgers) was born in 1766. In 1754, in order to train Native Americans to be missionaries to the Native tribes, a Puritan minister from Connecticut, Eleazar Wheelock, founded Moor's Charity School. In 1769 the school was moved to New Hampshire and re-established as Dartmouth College.[22]

One common trait runs throughout the early schools in America: virtually every school of the pre-colonial and the colonial period of the United States was founded by some branch of Christianity. Dr. Alvin J. Schmidt, in his book *Under the Influence: How Christianity Transformed Civilization*, points out that every college established in colonial America, except the University of Pennsylvania, was founded by some denomination of Christianity. He adds that, preceding the Civil War, 92 percent of the 182 colleges and universities in the U.S. were established by some branch of the church.[23]

The Puritans were at the forefront of the founding of higher education in the Colonial U.S., and they set the standard for such education. In fact, they set such a high standard that across the American Colonies, literacy was nearly universal.[24] Additionally, along with education, one of the most lasting legacies that Puritan influence had on America (though now it is sadly and tragically waning) is that of the value and importance of family. The Puritans practiced a form of parenting and courtship that resulted in an extremely high rate of stable and fruitful marriages. Puritan parents did not practice arranged marriages, but they did hold firmly to "veto" rights upon a courtship if they felt it was outside the will of God. They understood well that the family, consisting, of course, of mothers and fathers, rooted in Christ was the foundation of a moral and civil society. Thus, they lived their lives, quite fruitfully, reflecting this belief.

In fact, maybe they lived a bit too fruitfully. For as we look at the end of the seventeenth century and towards the dawn of the 1700s, the Puritan influence began to reside. Sadly, much of this can be attributed to the prosperity that many settlers were now experiencing. As Cotton Mather noted, "Religion begat prosperity, and the daughter devoured the mother."[25]

Children began to turn from the ways of their parents—from the Covenant Way—and go their own way. Practices of the occult began to be openly displayed and slothfulness crept in. Furthermore, conflicts with the Natives began to flourish. America needed a re-awakening. America needed a revival.

# CHAPTER 6

# Revival Lights a Fire

Between the colonial and Revolutionary periods of American history came what historians have dubbed the (first) "Great Awakening." Near the beginning of the eighteenth century, many churches under Puritan influence were beginning to be riddled with "comfortable pews." This does not mean that such churches were filled with comfortably padded pews that lulled congregants to sleep, but rather an absence of passionate Christianity.

One such church was Brattle Street Church in Boston. Brattle Street Church was an independent congregation filled with wealthy and influential Harvard College trustees. According to *A Wonderful Work of God: Puritanism and the Great Awakening*,

> Brattle Street Church became a society of nominal Christians who paid lip service to the Westminster Confession and who professed faith and obedience to Christ as a matter of common decency. An anonymous wag wrote of the Brattle Street Church:
>
> *"Our churches turn genteel*
> *Our parsons grow trim and trip*
> *With wealth, wine, and wig,*
> *And their heads are covered with meal."*
>
> But by the beginning of the eighteenth century other churches in the neighborhood of Boston were emulating the Brattle Street Church. Puritan practice was becoming more relaxed, much to the distress of the small conservative minority.[1]

Thus began a growing concern about the secularization of New England. The lack of passionate Christianity, along with the coinciding adoption of certain liberal interpretations of Scripture and a turn toward the secular, greatly concerned ministers such as Jonathan Edwards, Thomas Prince, and William Cooper.

By the 1730s, passionate and animated pleas for the souls of the lost became widespread. A common refrain was soon heard throughout the colonies: "God was an angry judge, and humans were sinners!"

The earliest principle figure of this period of spiritual revival was the brilliant and pious Puritan minister Jonathan Edwards. Born in 1703—the same year as John Wesley—to the Reverend Timothy and Esther Edwards, Jonathan showed signs of an unusually keen mind early on. He entered Yale just before he turned 13. He began his ministry at 23, alongside his maternal grandfather in Northampton, Massachusetts.

Edwards was literally born into Christian ministry. His father was a Congregationalist minister, and his mother, Esther Stoddard Edwards, was the daughter of renowned Massachusetts minister Solomon Stoddard. Stoddard succeeded Eleazer Mather as pastor of the Congregationalist Church in Northampton, Massachusetts. He was a firebrand of a preacher who abhorred alcohol and extravagance.

Though his theology was in conflict with many contemporary Puritan leaders, Stoddard was an extremely influential religious leader in the New England area for several decades.

> He was a Puritan of the old school and much
> disturbed by the decline in church attendance,
> and of religious concern generally…He was also
> concerned with the worldliness of so many of his
> parishioners, especially the young. During the
> late seventeenth and early eighteenth centuries it
> was common practice for families of the gentry
> in Northampton to meet socially on Sunday

evenings instead of going to church. Young
people were given the freedom to meet without
the supervision of their elders. There was also
much 'tavern haunting' and 'night walking' in
Northampton.[2]

Jonathan Edwards succeeded his grandfather as pastor of the
church at Northampton. He would later repudiate some of his
grandfather's theological views, an action which would cost him
his pulpit as he was dismissed from the Northampton church in
1750.[3] After this, Edwards accepted a role as pastor of a church in
Stockbridge, Massachusetts. During this period, Edwards was also
a missionary to the local Native American tribes.

Edwards was a prolific writer as well and is recognized as one of
the great intellectuals of his time. He produced such works as
*Freedom of the Will, The Great Christian Doctrine of Original Sin
Defended,* and *The Life of David Brainerd,* which inspired
countless missionaries of the nineteenth century. In 1758, Edwards
became the president of the College of New Jersey (Princeton). He
died weeks later from a smallpox inoculation. Edwards was the
grandfather of Aaron Burr, third Vice President of the United
States.

Jonathan Edwards loved the pulpit, and according to BJU Press,
was more teacher and preacher than pastor.[4] In late 1734 and early
1735, revival broke out in Northampton. By the summer of 1735, it
ended, but the seeds for something more lasting were planted.
Enter the mighty George Whitefield.

Whitefield is generally considered the "Father of the Great
Awakening." Born in England in 1714, Whitefield was an unruly
child. He described himself as,

> So brutish as to hate instruction and used
> purposely to shun all opportunities of receiving
> it. I soon gave pregnant proofs of an impudent
> temper. Lying, filthy talking, and foolish jesting,
> I was much addicted to, even when very young.

> Sometimes I used to curse, if not swear. Stealing
> from my mother I thought no theft at all, and
> used to make no scruple of taking money out of
> her pockets before she was up. I have frequently
> betrayed my trust, and have more than once
> spent money I took in the house in buying fruit,
> tarts, &c., to satisfy my sensual appetite.
> Numbers of Sabbaths have I broken, and
> generally used to behave myself very
> irreverently in God's sanctuary. Much money
> have I spent in plays, and in the common
> amusements of the age. Cards and reading
> romances were my heart's delight.[5]

Whitefield entered Pembroke College at Oxford at age 17. There he joined a group called the "Holy Club," where he befriended John and Charles Wesley. John Wesley led the group, and as a result of their "methodical" ways, critics took to calling them "Methodists." Of course, the name stuck.

Upon graduating and receiving his BA, Whitefield was ordained at 22. He began his preaching in the British towns of Bath, Bristol, and Gloucester. However, he felt the call to join General Oglethorpe's colony in Georgia. In 1738 Whitefield left for North America. Not long after arriving in Georgia, noting the hard conditions, high death rate, and an abundance of children who had lost their parents, he conceived the idea of an orphanage.

For the rest of his life, Whitefield raised money for the orphanage. Additionally, Whitefield acquired land in Pennsylvania where he intended to build a school for the education of blacks. He also continued to preach. Whitefield's message was one of salvation, a message which differed a bit from other Anglican ministers at the time who emphasized religiosity and moral living. It was not long before most of Georgia had heard of this young preacher with the booming voice and wild pulpit antics. News of Whitefield and his preaching soon spread throughout the colonies.

In 1739, after a brief return to England in hopes of securing land and funding for the orphanage in Georgia, Whitefield came back to America and would preach throughout the colonies. Jonathan Edwards invited Whitefield to preach in Northampton, Massachusetts. Whitefield's message resonated with rich and poor, farmers and tradesmen, church-goers and sinners—virtually everyone within earshot of Whitefield, which, according to Ben Franklin, in open space, was 30,000 people!

Whitefield was not alone. Along with Edwards, men like Isaac Backus, David Brainerd, James Davenport, Samuel Davies, Theodore Frelinghuysen, Jonathan Mayhew, Shubal Stearns, the Tennent brothers (Gilbert, John, William), and others implored settlers and Natives alike to trust in Christ and Christ alone for salvation. Their message of repentance caught fire up and down the American East Coast. In the words of Brainerd, the ongoing revival was like an "irresistible force of a mighty torrent or swelling deluge."

After the event at Pentecost as recorded in the Bible in Acts Chapter Two, and after the Protestant Reformation of the sixteenth century, many evangelicals of the eighteenth century considered the revival that was The Great Awakening as the third extraordinary outpouring of the Holy Spirit.

> The Great Awakening introduced a strong emphasis on the power of inspired preaching. Therefore, when the fervent Gilbert Tennent or the quiet Jonathan Edwards terrified their audiences with vivid, highly imaginative descriptions of the lake of fire, the agony of the damned, and the meaning of eternity, it was because the Holy Spirit flowed through their hearts and minds to be expressed in the rhetoric of the sermon. Charismatic preaching, therefore, was a major means of securing conviction and conversion. Some, however, like George Whitefield, experienced conversion by reading devotional books; others, like John Wesley,

while listening to a lecture on a passage by
Luther. Conviction can occur with or without the
medium of the preacher. However, it was the
view of Evangelical ministers that it was most
frequently effected through preaching.[6]

A letter written by Jonathan Edwards in December of 1743 notes
the positive practical effect revival was having on Northampton.
An excerpt reads:

> Ever since the great work of God that was
> wrought here about nine years ago, there has
> been a great abiding alteration in this town in
> many respects. There has been vastly more
> religion kept up in the town, among all sorts of
> persons, in religious exercises and in common
> conversation than used to be before. There has
> remained a more general seriousness and
> decency in attending the public worship. There
> has been a very great alteration among the youth
> of the town with respect to reveling, frolicking,
> profane and unclean conversation, and lewd
> songs. Instances of fornication have been very
> rare. There has also been a great alteration
> among both old and young with respect to tavern
> haunting. I suppose the town has been in no
> measure so free of vice in these respects for any
> long time together for this sixty years as it has
> been this nine years past.
>
> There has also been an evident alteration with
> respect to a charitable spirit to the poor (though I
> think with regard to this in this town, as the land
> in general, come far short of Gospel rules).[7]

Such results are exactly the kind of fruit that should be reaped
when real revival takes hold. So often in modern times we think of
revival—if it is thought of at all—as an annual or biannual week-

long church gathering, where there are morning and evening services, usually only attended by the already (at least somewhat) faithful, but with the entire focus of the preaching and teaching on bringing salvation to the lost. Salvation of the lost should certainly be part of the fruit of real revival, as the mighty George Whitfield himself emphasized, but too often today this is the complete message, and the real life struggles (sin)—such as those that occur with money, marriage, work, sexual immorality, and the like—are dealt with very little, if at all. Thus, as we see especially with sin such as divorce, the lives of many Christians don't look much different from those "of the world."

What's more, the fire of revival can spawn change that is felt world-wide. This was certainly the case with The First Great Awakening, for it was in the pulpits of American churches that the seeds of Revolution were sown. The British certainly thought so, as they blamed what they derisively described as the "Black Robed Regiment" for the thirst in the Colonies for American Independence.[8] Modern historians have noted, "There is not a right asserted in the Declaration of Independence which had not been discussed by the New England clergy before 1763."[9] The Great Awakening played no small role in helping to unite the American Colonies against the British.

For example, in 1750 the Rev. Jonathan Mayhew, a Harvard graduate, Congregationalist minister, and pastor of West Church in Boston, published *A Discourse Concerning Unlimited Submission and Non-Resistance to the Higher Powers*. Out of this was born a sermon entitled "The Morning Gun of the American Revolution." In this, Mayhew uses Romans 13 to justify throwing off the tyrannical yoke of England.

In the Discourse Mayhew concludes,

> Thus, upon a careful review of the apostle's reasoning in this passage, it appears that his arguments to enforce submission, are of such a nature, as to conclude only in favor of submission to such rulers as he himself

describes; i.e., such as rule for the good of
society, which is the only end of their institution.
Common tyrants, and public oppressors, are not
intitled to obedience from their subjects, by
virtue of any thing here laid down by the
inspired apostle.[10]

In 1765, Mayhew gave a powerful sermon railing against the evils
of King George III's hated Stamp Act. Mayhew declared,

The king is as much bound by his oath not to
infringe on the legal rights of the people, as the
people are bound to yield subjection to him.
From whence it follows that as soon as the
prince sets himself above the law, he loses the
king in the tyrant.[11]

According to historian Alice Mary Baldwin, joining Mayhew in
leading the opposition to the Stamp Act were the Reverends
Andrew Eliot, Charles Chauncey, and Samuel Cooper.[12] George
Whitefield accompanied Ben Franklin—whom he had
befriended—to Parliament to protest the Act. Franklin revealed to
Parliament that Americans would never willingly submit to the
Stamp Act. A month later, in March of 1766, celebrating the repeal
of the act, Whitefield recorded in his journal, *Stamp Act repealed,
Gloria Deo.*"[13]

John Witherspoon, Presbyterian minister, signer of the Declaration
of Independence, and president of the College of New Jersey
(Princeton)—in 1776, on a national day of prayer and fasting,
preached a sermon entitled *The Dominion of Providence over the
Passions of Men*. The sermon included the following:

There can be no true religion, till there be a
discovery of your lost state by nature and
practice, and an unfeigned acceptance of Christ
Jesus, as he is offered in the gospel. Unhappy are

they who either despise his mercy, or are ashamed of his cross. Believe it, "There is no salvation in any other." "There is no other name under heaven given amongst men by which we must be saved." Unless you are united to him by a lively faith, not the resentment of a haughty monarch, the sword of divine justice hangs over you, and the fulness of divine vengeance shall speedily overtake you...

If your cause is just, you may look with confidence to the Lord, and intreat him to plead it as his own. You are all my witnesses, that this is the first time of my introducing any political subject into the pulpit. At this season, however, it is not only lawful but necessary, and I willingly embrace the opportunity of declaring my opinion without any hesitation, that the cause in which America is now in arms, is the cause of justice, of liberty, and of human nature.[14]

Witherspoon was a mentor to many of America's founders and helped to educate many future leaders of the young United States of America. Among his students included James Madison, future U.S. President and "Father of the Constitution," Aaron Burr, future U.S. Vice President, twelve future Continental Congress members, forty-nine U.S. representatives, twenty-eight senators, three Supreme Court justices, and a secretary of state.[15] As America's Schoolmaster, Noah Webster, would later note, "The learned clergy...had great influence in founding the first genuine republican governments ever formed and which, with all the faults and defects of the men and their laws, were the best republican governments on earth."[16]

According to David Barton,

When Paul Revere set off on his famous ride, it was to the home of the Rev. [Jonas] Clark in Lexington that he rode. Patriot leaders John

> Hancock and Samuel Adams were lodging (as
> they often did) with the Rev. Clark. After
> learning of the approaching British forces,
> Hancock and Adams turned to Pastor Clark and
> inquired of him whether the people were ready to
> fight. Clark unhesitatingly replied, "I have
> trained them for this very hour!"[17]

As a result of this First Great Awakening, geographical barriers became no more significant than denominational ones. The country was beginning to unite. As Marshall and Manuel put it, "[Americans] were beginning to discover a basic truth which would be a major foundation stone of God's new nation, and which by 1776 would be declared self-evident: that in the eyes of their Creator, all men were of equal value."[18] Americans were beginning to rediscover the Covenant Way. One nation under God became the political as well as the spiritual legacy of The Great Awakening. It was now time for America to throw off the yoke of Great Britain.

# CHAPTER 7

# Let Freedom Ring, Part 1: Colonial Rebellion Builds

In 1772, to confront the unjust acts of Great Britain, citizens of Boston formed a Committee of Correspondence to coordinate their efforts with those of the other colonies. The citizens charged the Committee with several tasks, one of which was to create a statement of the rights of the colonists. This duty was given to none other than one of the leaders of the original Tea Party, the "Father of the American Revolution" himself, Samuel Adams.

"Among the natural rights of the Colonists," began Adams, "are these: First, a right to life; Secondly, to liberty; Thirdly, to property." On liberty, Adams later added that, "'Just and true liberty, equal and impartial liberty' …is a thing that all men are clearly entitled to by the eternal and immutable laws of God and nature, as well as by the law of nations and all well-grounded municipal laws, which must have their foundation in the former."[1]

Adams was a Congregationalist who was raised by devout Puritans. As the governor of Massachusetts, he was dubbed "the last Puritan." Adams was quite proud of his Puritan heritage, and as has been noted, rightly so. He understood well that for a new nation to succeed, "Under God" was the key. To be able to unite as men, without first being united with Christ, is one of the greatest lies ever perpetrated by Satan. (The bloody French Revolution is evidence of this.)

In 1773, a Crown-appointed governor wrote to the Board of Trade in England: "If you ask an American, who is his master? He will tell you he has none, nor any governor but Jesus Christ."[2] This may have given rise to the cry passed up and down the coast by the Committees of Correspondence: "No king but King Jesus!"[3]

Resistance sentiment continued to grow until one final event united the Colonies into the union that was necessary to stand up to England. In 1774, after the Boston Tea Party, the British decided to punish Boston by closing her port. They were attempting to end all trade in Boston and starve the inhabitants of the city. The Committees of Correspondence sent word to the rest of the Colonies and outrage swept through America. A day of fasting and prayer was declared, "to seek divine direction and aid." The rest of the Colonies began sending aid to Boston.

South Carolina sent barrels of rice. In North Carolina, 2000 pounds Sterling was raised in just a few days. A vessel and its crew were donated to carry provisions. Windham, Connecticut sent 258 sheep, and in Delaware plans were made for sending relief annually. Maryland and Virginia also contributed generously. George Washington personally donated 50 pounds Sterling (about $6,800 in 2011).

In October of 1774, Massachusetts held a Provincial Congress. John Hancock, the President of this Congress, declared:

> We think it is incumbent upon this people to humble themselves before God on account of their sins, for He hath been pleased in His righteous judgment to suffer a great calamity to befall us, as the present controversy between Great Britain and the Colonies. [And] also to implore the Divine Blessing upon us, that by the assistance of His grace, we may be enabled to reform whatever is amiss among us, that so God may be pleased to continue to us the blessings we enjoy, and remove the tokens of His displeasure, by causing harmony and union to be restored between Great Britain and these Colonies.[4]

There was still hope for a peaceful resolution to the growing conflict. Active resistance was only going to be entered into with great reluctance. In March of 1775, reluctance gave way to action as the Colonies unitedly responded to Patrick Henry's fiery words to the Virginia House of Burgesses:

> There is no longer room for hope. If we wish to be free, we must fight! An appeal to arms and to the God of Hosts is all that is left us!
>
> They tell me that we are weak, but shall we gather strength by irresolution? We are not weak. Three million people, armed in a holy cause of liberty and in such a country, are invincible by any force which our enemy can send against us. We shall not fight alone. God presides over the destinies of nations, and will raise up friends for us. The battle is not to the strong alone; it is to the vigilant, the active, the brave...
>
> Is life so dear, or peace so sweet, as to be purchased at the price of chains and slavery? Forbid it, almighty God! I know not what course others may take, but as for me, give me liberty or give me death![5]

The fire for revolution was lit.

On July 1, 1776, delegates of the Second Continental Congress entered what John Adams called, "the greatest debate of all." Even after over a year's worth of conflict against the mightiest military force on earth, declared independence from Great Britain was far from a foregone conclusion. Just weeks earlier, the majority of the men in the Congress were very much hoping that some formula for peace could be found with Great Britain.

These Congressmen knew very well what it would cost them personally to cast their votes openly with those few men who were calling for a declaration of independence. In the likely event of a military defeat, the men who signed such a declaration would be held personally responsible, and the penalty for instigating rebellion against the Crown was death.[6] Declaring independence required a unanimous vote from the Congress, and as Ben Franklin soberly put it, "We must indeed all hang together, or most assuredly we will all hang separately."[7]

During the debate on July 1, John Dickinson, representing Pennsylvania, made powerful and lengthy arguments against declaring independence. According to Daniel Webster, with quiet resolve, but equal conviction, John Adams answered him, concluding with,

> All that I have and all that I am, and all that I hope in this life, I am now ready here to stake upon it. And I leave off as I began, that live or die, survive or perish, I am for the Declaration. It is my living sentiment, and by the blessing of God it shall be my dying sentiment. Independence now, and Independence forever![8]

Shortly following this exchange, Congress voted. The majority supported independence, but it was not unanimous as required. Nine of the 13 colonies were ready officially to declare for freedom and the war necessary to achieve it. Pennsylvania and South Carolina voted no. Delaware's two delegates were split. The New York delegates abstained. Debate was to resume the next day, followed by another vote.

**Second Continental Congress Voting on the Declaration of Independence.**

On the following day, July 2, the South Carolina delegates, for the sake of unanimity, were swayed to support the Declaration. New Pennsylvania delegates voted for independence. With New York still abstaining, Delaware was the key. Its two delegates remained split. With a dramatic and grueling overnight ride through stormy weather, where often he had to dismount and lead his horse, an exhausted third Delaware delegate, Caesar Rodney, entered the State House in Philadelphia around 1:00 p.m., just as the final vote was about to occur. He had come to break the deadlock among his fellow statesmen.

Barely able to speak, he exclaimed, "As I believe the voice of my constituents and of all sensible and honest men is in favor of independence, my own judgment concurs with them. I vote for independence."[9] Therefore it was unanimously decided (New York would join with the other colonies officially on July 9th). The 13 colonies were now the United States of America.

John Winthrop prayed, others openly wept. Samuel Adams declared, "We have this day restored the Sovereign, to Whom alone men ought to be obedient. He reigns in heaven and from the rising to the setting of the sun, let His kingdom come."[10]

It was two days later on July 4 that an official Declaration of Independence document was actually signed, albeit only by two members of Congress: John Hancock, the President of Congress and Charles Thompson the Secretary of Congress. Most of the rest of the Congressmen would sign the Declaration about a month later.

On the same day that the Declaration of Independence became official, an extremely telling event further reveals that our founders understood well the "ancient principles" upon which our republic must be built. On July 4, 1776, the Second Continental Congress appointed a committee—consisting of Thomas Jefferson, Benjamin Franklin, and John Adams—to design an official seal for the United States. Adams proposed an image of Hercules contemplating the persuasions of Virtue and Sloth.

Franklin proposed a biblical theme:

> Moses standing on the Shore, and extending his Hand over the Sea, thereby causing the same to overwhelm Pharaoh who is sitting in an open Chariot, a Crown on his Head and a Sword in his hand. Rays from a Pillar of Fire in the Clouds reaching to Moses, to express that he acts by Command of the Deity. Motto: Rebellion to Tyrants is Obedience to God.[11]

**Nineteenth Century Artistic Rendition of Franklin's Proposed Design for the U.S. Seal**

Likewise, Jefferson preferred a biblical theme. According to a letter from John Adams to his wife Abigail, Jefferson proposed:

> The Children of Israel in the Wilderness, led by a Cloud by day, and a Pillar of Fire by night, and on the other Side Hengist and Horsa, the Saxon Chiefs, from whom We claim the Honour of being descended and whose Political Principles and Form of Government We have assumed.[12]

Our founders understood well that the story of Moses embodied what they hoped would be the story of America. (Of course, we now know their hope was well placed.) Bruce Feiler, author of *America's Prophet: Moses and the American Story*, says that, more than any other ancient figure, "Moses embodies the American story. He is the champion of oppressed people; he transforms disparate tribes in a forbidding wilderness into a nation of laws; he is the original proponent of freedom and justice for all."[13]

The committee agreed on an image of thirteen linked shields, each bearing the designation of a state and the motto "E Pluribus Unum," along with the all-seeing eye of the Creator inside a triangle. On the reverse side was the biblical scene and the motto "Rebellion to tyrants is obedience to God."

However, Congress tabled the matter for several years and eventually adopted the motto as we have it today: on the obverse, or front side, is our national coat of arms. It consists of an American bald eagle with raised wings. The breast of the eagle is covered by a red, white, and blue colored shield. In its right talon the eagle clutches an olive branch, which symbolizes peace, and in its left talon, the eagle clutches 13 arrows (representing the original 13 Colonies) which symbolizes war. The eagle faces the right which represents a preference for peace.

The mouth of the eagle holds a scroll containing the Latin phrase *E PLURIBUS UNUM* which means "Out of Many, One." This was a recognition of the wide array of (mostly) Europeans which made up the 13 Colonies, which made up the union that was the United States. Above the head of the eagle is a halo, or "glory," of 13 stars (again representing the 13 Colonies).

On the reverse side of the seal is a 13-step pyramid, with the year 1776 in Roman numerals along the base. At the top of the pyramid is the Eye of Providence with the Latin motto *ANNUIT COEPTIS* ("God has favored our undertakings") in the sky above. Below the pyramid is a scroll with another Latin phrase *NOVUS ORDO SECLORUM*. This is translated "New order of the ages," which is to imply that 1776 was the beginning of a new American era.

As the coming Revolutionary War would further prove, God had indeed "favored" the undertakings of the United States. Such favor was no doubt due to the firm faith demonstrated by those who sought to build a nation that, as Puritan leader John Winthrop would envision nearly a century-and-a-half earlier, would serve the world as a "City upon a Hill."

# CHAPTER 8

# Let Freedom Ring, Part 2: Revolution!

One of the surest places to find God at work is in the midst of human beings at war—especially among those who claim to know Him, and especially if their cause is just. As Screwtape, writing about World War I, put it to his demonic protégé in C.S. Lewis's *The Screwtape Letters*, "[If] we are not careful, we shall see thousands turning in this tribulation to the Enemy [God], while tens of thousands who do not go so far as that will nevertheless have their attention diverted from themselves to values and causes which they believe to be higher than the self."[1]

In examining the Revolutionary War, one can easily see the hand of God at work. Amazingly, most modern historians never even consider that God had anything to do with the Colonials' victory over the most powerful nation on earth. This, however, was not the view of the men leading the Revolution. These men were quick to give credit to the Lord for the amazing events that were taking place.

Soon after the victories at Lexington and Concord, a then loyal Colonel Benedict Arnold and Colonel Ethan Allen led forces to take Fort Ticonderoga. In the taking of the fort, Col. Allen shouted to the British commander, Capt. Delaplace: "Deliver this fort immediately!" Delaplace replied, "By what authority?" Allen answered, "In the name of the great Jehovah and the Continental Congress." The fort was taken without a shot being fired.

After a few early victories, the united Colonies began to swell with pride. Concerned American clergy saw this and knew that if this continued, God would no longer bless their efforts. A mature, humble, and steady hand was needed to lead the new Continental

Army. The Continental Congress unanimously chose George Washington.

As modern academics become more and more corrupted by the godless worldview that dominates today's schools, growing numbers question the faith of General Washington. As we examine our founding, these questions need to be answered, because according to Marshall and Manuel, only three other men played as pivotal a role as Washington in the first three centuries of American history—Columbus, Winthrop, and Whitefield.

A great insight into our first President's faith is revealed by an old book found in the Yale Divinity School library by Marshall and Manuel when they were doing their research for *The Light and The Glory*. The book was written by William Johnson and was entitled, *George Washington, the Christian*. In it were prayers hand written by Washington in a small manuscript book he called Daily Sacrifice. The first entry read,

> Let my heart, therefore, gracious God, be so affected with the glory and majesty of (Thine honor) that I may not do mine own works, but wait on Thee, and discharge those weighty duties which thou requirest of me...[2]

The next entry contained these words:

> O most glorious God, in Jesus Christ my merciful and loving father, I acknowledge and confess my guilt; in the weak and imperfect performance of the duties of this day. I have called on thee for pardon and forgiveness of sins, but so coldly and carelessly, that my prayers are become my sin and stand in need of pardon. I have heard thy holy word, but with such deadness of spirit that I have been an unprofitable and forgetful hearer...But, O God, who art rich in mercy and plenteous in

redemption, mark not, I beseech Thee, what I
have done amiss; remember that I am but dust,
and remit my transgressions, negligences and
ignorances, and cover them all with absolute
obedience of thy dear Son, that those sacrifices
which I have offered may be accepted by thee, in
and for the sacrifice of Jesus Christ offered upon
the Cross for me...[3]

There are many other entries which reveal the same thing: George
Washington was a devout Christian.

There is a very interesting story about Washington, told by David
Barton in a book he entitled *The Bulletproof George Washington.*
Marshall and Manuel also tell the story in their book. Also,
confirmation of it can be found in Bancroft's definitive nineteenth-
century history of the United States. The story goes:

Entering the Virginia militia as a young officer,
Washington distinguished himself in combat
during the French and Indian Wars. One of the
campaigns in which he served included the
Battle of the Monongahela, July 9, 1755. In this
action, the British forces were decimated, and his
commanding officer, General Edward Braddock,
was killed. Fifteen years after this battle,
Washington and his life-long friend Dr. Craik
were exploring wilderness territory in the
Western Reserve. Near the junction of the
Kanawha and Ohio Rivers, a band of Indians
came to them with an interpreter. The leader of
the band was an old and venerable chief, who
wished to have words with Washington. A
council fire was kindled, and this is what the
chief said:

*"I am a chief and ruler over my tribes. My
influence extends to the waters of the great lakes,
and to the far blue mountains. I have traveled a*

*long and weary path, that I might see the young warrior of the great battle. It was on the day when the white man's blood mixed with the streams of our forest, that I first beheld this chief. I called to my young men and said, 'Mark yon tall and daring warrior? He is not of the red-coat tribe—he hath an Indian's wisdom, and his warriors fight as we do—himself alone is exposed. Quick let your aim be certain, and he dies.' Our rifles were leveled, rifles which, but for him, knew not how to miss...Twas all in vain; a power mightier far than we shielded him from harm. He cannot die in battle. (One famous warrior reported firing 17 "fair" shots at Washington without one hit!) I am old, and soon shall be gathered to the great council fire of my fathers in the land of shades, but ere I go, there is something that bids me speak in the voice of prophecy: Listen! The Great Spirit protects that man, and guides his destinies—he will become the chief of nations, and a people yet unborn will hail him as the founder of a mighty empire.*"[4]

This prophecy, in 1770, from the old Native American chief would, of course, prove to be completely accurate. Additionally, the following story was included in American history textbooks until the year 1934:

On July 9, 1776, the Continental Congress authorized the Continental Army to provide chaplains for their troops. General Washington then issued the order and appointed chaplains to every regiment. On that same day, he issued the general order to his troops, stating:

*"The General hopes and trusts that every officer and man, will endeavor so to live, and act, as becomes a Christian Soldier defending the dearest Rights and Liberties of his country."*[5]

In March of 1776, after liberating occupied Boston with the aid of the cannons taken from Fort Ticonderoga, Washington and his aides attended church in order to thank God that the city was taken with little shedding of blood. Also, due to a hasty departure, the British left behind a treasure-trove in munitions and supplies.

While the American army was at Valley Forge, a Quaker by the name of Isaac Potts stumbled upon Washington in the woods, praying. Unnoticed, Potts listened in. Washington was interceding for his beloved country:

> With tones of gratitude that labored for adequate expression he adored that exuberant goodness which, from the depth of obscurity, had exalted him to the head of a great nation, and that nation fighting at fearful odds for all the world holds dear...[6]

Potts returned to his wife and reported the incident to her. He said,

> Till now I have thought that a Christian and a soldier were characters incompatible; but if George Washington be not a man of God, I am mistaken, and still more shall I be disappointed if God does not through him perform some great thing for this country.[7]

In a speech to the Delaware Nation (Native Americans) on May 12, 1779, Washington instructed them that they would "do well to wish to learn our arts and ways of life, and above all, the religion of Jesus Christ. These will make you a greater and happier people than you are."[8]

He charged his soldiers at Valley Forge that, "To the distinguished character of patriot, it should be our highest glory to add the more distinguished character of Christian."[9] The circumstances that led to the discovery of Benedict Arnold's treason were so miraculous that Washington was moved to declare, "The providential train of circumstances which led to it affords the most convincing proof that the Liberties of America are the object of divine Protection."[10]

In his inaugural address to Congress, President Washington said,

> It would be peculiarly improper to omit, in this
> first official act, my fervent supplication to that
> Almighty Being, who rules over the universe,
> who presides in the councils of nations, and
> whose providential aids can supply every human
> defect, that His benediction may consecrate to
> the liberties and happiness of the people of the
> United States…No people can be bound to
> acknowledge and adore the invisible hand which
> conducts the affairs of men more than the people
> of the United States. Every step by which they
> have advanced to the character of an independent
> nation seems to have been distinguished by some
> token of providential agency…We ought to be
> no less persuaded that the propitious smiles of
> Heaven can never be expected on a nation that
> disregards the eternal rules of order and right,
> which Heaven itself has ordained.[11]

On the back of Washington's tomb is engraved the verse from the Book of John, chapter 11: "'I am the Resurrection and the Life'; sayeth the Lord. 'He that believeth in Me, though he were dead yet shall he live. And whosoever liveth and believeth in Me shall never die.'"[12]

Led by General Washington, time and again the rag-tag American forces confronted the world's most elite army and snatched victory from the jaws of defeat. From Trenton to Princeton, Saratoga, Valley Forge, and on and on until Yorktown, American forces defied the odds and the "invisible hand" to which Washington referred was always there.

There were far too many "coincidences" that benefited the Colonial Army—at least for those who experienced or witnessed such events—for things to be written off simply as good fortune. Of course, that is exactly what many modern historians do. Thus for example, most Americans have never heard the "rest of the story" when it comes to the largest battle of the entire Revolutionary War.

The Battle of Long Island, the first major battle after the signing of the Declaration of Independence, was a victory for the British. However, the escape by the Americans was one of the most significant military achievements by the Colonial Army. It is also one of the greatest examples of divine intervention in American history.

Just prior to the American Declaration of Independence, in early June of 1776, the British began sending troop ships down from Canada with the intention of taking New York. The British ships dropped anchor just off Staten Island. Over the period of the next several weeks and months, the British had amassed a force of nearly 32,000 troops on Staten Island.

Washington had a force of about 19,000. However, about half were rag-tag groups of militia from various states. They were poorly equipped, poorly trained, and undisciplined. Moreover, Washington was unsure whether the British would invade at Long Island or Manhattan. Thus, he chose to divide his forces.

Beginning early in the morning on August 22, 1776, thousands of British troops launched from Staten Island and in the matter of a few hours landed on Long Island. Though Colonials were stationed on the shore, the British landing went unopposed. The Colonial forces, consisting of Colonel Edward Hand's Pennsylvanian Riflemen, retreated, and by noon there were about 15,000 Red Coats on the shores of Long Island.

Three days later, the Red Coats were reinforced by nearly 5,000 Hessians. Being misinformed of the British numbers, and thinking that perhaps the Long Island landing by the British was a ruse, Washington left his forces divided between Manhattan and Long

Island. When the fighting on Long Island commenced on August 27, the Colonial forces numbered about 10,000 troops. This was only about half the British and Hessian forces.

The fighting raged throughout the day, and soon the American forces were surrounded or overwhelmed. Two American regiments led by General William Alexander—known as Lord Stirling because of his Scottish ancestry—consisting of the First Delaware and the First Maryland Infantry, became cut off and trapped. Stirling ordered his forces to retreat behind the fortified American position on Brooklyn Heights.

A contingent of several hundred Maryland troops, known today as the Maryland 400 (which may have been only about 250), remained behind to protect the retreat. They battled British forces that were 10 times their number. Led by Lord Stirling and a young major named Mordecai Gist, they fought ferociously and heroically. Several times (maybe as many as six[13]), the Maryland 400 charged the British lines. They held the British off long enough for their comrades to reach safety. All but a handful would be killed or captured. Washington, observing the battle, remarked, "Good God, what brave fellows I must this day lose!"[14]

Surrounded, hopelessly outnumbered, and with the East River behind them, Washington and his army waited for what was surely to be the final British assault that would finish off the trapped Americans. All afternoon of the 27th they waited. Dusk turned to dark and inexplicably the British forces, led by General William Howe, a distinguished and capable commander, defied all military logic and held their ground.

By the morning of the 28th, overcast skies moved in. By the late afternoon rain began to fall. The British were settling in, digging trenches, and hoping for an American surrender. In addition to severely outnumbering the Americans, a significant contingent of the Royal Navy, led by General Howe's brother, Admiral Richard Howe, waited at the mouth of the East river ready to sail in and rain cannon fire upon the trapped colonials.

As J. Myers notes,

> Admiral Howe supported his brother with the
> largest expeditionary force Britain had ever
> dispatched — 10,000 sailors on 30 warships,
> with 1,200 guns and hundreds of supporting
> vessels. "Every thing breathes the Appearance of
> War," wrote the commander of one British
> frigate. "The Number of Transports are
> incredible. I believe there are more than 500 of
> different kinds, besides the King's ships — a
> Force so formidable would make the first Power
> in Europe tremble . . . ."[15]

However, the winds accompanying the storm that moved in kept the British ships safely away. As the night of the 28th came, General Howe continued to wait. All the waiting gave Washington time to develop a plan. It was desperate, and it was not popular among his senior officers. Washington had decided to evacuate his entire force of nearly 9,000 using small boats that he obtained from General William Heath who was stationed between Manhattan and what is now the Bronx.

The task was enormous and fraught with peril. At their current position, the East River was a mile wide. To be successful, the Americans needed stealth, time, deception, and wind to keep the Royal Navy away. In addition to getting the soldiers across, horses and cannons had to be moved as well. By chance—or what many would later deem as divine fortune—the last troops to reinforce Washington's position were Colonel John Glover's "Marvelous Men from Marblehead." This company of 1,200 men was disciplined and well trained. They were also mostly seamen and fishermen, which meant that they were expert oarsmen and quite capable of quietly rowing the necessary distance across the East River.

During the night, the storm moved out, and there was no rain to help drown out the noise of the withdrawal. Silence was ordered, and some forces had to remain in place to keep the British deceived. One unit of such men, led by Colonel Edward Hand, mistakenly received orders to head for the shore. This left a gap in the American line that the British could have easily exploited. However, it went unnoticed by the Red Coats and, catching the error, Washington sent Hand's men back into place.

As dawn was breaking, the evacuation was far from over. Major Ben Tallmadge, who would later become Washington's chief intelligence officer (and who is significantly portrayed in AMC's *Turn*, the TV series detailing what is hailed as "America's first spy ring"), and who was part of the rear guard protecting the retreat, noted,

> As the dawn of the next day approached, those of us who remained in the trenches became very anxious for our own safety, and when the dawn appeared there were several regiments still on duty. At this time a very dense fog began to rise [out of the ground and off the river], and it seemed to settle in a peculiar manner over both encampments. I recollect this peculiar providential occurrence perfectly well, and so very dense was the atmosphere that I could scarcely discern a man at six yards distance...we tarried until the sun had risen, but the fog remained as dense as ever.[16]

The fog remained until the last Colonial left Long Island. It then lifted, and the stunned British rushed to the river and began firing at the fleeing Americans, but it was too late: they were out of range and safely away. Virtually all Colonials who kept a diary of those events noted the fog and, like Tallmadge, gave credit where it was due. Nearly 9,000 Americans were evacuated with no loss of life or limb. According to witnesses, Washington was the last man to leave Brooklyn.[17] The capture of Washington and the large American contingent on Long Island likely would have ended the war. However, "providential aid" prevailed.

The miraculous fog, the dawdling and seemingly blind British, the timely arrival of skilled oarsmen, and a helpful northeast wind that kept British ships out of the East River—these were too many coincidences to give credit to mere chance. Though technically the British were the victors in the Battle of Long Island—when the news reached London there was tremendous celebration—the Americans could not deny that the "invisible hand" of the "Almighty Being" was clearly present on Long Island and had delivered them from what looked like certain defeat.

The battle that ended the Revolution occurred at Yorktown, Virginia. When the British were trapped and, like the Americans on Long Island, attempted to escape across the York River, hurricane-like winds rose up and blew the boats back to the Yorktown banks. After this incident, General Cornwallis, who led the British forces at Yorktown and who would soon after the attempted escape surrender to the Washington-led Americans, protested that it appeared that God was on Washington's side.[18] Thus, in the end, even the British had to acknowledge the "providential aid" given to the United States of America by that "Almighty Being" who "rules over the universe."

Whether in battles, escapes, provisions, the life of the Commander-in-Chief, the aid of the French, and so on, the period of the American Revolutionary War saw God work in amazing ways. The American victory over the British and the formation of the new United States of America were miraculous events that would forever change the world and bring to the earth one of the most powerful forces for truth and justice in the history of humanity.

# CHAPTER 9

# Let Freedom Ring, Part 3: Building the Constitution

Though the war ended, the trouble for the United States was far from over. The 13 colonies in America had existed as a confederation of states since late 1774. The Declaration of Independence united them as never before, and the Second Continental Congress, under the Articles of Confederation, governed the states during the Revolutionary War. For five years— seven until the Treaty of Paris, which officially ended the Revolutionary War, was signed—the Americans fought the British under the limitations of the weak Articles of Confederation.

John Dickinson, who during the debate over the Declaration, had opposed independence, was the author of the original draft of the Articles of Confederation. A significantly watered-down version of Dickinson's draft was accepted by Congress on November 15, 1777. It wasn't until 1781, near the end of the war, that all 13 states signed on to the Articles.

The states were not as "united" as many of us would like to believe, which had an effect on the war with the British. Along with lacking the power to impose a military draft, most significant was the fact that the Articles of Confederation did not provide the Continental Congress with the power to tax. Thus, funding the Revolution was an exercise in tremendous frustration. In fact, the Continental Congress had almost no enforcement power whatsoever, yet miraculously, the Americans held together for the time that it took to defeat the most powerful military force on earth.

With the Continental Congress lacking the power to tax, the Colonial Army relied on the voluntary generosity of the states to supply them. By the fall of 1777, the states had made no payments to Congress. The currency provided by the Continental Congress was first issued in June of 1775. It was paper money and was known as "Continental currency" or simply "Continentals." Paul Revere designed and made some of the early plates for the Continental.[1] The currency bore the inscription "The United Colonies," and was backed by nothing more than the promise of future tax revenues. The Continental existed in addition to the various state currencies that were issued during the Revolution. It was not long before Continentals were worth a fraction of their denoted value.

The weak value of the Continental was the result of several factors. In addition to Congress initially printing too much money, as part of the war effort, the British covertly produced counterfeit Continentals.[2] With a weak currency, inflation was a terrible problem during the Revolution.

As the war raged on, many states continued to shirk their responsibilities to support the Revolution financially. Throughout the war, soldiers not only went unpaid, but they were often poorly supplied—sometimes pitifully so, as in the case of Valley Forge. Rarely were there enough boots, blankets, or bullets. Some men even ended up going naked in the dead of winter. Congress eventually decided to authorize General Washington to confiscate from fellow Americans what he needed to supply his army.

Washington loathed the notion of such action, and he feared the discord that it could possibly sow. After all, Americans were in the midst of attempting to throw off one tyrant; they certainly were not going to be in the mood to surrender to another. However, Washington had no choice. If he and his army had to survive off of the land and the people working the land, so be it.

The future President of the United States was a gentleman and a statesman. If anyone could convince Americans to part with their resources for the sake of the cause, it was General Washington. Washington basically ended up issuing IOU's to those who were raided, or he paid them with near worthless Continentals. Again, miraculously, victory over the British was achieved before the complete collapse of the American army and the American currency.

However, winning a war was one thing; creating a functioning and thriving nation was quite another. It was becoming clear that the U.S. was not going to survive under the Articles of Confederation. After the Declaration of Independence, the United States of America would wait another 11 years (13 years before it would actually go into effect) for the strong charter of liberty called the U.S. Constitution. The Constitution would provide the enduring legal strength necessary for the U.S. to survive and thrive as a republic.

Prior to the Constitutional Convention, the states continued their squabbles. Whatever post-war euphoria existed soon was replaced by deep political and economic woes. In addition to refusing to pay any of the war debt, states began to coin their own money, send their own ambassadors abroad, and sought separate treaties with foreign nations. Many were beginning to wonder seriously if the union was going to hold together. This was so much the case that several foreign nations, including Britain and Spain, were taking steps to take advantage of such a collapse.

There was even talk among the Americans of a looming civil war. Moreover, mutiny began to brew in the military. In addition to Shay's Rebellion, which took place in Massachusetts, just months after Yorktown, one of General Washington's officers, Colonel Lewis Nicola, who was deeply dismayed at the treatment of the military by the states, sent Washington a letter which laid out his case for Washington as king of America. The army would back him, the Colonel assured Washington. It was with "great surprise and astonishment" that Washington read Nicola's letter. The General's reply declared, "Be assured Sir, no occurrence in the course of the War, has given me more painful sensations than your information of there being such ideas existing in the Army as you have expressed, and I must view with abhorrence, and reprehend with severity."[3] No matter how dire the financial and political situation of the young United States of America might be,

Washington wasn't about to undo what the Revolution had accomplished.

For five years after Yorktown, America continued to struggle under the Articles of Confederation. The situation even reached the level of "national humiliation," as Alexander Hamilton put it. In the *Federalist Papers* No. 15, Hamilton wrote of the "insufficiency of the present Confederation to preserve the Union." Hamilton lamented that, "We have neither troops, nor treasury, nor government."[4]

Bemoaning the lack of power to regulate commerce or form treaties, Samuel Adams wrote, "our friends are grieved, and our enemies insult us. Our ambassador at the court of London is considered as a mere cipher, instead of the representative of the United States."[5] Fisher Ames, one of the principal authors of the First Amendment, feared that the U.S. federal government was headed for dissolution. He asked, "Can liberty be safe without government?" He added, "The period of our political dissolution is approaching. Anarchy and uncertainty attend our future state."[6] Speaking of anarchy, a spirit of lawlessness gripped much of the nation. In other words, sin was prospering. Oliver Ellsworth of Connecticut, who helped draft the Constitution, exclaimed, "How have the morals of the people been depraved for the want of an efficient government, which might establish justice and righteousness! For the want of this, iniquity has come in upon us like an overflowing flood."[7]

In November of 1786 Washington wrote to James Madison, "We are fast verging to anarchy and confusion...What stronger evidence can be given of the want of energy in our government than these disorders?...A liberal and energetic constitution, well guarded and closely watched to prevent encroachments might restore us."[8] It was time for a Constitutional Convention.

As early as 1782, Alexander Hamilton got his state of New York to pass a resolution calling for a Constitutional Convention. However, no other state supported such action. When Hamilton was elected to Congress in 1783, he continued his call for a Constitutional Convention, but it fell on deaf ears. After Washington got the ominous letter from Nicola, he sent a letter to every state in the Union, begging them to call a Constitutional Convention. His pleadings went unheeded.

In 1785, Virginia and Maryland met in a conference to resolve their differences over fishing rights in the Potomac River and the Chesapeake Bay. The meetings went well, and both states were pleased with the results, so much so that both agreed to invite other states to a trade conference so that perhaps other issues could be similarly resolved.

The trade conference met at Annapolis in September of 1786. However, only five states were represented. Hamilton and Madison led the initiative to campaign for a Constitutional Convention. Congress was slow to act, but by February of 1787 an invitation was sent to all 13 states. They were invited to send delegates to Philadelphia on May 14 "for the sole and express purpose of revising the Articles of Confederation."

Most delegates were unable to arrive by the May 14 date. By May 25 a quorum of seven states was reached. Eventually every state except Rhode Island—referred to by many as "Rogue Island" because of its obstinate nature of opposition—would have their representative delegates in Philadelphia.

Of the 73 delegates appointed by the states, only 55 actually were able to attend. Since many states would not cover the expenses for their delegates to attend, some delegates simply could not afford the trip or the time away. John Adams and Thomas Jefferson were also unable to attend as they were both serving as American ambassadors in Europe.

However, the young United States was in good hands. As American historian Dr. Samuel Eliot Morison noted,

> Practically every American who had useful ideas on political science was there except John Adams and Thomas Jefferson, on foreign missions, and John Jay, busy with the foreign

relations of the Confederation. Jefferson
contributed indirectly by shipping to Madison
and Wythe from Paris sets of Polybius and other
ancient publicists who discoursed on the theory
of "mixed government" on which the
Constitution was based.[9]

Washington was unanimously elected president of the convention.
Other notable figures present were Alexander Hamilton, Ben
Franklin, Charles Pinckney, Edmund Randolph, Elbridge Gerry,
James Madison, James Wilson, Robert Morris, and Roger
Sherman. The convention began on May 25 and began cordially
enough. However, it soon became clear that the delegates were not
in Philadelphia merely to amend the Articles of Confederation. A
new form of government, unique in the history of the world, was in
the works.

Presented were the Virginia Plan, the New Jersey Plan, and the
Hamilton Plan. The Virginia Plan was put forth first on May 29.
With the Virginia delegates present on May 15 and while waiting
on the delegates from the other states to arrive, Madison drafted
the Virginia Plan. Among other things, it called for two legislative
branches—each with representation determined by state
population, a single executive, and establishment of federal courts.

The Virginia Plan was popular with the larger states (Virginia was
the largest state in the Union at that time) mainly because
representation in both branches of the legislature would be
determined by a state's population. The less populous southern
states were particularly opposed to this. Under the Articles of
Confederation, there was one legislature and each state had one
vote; thus, a small state had just as much voting power as a large
one. The small states wanted to hang on to this power. Smaller
states wanted to abandon the Virginia Plan and return to re-
working the Articles of Confederation. The New Jersey Plan—the
small state answer to the Virginia Plan—was presented on June 15.
Among other things, it recommended a single legislative body—
each state with one vote and multiple executives.

While the Convention was hashing out these two plans, Alexander Hamilton presented his plan which proposed a government very similar to the government in Great Britain. It was abandoned almost as soon as it was presented.

By late June there was still no agreement, and the debate was becoming bitter. Things became so bad that some delegates left the Convention, never to return. According to James Madison's detailed records, on June 28 the senior member of the Convention, Ben Franklin—at 81 years old—arose and gave a speech that helped changed the course of the Convention:

> Mr. President [to George Washington]
>
> The small progress we have made after 4 or five weeks close attendance & continual reasonings with each other—our different sentiments on almost every question, several of the last producing as many noes as ays, is methinks a melancholy proof of the imperfection of the Human Understanding.
>
> We indeed seem to feel our own want of political wisdom, since we have been running about in search of it. We have gone back to ancient history for models of Government, and examined the different forms of those Republics which having been formed with the seeds of their own dissolution now no longer exist. And we have viewed Modern States all round Europe, but find none of their Constitutions suitable to our circumstances.
>
> In this situation of this Assembly, groping as it were in the dark to find political truth, and scarce able to distinguish it when presented to us, how has it happened, Sir, that we have not hitherto once thought of humbly applying to the Father of lights to illuminate our understandings?

In the beginning of the Contest with G. Britain, when we were sensible of danger we had daily prayer in this room for the divine protection.- Our prayers, Sir, were heard, & they were graciously answered. All of us who were engaged in the struggle must have observed frequent instances of a superintending providence in our favor.

To that kind providence we owe this happy opportunity of consulting in peace on the means of establishing our future national felicity. And have we now forgotten that powerful friend? or do we imagine that we no longer need his assistance?

I have lived, Sir, a long time, and the longer I live, the more convincing proofs I see of this truth—that God Governs in the affairs of men. And if a sparrow cannot fall to the ground without his notice, is it probable that an empire can rise without his aid?

We have been assured, Sir, in the sacred writings, that "except the Lord build the House they labour in vain that build it." I firmly believe this; and I also believe that without his concurring aid we shall succeed in this political building no better, than the Builders of Babel: We shall be divided by our little partial local interests; our projects will be confounded, and we ourselves shall become a reproach and bye word down to future ages. And what is worse, mankind may hereafter from this unfortunate instance, despair of establishing Governments by Human wisdom and leave it to chance, war and conquest.

I therefore beg leave to move—that henceforth prayers imploring the assistance of Heaven, and its blessings on our deliberations, be held in this

Assembly every morning before we proceed to
business, and that one or more of the Clergy of
this City be requested to officiate in that
Service.[10]

Franklin's rebuke and call for prayer were powerful and
authoritative. The noted statesmen—a man respected by every
delegate at the Convention—not only acknowledged the miracles
which God had performed in creating the United States of
America, but he called for his fellow statesmen to continue to seek
God's wisdom and favor as a unprecedented form of government
was in the works. Jonathan Dayton, a delegate from New Jersey,
reported the reaction of Congress to Dr. Franklin's speech:

> The Doctor sat down; and never did I behold a
> countenance at once so dignified and delighted
> as was that of Washington at the close of the
> address; nor were the members of the convention
> generally less affected. The words of the
> venerable Franklin fell upon our ears with a
> weight and authority, even greater than we may
> suppose an oracle to have had in a Roman
> senate![11]

Following the address, Roger Sherman seconded the motion that
Franklin's appeal for prayer be enacted. However, because the
Convention had no money to pay for a minister, Franklin's motion
did not pass. However, Edmund Randolph, a delegate from
Virginia, further moved "that a sermon be preached at the request
of the convention on the 4th of July, the anniversary of
Independence; and thenceforward prayers be used in ye
Convention every morning."[12]

As historian David Barton notes,

> As it turns out, after the Convention, and nine
> days after the first Constitutional Congress
> convened with a quorum (April 9, 1789), they
> implemented Franklin's recommendation. Two
> chaplains of different denominations were
> appointed, one to the House and one to the
> Senate, with a salary of $500 each. This practice
> continues today, posing no threat to the First
> Amendment.[13]

It's also interesting to note that, as author Tim LaHaye points out,
Congress has opened both houses with prayer ever since.[14]

Per Randolph's motion, the entire Convention met at the Reformed
Calvinistic Church to hear a sermon from the Rev. William
Rogers. Following this service, a greater spirit of humility and
cooperation was present at the Convention. The delegates returned
to the monumental task of creating a new government.

By July 16, a significant hurdle was overcome. The small states
and the large states reached a compromise over the manner in
which the states would be represented in Congress. The formula
for representation was devised by Roger Sherman of Connecticut,
a plan which has stood the test of time. Congress would consist of
two houses: a Senate where states would have equal representation
and a House of Representatives where representation would be
apportioned according to population.

By late July there was general agreement on the rough form of the
Constitution. In the next several weeks many other important
details were worked out. By early September the final rewrite
began. On Monday, September 17, 1787, the remaining delegates
gathered to sign the final draft. There were still objections—mainly
that the Constitution lacked a Bill of Rights—and thus three
delegates, Elbridge Gerry, George Mason, and Governor Edmund
Randolph, refused to sign. However, 55 delegates, a majority of
each state's delegation, did sign. Nine out of 13 states needed to

ratify the Constitution for it to take effect. Initially, the reaction to this brand new form of government—a "three-headed monstrosity"—was not encouraging. Most had expected simple changes to the Articles of Confederation. Also, the fact that the esteemed George Mason, along with Elbridge Gerry and Virginia Governor Edmund Randolph refused to sign the Constitution troubled many people.

Such apprehension was unsurprising to most of the Constitutional delegates. After all, the Constitution was years in the making. To quickly have the necessary support of nine states was unlikely and unreasonable. The debates within the state legislatures was vigorous. Studious attention was given to every detail within the groundbreaking document.

In order to make sure that the Constitution was properly understood and to expedite the ratification process, over the next year, under the pseudonym "Publius," James Madison, Alexander Hamilton, and John Jay set about writing the Federalist Papers. Published as a series of 85 newspaper articles, virtually every phrase of the Constitution was addressed.

On December 6, 1787, by unanimous consent, Delaware became the first state to ratify the new Constitution. New Jersey and Georgia soon followed, also by unanimous consent. On December 12, 1787, by a vote of 46 to 23, Pennsylvania approved the Constitution. In 1788, Connecticut, Massachusetts (by a close 187 to 168 vote), Maryland, and South Carolina made it eight states. New Hampshire was the state that put the Constitution into effect.

Christian ministers played no small role in the matter. Samuel Langdon was a distinguished theologian and scholar. He graduated from Harvard in 1740, went on to become a prominent Congregational minister, and was president of Harvard University from 1774 to 1780. He was also a delegate to the New Hampshire convention that ratified (by the slim margin of 57 to 46) the U.S. Constitution in 1788. New Hampshire was the last of the necessary nine states needed to ratify the Constitution. In order to persuade his fellow delegates to vote in favor of the U.S. Constitution,

Langdon delivered an "election sermon" entitled, *The Republic of the Israelites an Example to the American States.*

After beginning by quoting Deuteronomy 4:5-8 in his sermon, Langdon noted,

> [T]he Israelites may be considered as a pattern to the world in all ages; and from them we may learn what will exalt our character, and what will depress and bring us to ruin. Let us therefore look over their constitution and laws, enquire into their practice, and observe how their prosperity and fame depended on their strict observance of the divine commands both as to their government and religion.[15]

Langdon then gave an account of how Moses, upon the wise counsel of his father-in-law Jethro, "the priest of Midian," set up a republican form of government, with representatives ("leaders," "rulers," "judges," depending on the biblical translation) from groups of thousands, hundreds, fifties, and tens. In addition, 70 elders, or wise-men—a type of national Senate as described by biblical and Jewish scholars—were selected by Moses and approved by the consent of the people.

Langdon added,

> A government thus settled on republican principles, required laws; without which it must have degenerated immediately into aristocracy, or absolute monarchy. But God did not leave a people, wholly unskilled in legislation, to make laws for themselves: he took this important matter wholly into His own hands, and beside the moral laws of the two tables, which directed their conduct as individuals, gave them by Moses a complete code of judicial laws.[16]

Langdon goes on to describe how this republican form of government helped the nation of Israel grow from a "mere mob" (if only the eighteenth century French had taken notice) to a "well regulated nation, under a government and laws far superior to what any other nation could boast!" After detailing Israel's later struggles—they would eventually "[neglect] their government, [corrupt] their religion, and [grow] dissolute in their morals"—Langston exhorted his fellow citizens to learn from the nation of Israel.

That as God in the course of his kind providence hath given you an excellent constitution of government, founded on the most rational, equitable, and liberal principles, by which all that liberty is secured which a people can reasonably claim, and you are empowered to make righteous laws for promoting public order and good morals; and as he has moreover given you by his son Jesus Christ, who is far superior to Moses, a complete revelation of his will, and a perfect system of true religion, plainly delivered in the sacred writings; it will be your wisdom in the eyes of the nations, and your true interest and happiness, to conform your practice in the strictest manner to the excellent principles of your government, adhere faithfully to the doctrines and commands of the gospel, and practice every public and private virtue. By this you will increase in numbers, wealth, and power, and obtain reputation and dignity among the nations: whereas, the contrary conduct will make you poor, distressed, and contemptible.[17]

On September 21, 1788 the Constitution and the new government of the United States went into effect. Just over three years later, the Bill of Rights would be added. By 1790, when Rhode Island, by a vote of 34 to 32, joined the Union, it was unanimous.

On July 4, 1837, in a speech delivered in the town of Newburyport, Massachusetts, John Quincy Adams, son of John Adams, and the sixth U.S. President, proclaimed,

> Why is it that, next to the birthday of the Savior of the World, your most joyous and most venerated festival returns on this day? Is it not that, in the chain of human events, the birthday of the nation is indissolubly linked with the birthday of the Savior? Is it not that the Declaration of Independence first organized the social compact on the foundation of the Redeemer's mission upon earth?[18]

Witnessing the events of the Revolution as a boy, and no-doubt hearing from his father of the raucous debates that gave us the Constitution and the Bill of Rights, and then going on to serve his country in many various capacities, John Quincy Adams saw that Christmas and Independence Day were fundamentally linked. He understood well that the Founders took the principles that Christ brought to the world and incorporated them into civil government. This is what makes the U.S. government so distinctive, why it has been so durable, and why, to this day, we are the greatest nation the world has ever known.

# CHAPTER 10

# America Confronts the Sin of Slavery, Part 1: A Nation Divided

From 1790 until the dawn of the U.S. Civil War, America would experience amazing growth. The powerful and innovative industrialization of America that took place during this period would cause the world to look on with amazement. (This astonishing period of American history will be addressed in later chapters.) As the new United States of America was on the rise to unprecedented heights among the nations of the world, a dire wickedness would nearly tear her apart. In the history of our nation, the greatest challenge to the United States as we know her today was the institution of slavery.

Slavery was hotly debated from before the founding of the United States. According to David Barton, "prior to the American Revolution some of the Colonies had voted to end slavery in their State, but those State laws had been struck down by the King."[1] The vast majority of Colonial and Revolutionary Americans, including the political leadership, did not own slaves. Having achieved independence from Great Britain in the name of freedom and liberty, many who did own slaves set them free after the Revolutionary War.

Many Founding Fathers were ardent opponents of the American slave trade. Thomas Jefferson's original draft of the Declaration of Independence contained a strong repudiation of slavery and included King George's continuation of the slave trade as one of the justifications for American Independence. It read,

> He [King George III] has waged cruel war
> against human nature itself, violating its most
> sacred rights of life and liberty in the persons of
> a distant people who never offended him,
> captivating and carrying them into slavery in
> another hemisphere. . . . Determined to keep
> open a market where MEN should be bought and
> sold, he has prostituted his negative for
> suppressing every legislative attempt to prohibit
> or restrain this execrable commerce.[2]

In 1773, Ben Franklin wrote,

> A disposition to abolish slavery prevails in North
> America, that many of Pennsylvanians have set
> their slaves at liberty, and that even the Virginia
> Assembly have petitioned the King for
> permission to make a law for preventing the
> importation of more into that colony. This
> request, however, will probably not be granted as
> their former laws of that kind have always been
> repealed...[3]

Benjamin Rush, the "Father of American Medicine," signed the
Declaration of Independence, attended the Continental Congress,
and served as the Surgeon General of the Continental Army. In
1794, speaking to a convention of delegates from the Abolition
Societies in Philadelphia, Rush said,

> Domestic slavery is repugnant to the principles
> of Christianity...It is rebellion against the
> authority of a common Father. It is a practical
> denial of the extent and efficacy of the death of a
> common Savior. It is an usurpation of the
> prerogative of the great Sovereign of the
> universe who has solemnly claimed an exclusive
> property in the souls of men.[4]

Acting to abolish slavery, Rush and Franklin started the first anti-slavery society in America. John Jay was also president of such a society. In 1793, Noah Webster published *Effects of Slavery on Morals and Industry*. In it he wrote, "Justice and humanity require it (the end of slavery)—Christianity commands it. Let every benevolent... pray for the glorious period when the last slave who fights for freedom shall be restored to the possession of that inestimable right."[5]

More than any other single issue, slavery was the cause of the U.S. Civil War. Though most Southerners did not own slaves (about one-fifth lived in households who owned slaves), according to noted historian Sidney Ahlstrom, "Had there been no slavery, there would have been no war. Had there been no moral condemnation of slavery, there would have been no war."[6]

Historian David Barton notes that it is revisionist history to conclude that the South did not go to war over slavery. He concludes that, "the South's desire to preserve slavery was indisputably **the** driving reason for the formation of the Confederacy."[7]

After Lincoln's divisive election in November of 1860, the southern states began meeting individually in their respective state conventions in order to decide whether to secede from the Union. On December 20, 1860, South Carolina became the first state to make the decision to leave the United States of America. Throughout its secession document, South Carolina's leaders repeatedly declared that they were leaving the U.S. in order to preserve the institution of slavery.

> [A]n increasing hostility on the part of the non-slaveholding [i.e., northern] states to the institution of slavery has led to a disregard of their obligations. . . . [T]hey have denounced as sinful the institution of slavery. . . . They have encouraged and assisted thousands of our slaves to leave their homes [through the Underground Railroad]. . . . A geographical line has been

drawn across the Union, and all the states north
of that line have united in the election of a man
to the high office of President of the United
States [Abraham Lincoln] whose opinions and
purposes are hostile to slavery. He is to be
entrusted with the administration of the common
government because he has declared that
"Government cannot endure permanently half
slave, half free," and that the public mind must
rest in the belief that slavery is in the course of
ultimate extinction. . . . The slaveholding states
will no longer have the power of self-
government or self-protection [over the issue of
slavery]...[8]

The second state to secede was Mississippi. On January 9, 1861,
Mississippi announced,

Our position is thoroughly identified with the
institution of slavery – the greatest material
interest of the world. . . . [A] blow at slavery is a
blow at commerce and civilization. That blow
has been long aimed at the institution and was at
the point of reaching its consummation. There
was no choice left us but submission to the
mandates of abolition or a dissolution of the
Union, whose principles had been subverted to
work out our ruin. That we do not overstate the
dangers to our institution [slavery], a reference to
a few facts will sufficiently prove. The hostility
to this institution commenced before the
adoption of the Constitution and was manifested
in the well-known Ordinance of 1787.[9]

Barton also notes that,

> On July 13, 1787, when the nation still governed itself under the Articles of Confederation, the Continental Congress passed the Northwest Ordinance (which Mississippi here calls the 'well-known Ordinance of 1787'). That Ordinance set forth provisions whereby the Northwest Territory could become states in the United States, and eventually the states of Ohio, Indiana, Illinois, Michigan, Wisconsin, and Minnesota were formed from that Territory. As a requirement for statehood and entry into the United States, Article 6 of that Ordinance stipulated: 'There shall be neither slavery nor involuntary servitude in the said territory.' When the Constitution replaced the Articles of Confederation, the Founding Fathers re-passed the 'Northwest Ordinance' to ensure its continued effectiveness under the new Constitution. Signed into law by President George Washington on August 7, 1789, it retained the prohibition against slavery. As more territory was gradually ceded to the United States (the Southern Territory – Mississippi and Alabama; the Missouri Territory – Missouri and Arkansas; etc.), Congress applied the requirements of the Ordinance to those new territories. Mississippi had originally entered the United States under the requirement that it not allow slavery, and it is here objecting not only to that requirement of its own admission to the United States but also to that requirement for the admission of other states.[10]

Mississippi continued:

> It has grown until it denies the right of property
> in slaves and refuses protection to that right on
> the high seas [Congress banned the importation
> of slaves into America in 1808], in the territories
> [in the Northwest Ordinance of 1789, the
> Missouri Compromise of 1820, the Compromise
> of 1850, and the Kansas-Nebraska Act of 1854],
> and wherever the government of the United
> States had jurisdiction. . . . It advocates Negro
> equality, socially and politically. . . . We must
> either submit to degradation and to the loss of
> property [i.e., slaves] worth four billions of
> money, or we must secede from the Union
> framed by our fathers to secure this as well as
> every other species of property.[11]

Florida and Alabama were the third and fourth states to secede.
Both cited slavery as a reason. Alabama's secession document
read:

> ...the election of Abraham Lincoln and Hannibal
> Hamlin to the offices of President and Vice-
> President of the United States of America by a
> sectional party [the Republican Party], avowedly
> hostile to the domestic institutions [slavery] and
> to the peace and security of the people of the
> State of Alabama...[12]

With the election of Lincoln in 1860, the Republicans controlled
the U.S. House, Senate, and the presidency. As the fifth state to
secede, Georgia also cited the election of Lincoln and the
Republicans:

> A brief history of the rise, progress, and policy
> of anti-slavery and the political organization into

whose hands the administration of the federal
government has been committed [the
republicans] will fully justify the pronounced
verdict of the people of Georgia [who voted to
secede]. The party of Lincoln, called the
Republican Party under its present name and
organization, is of recent origin. It is admitted to
be an anti-slavery party. . . . The prohibition of
slavery in the territories, hostility to it
everywhere, the equality of the black and white
races, disregard of all constitutional guarantees
in its favor, were boldly proclaimed by its
leaders and applauded by its followers. . . . [T]he
abolitionists and their allies in the northern states
have been engaged in constant efforts to subvert
our institutions.[13]

The Confederate States of America was formed at the Montgomery
Convention in February of 1861. For the southern states—and
anyone else in the world paying attention—the agenda of the
newly formed (and electorally victorious) Republican Party agenda
was clear. Every party platform since the creation of the
Republican Party had forcefully denounced slavery. After the
infamous Dred Scott ruling by the U.S. Supreme Court in 1857, the
subsequent Republican platform strongly condemned the ruling
and reaffirmed the right of Congress to ban slavery in the
territories. Tellingly, the corresponding Democrat platform praised
the Dred Scott ruling and condemned all efforts to end slavery in
the U.S.

The Republican Party platform of 1856 read,

That, with our Republican fathers, we hold it to
be a self-evident truth, that all men are endowed
with the inalienable right to life, liberty, and the
pursuit of happiness, and that the primary object
and ulterior design of our Federal Government
were to secure these rights to all persons under
its exclusive jurisdiction; that, as our Republican

fathers, when they had abolished Slavery in all our National Territory, ordained that no person shall be deprived of life, liberty, or property, without due process of law, it becomes our duty to maintain this provision of the Constitution against all attempts to violate it for the purpose of establishing Slavery in the Territories of the United States by positive legislation, prohibiting its existence or extension therein. That we deny the authority of Congress, of a Territorial Legislation, of any individual, or association of individuals, to give legal existence to Slavery in any Territory of the United States, while the present Constitution shall be maintained.[14]

The Republican Party platform of 1860 included:

7. That the new dogma that the Constitution, of its own force, carries slavery into any or all of the territories of the United States, is a dangerous political heresy, at variance with the explicit provisions of that instrument itself, with contemporaneous exposition, and with legislative and judicial precedent; is revolutionary in its tendency, and subversive of the peace and harmony of the country.

8. That the normal condition of all the territory of the United States is that of freedom: That, as our Republican fathers, when they had abolished slavery in all our national territory, ordained that "no persons should be deprived of life, liberty or property without due process of law," it becomes our duty, by legislation, whenever such legislation is necessary, to maintain this provision of the Constitution against all attempts to violate it; and we deny the authority of Congress, of a territorial legislature, or of any

individuals, to give legal existence to slavery in any territory of the United States.

9. That we brand the recent reopening of the African slave trade, under the cover of our national flag, aided by perversions of judicial power, as a crime against humanity and a burning shame to our country and age; and we call upon Congress to take prompt and efficient measures for the total and final suppression of that execrable traffic...[15]

The 1864 platform read:

3. Resolved, That as slavery was the cause, and now constitutes the strength of this Rebellion, and as it must be, always and everywhere, hostile to the principles of Republican Government, justice and the National safety demand its utter and complete extirpation from the soil of the Republic; and that, while we uphold and maintain the acts and proclamations by which the Government, in its own defense, has aimed a deathblow at this gigantic evil, we are in favor, furthermore, of such an amendment to the Constitution, to be made by the people in conformity with its provisions, as shall terminate and forever prohibit the existence of Slavery within the limits of the jurisdiction of the United States.

5. Resolved, That we approve and applaud the practical wisdom, the unselfish patriotism and the unswerving fidelity to the Constitution and the principles of American liberty, with which ABRAHAM LINCOLN has discharged, under circumstances of unparalleled difficulty, the great duties and responsibilities of the Presidential office; that we approve and indorse,

as demanded by the emergency and essential to the preservation of the nation and as within the provisions of the Constitution, the measures and acts which he has adopted to defend the nation against its open and secret foes; that we approve, especially, the Proclamation of Emancipation, and the employment as Union soldiers of men heretofore held in slavery; and that we have full confidence in his determination to carry these and all other Constitutional measures essential to the salvation of the country into full and complete effect.[16]

However, the abolition movement in the United States did not have its roots in the Republican Party. As was the case with the "Black Robed Regiment" and the American Revolution, it was the Christian clergy in America who lit the moral fire beneath the abolition movement in the U.S.

Colonel Granville Moody, "the fighting Methodist parson," said, "We [abolitionist preachers] are charged with having brought about the present crisis. I believe it is true that we did bring it about, and I glory in it, for it is a wreath of glory around our brow."[17]

Writing on how "Christians ended slavery," Dinesh D'Souza notes,

The anti-slavery movements led by [William] Wilberforce in England and abolitionists in America were dominated by Christians. These believers reasoned that since we are all created equal in the eyes of God, no one has the right to rule another without consent. This is the moral basis not only of anti-slavery but also of democracy.[18]

Author and historian David Goldfield ties slavery to western expansion as a significant factor in the U.S. Civil War. Goldfield says,

> The Westward Movement certainly was an important part of it because evangelicals believed that we were a God blessed nation. We were unique in the world in spreading the Gospel not only of Jesus Christ but also the gospel of democracy across the land ordained to conquer a continent from sea to shining sea. We were in effect the new Israel; that is we were God's chosen people for this particular task. Northern evangelicals believed that in order to achieve this great effort of fulfilling God's prophecy that the nation had to rid itself of its sin.[19]

One of the early leaders in the American abolition movement was the Quaker John Woolman. In 1754 he published *Some Considerations on the Keeping of Negroes*. Woolman presented it at a Quaker convention in Philadelphia. It began with Matthew 25:40: "The King will reply, 'I tell you the truth, whatever you did for one of the least of these brothers of mine, you did for me.'" It concluded that slavery was "neither consistent with Christianity nor common justice." Quaker abolitionists began to purchase the freedom of slaves. Other Christian organizations and denominations were inspired, and the abolition movement began to spread.

In 1833 William Lloyd Garrison formed the American Anti-Slavery Society (AASS). Garrison authored the "Declaration of Sentiments" for the group. It read:

> More than fifty-seven years have elapsed, since a band of patriots convened in this place, to devise measures for the deliverance of this country from a foreign yoke. The corner-stone upon which they founded the Temple of Freedom was broadly this—"that all men are created equal;

that they are endowed by their Creator with certain inalienable rights; that among these are life, LIBERTY, and the pursuit of happiness." At the sound of their trumpet-call, three millions of people rose up as from the sleep of death, and rushed to the strife of blood; deeming it more glorious to die instantly as freemen, than desirable to live one hour as slaves. They were few in number—poor in resources; but the honest conviction that Truth, Justice and Right were on their side, made them invincible...

Their measures were physical resistance—the marshalling in arms—the hostile array—the mortal encounter. Ours shall be such only as the opposition of moral purity to moral corruption—the destruction of error by the potency of truth—the overthrow of prejudice by the power of love—and the abolition of slavery by the spirit of repentance...

We further maintain—that no man has a right to enslave or imbrute his brother—to hold or acknowledge him, for one moment, as a piece of merchandise—to keep back his hire by fraud—or to brutalize his mind, by denying him the means of intellectual, social and moral improvement...

The right to enjoy liberty is inalienable. To invade it is to usurp the prerogative of Jehovah. Every man has a right to his own body—to the products of his own labor—to the protection of law—and to the common advantages of society. It is piracy to buy or steal a native African, and subject him to servitude. Surely, the sin is as great to enslave an American as an African.

Therefore we believe and affirm—that there is no difference, in principle, between the African slave trade and American slavery:

That every American citizen, who detains a
human being in involuntary bondage as his
property, is, according to Scripture, (Ex. xxi. 16,)
a man-stealer:

That the slaves ought instantly to be set free, and
brought under the protection of law...[20]

Rodney Stark, Distinguished Professor of the Social Sciences at
Baylor University, who has authored over 30 books, including *The
Rise of Christianity* (1996), states that Christian clergymen were
the "vital spine" of AASS, and its statements and declarations
"rang high of scripture." By 1840, AASS had nearly 200,000
members. Garrison's call to abolish slavery paralleled the struggle
of the Colonists to throw off the bondage of English oppression.
Like the clergy of the middle of the eighteenth century who were
calling for a revolution, Garrison invoked God as the giver of life
and liberty, and thus it was an affront to the eternal truths of our
Creator to enslave another human being.

However, Garrison would change his views on the authority of
Scripture. In 1845 he "paid homage in the *Liberator* to Thomas
Paine for providing him with intellectual resources for getting
beyond the Bible."[21] While Garrison never achieved Paine's level
of skepticism when it came to Scripture, he no longer viewed the
Bible as the inerrant and irrefutable Word of God. Garrison wrote,
"To say that everything contained within the lids of the bible is
divinely inspired, and to insist upon the dogma as fundamentally
important, is to give utterance to a bold fiction and to require the
suspension of the reasoning faculties."[22]

Garrison's willingness to abandon Scripture worked to the
advantage of those who would use the Bible as a defense of the
institution of slavery in America. It also made it more difficult for
those who were using the Bible to identify slavery for the terrible
sin that it was (and is). (We see the same things going on today in
the debate over sexual sins—abortion, adultery, fornication,
homosexuality, pornography, human trafficking, transgenderism,
and the like—raging in modern America.)

Also, many Christian abolitionists who longed to nail the institution of slavery to the cross were determined to do so by reasoning strictly from the Scriptures, using the Bible as their only authoritative source. Although not to the extent of Garrison, and because of the arguments in support of slavery—in many cases very well-reasoned—that relied heavily on what the Bible said, some abolitionists had taken to extra-biblical arguments in order to attempt to end slavery in America.

Such reasoning greatly troubled men like Connecticut Congregationalist Leonard Woolsey Bacon, who desperately wanted to oppose slavery as a sin.

> In Bacon's view, the well-intentioned souls who [torture the Scriptures into saying that which the anti-slavery theory requires them to say] did great damage to the Scriptures themselves. To Bacon and many others who were tempted to move from the Bible's [letter] of sanction for slavery to its [spirit] of universal liberation, the facts of American experience may have been the great stumbling block. Precisely by following the Bible strictly, by tending to its [letter] when heretics of various kinds were running after its [spirit,] the churches had prospered, and the balm of the gospel had reached unprecedented numbers of spiritually needy men and women.[23]

Nevertheless, the tactic of combining the republican principles as laid out in the U.S. Constitution (all men are created equal, with certain inalienable rights to life, liberty, property, and the pursuit of happiness) with the broad spiritual message of the Bible (love God, and love your neighbor as yourself), became a common refrain among American abolitionists.

We see this as early as 1776, when Samuel Hopkins, a Congregationalist theologian from Newport, Rhode Island, and a student and close friend of Jonathan Edwards, published the groundbreaking pamphlet *A Dialogue Concerning the Slavery of the Africans.* Hopkins was one of the first Congregationalists to denounce slavery openly. His efforts helped lead to a 1774 law that banned the importation of slaves into Rhode Island. He also started a school for Negro missionaries to Africa.

By the turn of the nineteenth century, frustrated that the independent United States had yet to halt slavery, "Hopkins returned to the subject. This time he insisted, with a combination of republican and Christian language, that [tyranny and slavery] were [evils] that [the gospel] thoroughly opposed."[24]

Similarly, in 1816, George Bourne published *The Book and Slavery Irreconcilable*, which "dealt at length with individual texts of Scripture, even as it leaned even harder on what Bourne obviously considered the humanitarian agreement of biblical and republican principles."[25] Bourne considered slavery a sin and questioned whether those who owned slaves should be considered Christians.

He wrote,

> Every man who holds Slaves and who pretends to be a Christian or a Republican, is either an incurable Idiot who cannot distinguish good from evil, or an obdurate sinner who resolutely defies every social, moral, and divine requisition.... Every ramification of the doctrine, *that one rational creature can become the property of another*, is totally repugnant to the rule of equity, the rights of nature, and the existence of civil society.[26]

Jonathan Blanchard, a Presbyterian minister in Ohio and a member of Theodore Dwight Weld's "Seventy"—famous trained "agents" who preached abolition across the U.S. (Don't we need such in the marriage debate!)—helped publish the abolition newspaper *The Philanthropist* and in 1843 represented Ohio at the World Anti-Slavery Convention.

In 1845, for eight hours a day over a four day period, Blanchard debated the "moderate emancipationist," Nathanial Rice, who advocated that, although the Bible didn't explicitly forbid slavery, the South should nonetheless voluntarily abandon it. Early in the debate, mingling Scripture with American principles of republicanism, Blanchard exclaimed,

> Abolitionists take their stand upon the New Testament doctrine of the natural equity of man. The one-bloodism of human kind [from Acts 17:26]:—and upon those great principles of human rights, drawn from the New Testament, and announced in the American Declaration of Independence, declaring that all men have natural and *inalienable* rights to person, property and the pursuit of happiness.[27]

Theodore Dwight Weld, whose father and grandfather were Congregational ministers, as a young man witnessed slavery firsthand. He studied at Hamilton College (later Colgate University) where he became a disciple of Charles Finney. By the mid-1830s Weld was an enthusiastic abolitionist, becoming a member of Garrison's American Anti-Slavery Society, and became a leader in the movement. He converted famous abolitionists Henry Ward Beecher and Harriet Beecher Stowe.

Weld would split with Garrison and help form the American and Foreign Anti-Slavery Society. He would also become politically active with the anti-slavery Liberty Party, a forerunner of the Republican Party. In 1838, Weld published *The Bible Against Slavery*. In 1839, along with his wife, Angela Grimké, and his wife's sister, Sarah Grimké, Weld published the extremely influential *American Slavery As It Is: Testimony of a Thousand Witnesses*. After *Uncle Tom's Cabin*, this work is widely considered to be the second most influential piece of anti-slavery literature of its time.

# CHAPTER 11

# America Confronts the Sin of Slavery, Part 2: Dueling Sermons

In addition to the abolition efforts that combined the message of the Bible with the American ideal of liberty, there were also successful and influential abolitionists who used nothing but biblical arguments. Many pulpits stuck to the notion that opposition to slavery was not merely a political issue, but a moral one. The Second Great Awakening helped give rise to such preaching.

After the First Great Awakening waned, there occurred a discouraging rise of religious groups—Unitarians, Universalists, Deists, et al—that denied the basic tenets of Christianity. According to the Christian History Institute, "These 'infidels' caused a widespread drift from the settled religious customs and practices in New England and throughout the colonies after 1750."[1]

In 1789, not even a year after the U.S. Constitution went into effect, the bloody French Revolution began. Initially, for the most part, Americans approved. However, soon word of widespread murder, mayhem, and lawlessness revealed that the revolution in France little resembled what occurred in America. It was not long before the clergy in America saw the connection between the French Revolution and deism.

In 1793, writing for the French, Thomas Paine, who aided in the American Revolution, wrote his notorious *The Age of Reason*. Paine's book was pure deism and ridiculed religion, especially

Christianity. On the Bible, Paine wrote, "…It would be more consistent that we called it the word of a demon than the word of God."[2] Unfortunately, *The Age of Reason* was a best-seller in America, and it sparked a bit of a deistic "revival." Such a turn from the truth drew the attention of many people who were desperate for another "awakening" of the Spirit of God.

In the early to mid-1800s, as the U.S. population soared from five million to 30 million, revival meetings became one of the primary means by which Christianity was spread. On the American frontier, these revivals were known as "camp meetings."

According to Christianity.com,

> The first camp meeting revival was in south central Kentucky. At a meeting in June, 1800, Presbyterian James McGready and two other pastors preached for 3 days; on the fourth day, two traveling Methodist ministers officiated and concluded with an emotional exhortation. Many physically collapsed at what they called conviction of sin. People were convinced they were experiencing a visitation of the Holy Spirit such as the early church had known at Pentecost.[3]

Led by Barton W. Stone, the most famous camp meeting of that time was held in Cane Ridge, Kentucky, in August of 1801. The meeting lasted over a week and was attended by more than 20,000 people. The revival was characterized by strong emotional responses by those who were "saved" (surrendered to Christ). Some fell to the ground ("slain in the spirit"), others shook, seemingly out-of-control, there was also "dancing, running, and singing." These revivals spread throughout Kentucky and into Tennessee, the rest of the South, and eventually all over the U.S.

Charles Finney, the "Father of Revivalism" in America, was a leader in the Second Great Awakening. Finney was a passionate evangelist who, along with a desire to see people surrender to

Christ, wanted to see broad social change in America's culture. Finney had a vision for a "Christian America," which he regularly promoted. He desired a nation that was "ruled by the moral government of God."[4] Contemporary Christians would do well to look to the words and the tactics of Finney and his spiritual cohorts as we battle the evils (abortion, homosexuality, promiscuity, same-sex "marriage," and the like) that plague modern American culture.

The Benevolent Empire—a missionary movement organized by Finney and other protestant leaders that was devoted to "Christianizing America"—became an instrument by which Finney, and others who shared his vision, hoped to attack America's social problems. There were dozens of volunteer organizations in the Benevolent Empire. The most important were the "Great Eight" benevolent societies. Among this group was the *American Bible Society*, founded in 1816; the *American Board of Commissioners for Foreign Missions*, founded in 1810; the *American Sunday School Union*, founded in 1817; the *American Tract Society*, founded in 1826; the *American Temperance Society*, founded in 1826; and the *Americans Home Missionary Society*, founded in 1826.[5]

In addition to his temperance, anti-tobacco, anti-prostitution efforts, Finney was well-known as an ardent anti-slavery agitator. Finney's revivals were very important to the abolition movement. In fact, in 1933, Gilbert Barnes in his book *The Anti-Slavery Impulse: 1830-1844*, concluded that, to a significant extent, the origin for the abolition movement in the U.S. lay in the revivals of Charles Finney. In his preface, Barnes writes that "a different and incomparably more significant tale of a religious impulse which began in the West of 1830, was translated for a time into antislavery organization, and then broadened into a sectional crusade against the South."[6]

Barnes also makes the case that it was no mere coincidence that the abolition movement in the U.S. was in conjunction with the "Great Revival." He concludes that, "In leadership, in method, and in objective, the Great Revival and the American Anti-Slavery Society now were one."[7]

129

To end slavery, or any of the other sins that infected the American culture—alcoholism, prostitution, greed, apathy, and the like—Finney always emphasized revival. He believed—quite correctly—that true repentance and salvation were the cure for all that ails us. However, by the 1830s he began to take serious specific steps to combat slavery. "On November 3, 1834, Finney and his congregation voted to ban slaveholders and slave traders from communion in the congregation. He was one of the first to take such an action, believing that such a stance would help to bring about slavery's downfall."[8]

In 1835, Finney took a position as a professor at Oberlin College. He served as president of Oberlin from 1851 to 1866. In quite a contrast to the perversions (full embrace of the homosexual agenda, and the like) that so corrupt Oberlin College today, during his tenure as president, Finney regularly challenged his students to make revivalism their first priority.

Theodore Dwight Weld was probably Finney's most notable convert. Weld's work, *American Slavery As It Is: Testimony of a Thousand Witnesses*—again, widely considered to be the second most significant piece of abolition literature—gave rise to the most influential document in the American abolition movement: Harriet Beecher Stowe's book, *Uncle Tom's Cabin*.

*Uncle Tom's Cabin* was the best-selling novel of the nineteenth century and was second only to the Bible as the best-selling book overall. The notion of the Bible's opposition to slavery was a theme that ran throughout Stowe's book. Stowe was a dedicated Christian, who, when she was fourteen years old and struggling with her faith, "cried out to her father that she had given herself to Christ."[9]

Though *Uncle Tom's Cabin* is a piece of fiction, parts of the book are based on actual accounts of desperate fugitive slaves. The book was moving and vivid and became a worldwide sensation. Tellingly, it was banned in the South. (Ironically, today we see similar efforts toward censorship from the modern homosexual agenda as it seeks to redefine marriage, proper sexuality, and family throughout America.)

In the biblical debate over slavery, Stowe's *Uncle Tom's Cabin* possessed significant emotional power. "More effectively than debaters like Jonathan Blanchard or Francis Wayland, Stowe exemplified rather than just announced the persuasive force of what she regarded as the Bible's overarching general message."[10] Reportedly, when President Abraham Lincoln met Stowe during the Civil War he said to her, "So you're the little woman who [started] this big war."[11]

Many other American pastors took Finney's approach to Scripture and slavery. In spite of the fact that slavery was still legal, in their repudiation of this wicked institution, hundreds of Northern preachers began to appeal to higher law. For example, in a sermon entitled "The Limits of Civil Disobedience," Nathaniel Hall, a Congregationalist from Dorchester, Massachusetts, proclaimed that "we are bound to obey the requisitions of human law, except where they conflict with the law of God, as made known in our souls and in His Word."[12]

Representative of the sermons preached in the North during this time were two sermons delivered by the Reverend Elijah Porter Barrows. Barrows was a graduate of Yale and was pastor at the First Free Presbyterian Church in New York City. After accepting his appointment as pastor, like so many other pastors—North and South—Barrows soon found out that his congregation was divided on the issue of slavery.

> Two sermons were prepared and delivered to this congregation for the purpose of bringing about a unified opposition to slavery. After carefully defining slavery, Barrows presented his arguments as to why slavery was a violation of love, was unjust and evil, and did great moral and mental harm to both slaves and masters. Opposing violence, he asked for a peaceful abolition of slavery. Then he presented a biblical basis for his antislavery position, saying that abolitionism was based upon broad biblical

principles rather than specific texts. Barrows was
aware that defenders of slavery often appealed to
specific biblical texts.[13]

Similarly,

> In July of 1834 James Taylor Dickinson from
> Connecticut delivered a sermon in which he
> supported the abolitionist position with many
> references from the Scriptures. Guilt for the sin
> of slavery, he emphasized, must be shared by the
> entire nation which had permitted the
> perpetuation of the institution. Non-slaveholding
> Christians had a duty to warn slaveholders of
> God's certain judgment and punishment if
> slavery persisted. Laws protecting slavery should
> be nullified by obedience to the higher law of
> God.[14]

If only such sermons were prevalent in today's churches as we
debate the moral issues of our time!

Because of the danger of slavery expanding into western territories
of the U.S., anti-slavery sermons became more impassioned and
grew in frequency. Some pastors also passionately spoke out
against the Mexican-American War that took place from 1846 to
1848 because they saw the conflict as a means to spread slavery.
The Mexican-American War had popular support among the
American public in general, and pastors who preached against it
were sometimes labeled "unpatriotic." President Polk himself
resorted to such rhetoric.

By the time the 1850s arrived, Americans were deeply divided
over slavery. Several actions of the 1850s hastened the U.S. toward
civil war: The Fugitive Slave Law, the Kansas-Nebraska Act
(which essentially reversed the Missouri Compromise of 1820 and
also paved the way for the Transcontinental Railroad), the Dred
Scott decision, and so on.

Henry Ward Beecher was so angry over the Fugitive Slave Law that he openly preached of defying it. In an 1859 sermon he thundered: "If he [the slave] has escaped and comes to me, I owe him shelter, succor, defense, and God-speed to a final safety. If there were as many laws as there are lines in the Fugitive Slave Law ... I would disregard every law but God's, and help the fugitive!"[15]

Henry Ward Beecher was a younger brother of Harriet Beecher Stowe, and the son of outspoken Presbyterian minister Lyman Beecher, who was considered by some during this time, "America's most famous preacher." Henry attended Amherst College and later Lane Theological Seminary where his father was president. He would pastor both Presbyterian and Congregational churches. Henry Ward Beecher would become, according to Debby Applegate—who won the Pulitzer Prize for her biography of Beecher—"The Most Famous Man in America."

Beecher became a powerful voice for women's rights and the end of slavery. "During the battle over slavery in Kansas, he used his power of the pulpit to raise money for the purchase of rifles ('Beecher's Bibles') for protection of anti-slavery Northern settlers relocating in Kansas."[16]

About three weeks after Lincoln's election as U.S. President, which was about two weeks before the first state—South Carolina—was to secede from the Union, and about five months before the Civil War began, governors across America proclaimed Thursday November 29, 1860, a "Day of Thanksgiving." Henry Ward Beecher took the opportunity to present a lengthy sermon on a wide-range of moral issues. In the sermon, "Against a Compromise of Principle," Beecher railed against the "rank infidelity" and "stupendous infatuation" that supposed "that the greatness of this nation ever sprung from the wisdom of expediency, instead of the power of settled principles."

He concluded that,

> Your harbor did not make you rich; you made
> the harbor rich. Your ships did not create your
> commerce; your commerce created your ships;
> and you created your commerce. Your stores did
> not make traffic. Your factories did not create
> enterprise. Your firms, your committees, your
> treaties, and your legislation did not create
> national prosperity. Our past greatness sprung
> from our obedience to God's natural and moral
> law.[17]

Quite a contrast from the infamous words of President Obama:
"You didn't build that!"

Beecher spent a significant portion of the sermon preaching against
slavery. He declared,

> The Southern States and the Northern alike
> found poisonous seed sown in colonial days. The
> North chose to weed it out. The South
> determined to cultivate it, and see what it would
> bear. The harvest- time has now come. We are
> reaping what we sowed. They sowed the wind,
> and they are about to reap the whirlwind. Let us
> keep in view the causes of things. Our prosperity
> is the fruit of the seed that we sowed, and their
> fears, their alarms, their excitements, their
> fevers, their tumults, and their rages are the fruit
> of the seed that they sowed. Ours is wholesome;
> theirs is poisonous. All, now, that we demand is,
> **that each side shall reap its own harvest.**
> (Emphasis his.)
>
> It is this that convulses the South. They wish to
> reap fruits of liberty from the seed of slavery.
> They wish to have an institution which sets at
> naught the laws of God, and yet be as refined and

prosperous and happy as we are, who obey these laws; and since they cannot, they demand that we shall make up to them what they lack. The real gist of the controversy, as between the greatest number of Southern States and the North, is simply this. The South claims that the United States government is bound to make slavery as good as liberty for all purposes of national life. That is the root of their philosophy. They are to carry on a wasting system, a system that corrupts social life in its very elements, to pursue a course of inevitable impoverishment, and yet, at every decade of years, the government is, by some new bounty and privilege, to make up to them all the waste of this gigantic mistake! And our national government has been made a bribed judge, sitting on the seat of authority in this land, to declare bankruptcy as good as honesty; to declare wickedness as good as virtue; and to declare that there shall be struck, from period to period, a rule that will bring all men to one common municipal and communal prosperity, no matter what may be the causes that are working out special evils in them.

The Southern States, then, have organized society around a rotten core, —slavery: the North has organized society about a vital heart, — liberty. At length both stand mature. They stand in proper contrast. God holds them up to ages and to nations, that men may see the difference.[18]

He continued,

Whether men have acted well or ill, is not now the question; but simply this: **On which side will you be found?** (Emphasis his.) This controversy will go on. No matter what you do, God will

carry out his own providences with you or
without you, by you or against you. You cannot
hide or run away, or shift the question, or stop
the trial. Complaints are useless, and
recriminations foolish and wicked. The
distinctive idea of the Free States is Christian
civilization, and the peculiar institutions of
civilization. The distinctive idea of the South is
barbaric institutions. In the North mind, and in
the South force, rules. In the North every shape
and form of society in some way represents
liberty. In the South every institution and
element of society is tinged and pervaded with
slavery. The South accepts the whole idea of
slavery, boldly and consistently. The North will
never have peace till she with equal boldness
accepts liberty.[19]

In spite of the efforts of Beecher, Finney, Stowe, Weld, Blanchard,
Bourne, and many others, Americans remained bitterly divided
over slavery. To a significant extent, the division remained because
of the skillfulness of those who made biblical arguments in favor
of slavery. Additionally, the pro-slavery position of the Southern
clergy is even more astonishing when one discovers that most of
the Southern churches—mainly the Baptists, Methodists, and
Presbyterians which comprised the vast majority of Southern
worshippers—all opposed slavery in the eighteenth century.

In 1784 the Methodists had passed a series of
strict rules for the purpose of eliminating slavery
from their churches. In 1790 the Virginia
General Committee (Baptist) declared slavery to
be "a violent deprivation of the rights of nature,
and inconsistent with a republican government,"
and recommended "every legal measure to
extirpate the horrid evil from the land."[20]

Around the turn of the nineteenth century, Southern churches adopted the position of silence. They began to assert the idea that slavery was not a religious matter but a civil one. The prevailing opinion was that, as Donald G. Mathews has written, "Slaveholding is a civil institution; and we [churches and ministers] will not interfere. The character of civil institutions is governed by politics; and we will not interfere. Politics are beyond the scope of the church; and we will not interfere."[21]

Moreover, as author Anne Loveland puts it,

> The churches' retreat from antislavery would not
> have been so important a factor in shaping the
> southern evangelical view had some ministers in
> the South continued to voice anti-slavery
> opinions. But in the early nineteenth century,
> preachers who opposed slavery either left the
> South or fell silent.[22]

Likewise, three significant Northern denominations—Roman Catholic, Protestant Episcopal, and Lutheran—were almost completely silent on the subject of slavery during the decade preceding the Civil War. During the Civil War the Lutherans finally took a stand in opposition to slavery; however, the Catholics and Episcopalians still remained mostly silent.

The Southern position of silence did not prevail, at least for those in the South who supported slavery. In fact, the Southern pulpits became the primary voice for the defense of slavery. Pro-slavery apologists firmly maintained that slavery was an institution ordained and protected by God. Presbyterian pastor James Henley Thornwell—described by noted nineteenth century historian George Bancroft as "the most learned of the learned," and whom Eugene Genovese and Elizabeth Fox-Genovese called the antebellum South's "most formidable theologian"—was well-known for his biblical defense of slavery and for making the constitutional case for secession.

Thornwell was also known for his attempts at reconciling biblical truths with what "modern science" (a reference to Darwin's *Origin of Species* published in 1859) was saying about the fossil record and the age of the earth. "Thornwell argued that Christians could reconcile the apparent old age of the earth with the 'days' of Genesis 1 by interpreting the days as longer periods of time."[23] (Imagine that. One of the foremost apologists for slavery in America was also willing to compromise long-held truths of Scripture with Darwinian evolution.)

In 1857, Frederick A. Ross, pastor of the First Presbyterian Church in Huntsville, Alabama, published a book entitled *Slavery Ordained of God.* In the preface Ross wrote,

> Let the Northern philanthropist learn from the Bible that the relation of master and slave is not sin per se. Let him learn that God says nowhere it is sin. Let him learn that sin is the transgression of the law; and where there is no law there is no sin, and that **the Golden Rule** may exist in the relations of slavery. Let him learn that slavery is simply an evil **in certain circumstances**. Let him learn that **equality** is only the highest form of social life; that **subjection** to authority, even **slavery**, may, in **given conditions**, be **for a time** better than freedom to the slave of any complexion. Let him learn that **slavery**, like **all evils**, has its **corresponding** and **greater good**; that the Southern slave, though degraded **compared with his master, is elevated and ennobled compared with his brethren in Africa.**
> (Emphases his.)[24]

Robert Lewis Dabney, the famous biographer of Stonewall Jackson, was another prominent theological voice in the South. Dabney was a chaplain in the Confederate Army and also served as Jackson's chief of staff. In an attempted moral defense of Southern politics and social order, Dabney wrote *A Defense of Virginia, and Through Her, of the South.*

An excerpt reads,

> One of these general objections to our New Testament argument is the following. They say, Christ could not have intended to authorize slavery, because the tenour and spirit of His moral teachings are opposed to it. The temper He currently enjoins is one of fraternity, equality, love, and disinterestedness. But holding a fellow-being in bondage is inconsistent with all these. Especially is the great "Golden Rule" incompatible with slavery. This enjoins us to do unto our neighbour as we would that he should do unto us. Now, as no slaveholder would like to be himself enslaved, this is a clear proof that we should not hold others in slavery. Hence, the interpretations which seem to find authority for slavery in certain passages of the New Testament, must be erroneous, and we are entitled to reject them without examination.
>
> Abolitionists usually advance this with a disdainful confidence, as though he who does not admit its justice were profoundly stupid. But it is exceedingly easy to show that it is a bald instance of **petitio principia** [circular reasoning], and it is founded on a preposterous interpretation of the Golden Rule, which every sensible Sabbath-school boy knows how to explode. Its whole plausibility rests on the a priori assumption of prejudice, that slaveholding cannot but be wicked, and on a determination not to see it otherwise. (Emphasis his.)[25]

When it became clear that the issue of slavery was dividing the Union of American States beyond repair, some in the North were willing to allow the southern states to secede peacefully. This initially was the case with Henry Ward Beecher. However, on April 14, 1861, the day the Union surrendered Fort Sumter, Beecher preached a sermon that revealed his change of heart on the matter of war with the South.

Beecher declared,

> The war is brought to us. Shall we retreat, or shall we accept the hard conditions on which we are to maintain the grounds of our fathers? Hearing the voice of God in his providence saying, 'Go Forward!' shall we go?

> I go with those that go furthest in describing the wretchedness and wickedness and monstrosity of war. The only point on which I should probably differ from any is this: that while war is an evil so presented to our senses that we measure and estimate it, there are other evils just as great and much more terrible, whose deadly mischiefs have no power upon the senses. I hold that it is ten thousand times better to have war than to have slavery.[26]

Beecher's voice became so prominent that, in 1863, President Lincoln sent Beecher on a speaking tour of Europe in order to promote and build support for the Union cause.

# CHAPTER 12

# America Confronts the Sin of Slavery, Part 3: War and the *Divine Will*

The die was cast. America was now embroiled in a "great civil war" that would last four long years. As both sides were convinced that their view of slavery was in line with God's Word, both sides were also convinced that their cause was just and that God would be with them throughout the war and would bring them victory.

As historian and author Mark Noll puts it,

> With debate over the Bible and slavery at such a pass, and especially with the success of the proslavery biblical argument manifestly (if also uncomfortably) convincing to most Southerners and many in the North, difficulties abounded. The country had a problem because its most trusted religious authority, the Bible, was sounding an uncertain note. The evangelical Protestant churches had a problem because the mere fact of trusting implicitly in the Bible was not solving disagreements about what the Bible taught concerning slavery. The country and the churches were both in trouble because the remedy that finally solved the question of how to interpret the Bible was recourse to arms. The supreme crisis over the Bible was that there

existed no apparent biblical resolution to the
crisis. As I have written elsewhere, it was left to
those consummate theologians, the Reverend
Doctors Ulysses S. Grant and William Tecumseh
Sherman, to decide what in fact the Bible
actually meant.[1]

After the Civil War began, it was also not unusual for the Northern
clergy to cast the war in apocalyptic and millennialistic language.
In January of 1861, Yale graduate and noted Congregationalist
minister Heman Humphrey asked, "Would [God] have brought us
hither and given us so much work in prospect for bringing in the
millennium, if He had intended to pluck us up, just as we are
entered upon the work?"[2]

Also, much like Columbus in his conquest of the New World, and
as we saw during the Colonial and Revolutionary period of
America, throughout the Civil War many American theologians
continued to see the United States as a new Israel. And as it was
with the Israelites, Civil War pastors preached that America was
under the "paternal care of God."

On May 11, 1861 the Rev. G.D. Carrow of Wharton Street
Methodist Episcopal Church (Philadelphia) delivered the sermon,
*The Divine Right of the American Government.* Through no
shortage of words, Carrow goes to great lengths to point out that
"the care of Divine Providence, in a marked, pre-eminent degree,
has been exercised over this nation, from the birth of its first
child…"[3]

"God has cared for the American people, as a father cares for his
children," Carrow wrote, and thus, "Rebellion against the
American government, is rebellion against God."[4]

Carrow continued,

The second critical and decisive period in the
history of the American people, is that which
stood between the first gun fired at Lexington,
and the last one fired at Yorktown. The

142

American people have not studied the history of
that momentous period with sufficient care. It
ought to have greater prominence in American
school-rooms. And if American Christians would
more thoroughly regard it, their increased
attention to, and interest in it, would at the same
time increase their patriotic devotion, and their
faith in the providence of God. For, as surely as
there was ever a providence over any people,
was there a providence over the American people
during the years of their great struggle for
freedom and national independence. As surely as
God was in the pillar of cloud by day, and the
pillar of fire by night, that guided and saved the
hosts of Israel, so surely was He in the cabinet
councils, the tented fields, the toilsome marches,
and bloody battles, which marked the
revolutionary career of our patriotic, gallant, and
noble sires.[5]

Likewise, on May 16, 1862, the Rev. J.W. Tucker of Fayetteville,
North Carolina delivered to his congregation the sermon "God's
Providence in War." Rev. Tucker's message spoke often of God's
"divine purpose" in the United States:

As a Christian people, we look not to fortune nor
to accidents for help in this hour of our country's
peril, but to the God of battles and of nations.
The reason is apparent: If the teaching of the
Bible, and the revelation of the Christian religion
be true, there is no such thing as fortune; there
can be no accidents... All acts are provided for
in God's plan and over-ruled by his providence,
for the advancement of his glory and the well-
being of his people... it is evident that God has a
plan and a purpose in reference to all nations,
revolutions and wars. All these things are
brought about in accordance with the divine
plan, and in fulfillment of the divine purpose,

143

which was drafted in the mind of God before the
world was called into being. He has a providence
in all national revolutions...

God has without question been with his church
in every age of the world; but he has found it
necessary to preserve his people with the salt,
and purify them by the fires of persecution. God
was with our Revolutionary fathers in their
struggle for independence; but he suffered them
often to be defeated in their seven years conflict
with the mother country; but the eagle bird of
Liberty gathered strength while rocked by the
storms and tempests of a bloody Revolution.[6]

In the early going, when Southern victories were mounting, each
side took this as a sign. Rev. Tucker noted,

Our victories indicate the presence of God with
our [Confederate] armies in this conflict. Who
can read the reports of the battles of Bethel, Bull
Run, Manassas Plains, Ball's Bluff, Springfield,
Shiloh and Williamsburg, without being
convinced that God gave us the victory, and that
to him we should render thanksgiving for the
glorious triumph of our arms. Every soldier who
moved amid the perils and dangers of these
bloody conflicts, must feel that the "Lord of host
is with us; and the God of Jacob is our refuge."[7]

Near the end of the sermon, Rev. Tucker boldly encouraged the
Confederates,

Soldiers of the South, be firm, be courageous, be
brave; be faithful to your God, your country and
yourselves, and you shall be invincible. Never
forget that the patriot, like the Christian, is

immortal till his work is finished. You are
fighting for everything that is near and dear, and
sacred to you as men, as Christians and as
patriots; for country, for home, for property, for
the honor of mothers, daughters, wives, sisters,
and loved ones. Your cause is the cause of God,
of Christ, of humanity. It is a conflict of truth
with error--of the Bible with Northern infidelity -
-of a pure Christianity with Northern fanaticism-
-of liberty with despotism--of right with might.[8]

Notice the lack of any mention of slavery.

In the light of the many early victories by the Confederates, some
Northern preachers noted that it was because too much attention
was given to preserving the union instead of ending slavery.
President Lincoln himself had given priority to preserving the
Union.

According to Michael P. Johnson,

Again and again Lincoln promised, as he put it in
his first inaugural address, "I have no purpose,
directly or indirectly, to interfere with the
institution of slavery in the States where it exists.
I believe I have no lawful right to do so, and I
have no inclination to do so." Lincoln followed
this unambiguous statement that he did not have
an emancipationist card up his inaugural coat-
sleeve by professing, "I take the official oath
today, with no mental reservations, and with no
purpose to construe the Constitution or laws, by
any hypercritical rules." This declaration was no
meaningless rhetorical gesture. Near the end of
his inaugural address, Lincoln announced that he
had "no objection' to the Thirteenth Amendment
recently sent to the states with two-thirds
majorities from the House and Senate. The

145

proposed amendment guaranteed that the federal government would never interfere with slavery in the states. Lincoln explained that because he believed 'such a provision to now be implied constitutional law," he had "no objection to its being made express, and irrevocable."[9]

David Chesebrough notes,

> On November 21, 1861, the Rev. Henry Kimball delivered a sermon in the First Congregational Church of Sandwich, Massachusetts, where he announced that Union defeats were due to the federal government's failure to take a stand against slavery. The ship of state had come upon a storm that would not abate until "Jonah" (slavery) was thrown overboard. Kimball proclaimed: "It is preposterous for us to suppose that we can keep up long before a civilized world, and nourish the very cause of all our disasters. The venom of slavery is in the fang of treason; let us extract the poison, and the teeth of rebellion will be drawn."[10]

As the calendar turned to 1862, it was clear that the Confederacy had the early upper hand in the war. The year would be a particularly dark time for President Lincoln. In late August, the Union suffered a major tactical loss to the Confederates at the Second Battle of Bull Run. The already low morale in the North got even lower. Earlier that year, President and Mrs. Lincoln endured the tragic death of their eleven-year-old son, William Wallace (Willie) Lincoln, the Lincolns' third son.

Both parents were particularly devastated. Mary Lincoln's friend and seamstress, Elizabeth Keckley, described Willie as "his mother's favorite child." A family friend added that Willie was "the most lovable boy I ever knew, bright, sensible, sweet-tempered and gentle-mannered." As he first glanced upon his dead son, President Lincoln mumbled, "My poor boy. He was too good for this earth. God has called him home. I know that he is much better off in heaven, but then we loved him so. It is hard, hard to have him die!"[11] President Lincoln remained out of work for three weeks. Mary Lincoln fell into a deep depression. She was so distraught that those close to her feared for her sanity.

The Rev. Phineas Gurley (who also preached the funeral of President Lincoln) presided over the funeral of young Willie. During the eulogy, Rev. Gurley declared,

> It is well for us, and very comforting, on such an occasion as this, to get a clear and a scriptural view of the providence of God.
>
> His kingdom ruleth over all. All those events which in anywise affect our condition and happiness are in his hands, and at his disposal. Disease and death are his messengers; they go forth at his bidding, and their fearful work is limited or extended, according to the good pleasure of His will.
>
> Not a sparrow falls to the ground without His direction; much less any one of the human family, for we are of more value than many sparrows.
>
> We may be sure, -- therefore, bereaved parents, and all the children of sorrow may be sure, -- that their affliction has not come forth of the dust, nor has their trouble sprung out of the ground.
>
> It is the well-ordered procedure of their Father and their God.
>
> A mysterious dealing they may consider it, but still it is His dealing; and while they mourn He is saying to them, as the Lord Jesus once said to his Disciples when they were perplexed by his conduct, "What I do ye know not now, but ye

shall know hereafter." What we need in the hour
of trial, and what we should seek by earnest
prayer, is confidence in Him who sees the end
from the beginning and doeth all things well.

Only let us bow in His presence with an humble
and teachable spirit; only let us be still and know
that He is God; only let us acknowledge His
hand, and hear His voice, and inquire after His
will, and seek His holy spirit as our counsellor
and guide, and all, in the end, will be well. In His
light shall we see light; by His grace our sorrows
will be sanctified -- they will be made a blessing
to our souls -- and by and by we shall have
occasion to say, with blended gratitude and
rejoicing, "It is good for us that we have been
afflicted."[12]

President Lincoln was so moved that he asked for a copy of the
eulogy. Lincoln biographer Ronald C. White noted, "This sermon
is a real pivotal moment in Lincoln's life. Your son has died; you
listen to this sermon; this pastor whom you have respected comes
into the White House and suggests to you that you need to trust in
a loving God with personality, who acts in history."[13]

Along with the death of his beloved son, two years of the Civil
War had resulted in President Lincoln losing other relatives and
close friends. Combine this with the deaths of tens-of-thousands of
American soldiers, which weighed heavily on the President, and
Abraham Lincoln was literally stalked by death. President Lincoln
could've easily shaken his fist at God and surrendered to despair.
On the contrary, upon hearing the words of Dr. Gurley, Lincoln's
faith deepened. According to Lincoln biographer William E.
Barton,

Mr. Lincoln was not conscious of any radical
change; but Mrs. Lincoln noticed a change in
him after Willie's death, which grew more
pronounced after his visit to Gettysburg, and his

own faith, while undergoing no sudden and radical transformation, manifests a consistent evolution.[14]

Author William Wolfe notes that, "[T]he personal anguish of the death of friends and the tragic loss of his beloved Willie... turned Lincoln toward a deeper piety than he had known before."[15]

In September of 1862, just after the Union defeat at the Second Battle of Bull Run, Lincoln penned his *Meditation on the Divine Will*, which his secretaries would later reveal were originally written for Lincoln's eyes only:

> The will of God prevails. In great contests each party claims to act in accordance with the will of God. Both may be, and one must be, wrong. God cannot be for and against the same thing at the same time. In the present civil war it is quite possible that God's purpose is something different from the purpose of either party -- and yet the human instrumentalities, working just as they do, are of the best adaptation to effect His purpose.
>
> I am almost ready to say that this is probably true -- that God wills this contest, and wills that it shall not end yet. By his mere great power, on the minds of the now contestants, He could have either saved or destroyed the Union without a human contest. Yet the contest began. And, having begun He could give the final victory to either side any day. Yet the contest proceeds.[16]

Perhaps more than at any other point prior in his life, it seems that God had the attention of the heart and mind of Abraham Lincoln. On September 17, 1862, the bloodiest day in U.S. military history, Union forces defeated Robert E. Lee and the Confederate Armies at Antietam in Maryland. At the battle's end, approximately 25,000

American men were killed, wounded, or missing. The victory held special significance for Lincoln.

A few days later, in the cabinet meeting on September 22, Lincoln announced his decision to issue the Preliminary Emancipation Proclamation. The best account of the event comes from the diary of Lincoln's Secretary of the Navy, Gideon Welles. According to Welles,

> [Lincoln] remarked that he had made a vow, a covenant, that if God gave us the victory in the approaching battle, he would consider it an indication of Divine will, and that it was his duty to move forward in the cause of emancipation. It might be thought strange, he said, that he had in this way submitted the disposal of matters when the way was not clear to his mind what he should do. God had decided this question in favor of the slaves. He was satisfied it was right, was confirmed and strengthened in his action by the vow and the results.[17]

This proclamation announced that, on January 1, 1863, Lincoln would free all slaves in states still in rebellion, and of course, Lincoln followed through. Since the Emancipation Proclamation only applied to states in the Confederacy, it effectively freed no one immediately. However, in addition to the important moral significance of such an action, what the Emancipation Proclamation did serve to do is further isolate the Confederacy.

European nations now largely viewed the American Civil War as an effort to free American slaves. Thus, nations such as Great Britain were now almost certain not to recognize the Confederate States as a nation.

A few weeks after his September cabinet meeting, Lincoln confided in Eliza Gurney, the widow of English Quaker Joseph A. Gurney. Lincoln wrote,

If I had my way, this war would never have been commenced. If I had been allowed my way, this war would have ended before this. But we find it still continues; and we must believe that He permits it for some wise purpose of His own, mysterious and unknown to us; and though with our limited understanding we may not be able to comprehend it, yet we cannot but believe, that He who made the world still governs it.

We are indeed going through a great trial—a fiery trial. In the very responsible position in which I happened to be placed, being a humble instrument in the hands of our Heavenly Father, as I am, and as we all are, to work out His great purposes, I have desired that all my works and acts may be according to His will, and that it might be so, I have sought His aid.[18]

On December 1, 1862, exactly one month prior to the effective date of the Emancipation Proclamation, Lincoln ended his Second Annual Address to Congress declaring,

Fellow-citizens, we cannot escape history. We of this Congress and this Administration will be remembered in spite of ourselves. No personal significance or insignificance can spare one or another of us. The fiery trial through which we pass will light us down in honor or dishonor to the latest generation. We say we are for the Union. The world will not forget that we say this. We know how to save the Union. The world knows we do know how to save it. We, even we here, hold the power and bear the responsibility. In giving freedom to the slave we assure freedom to the free--honorable alike in what we give and what we preserve. We shall nobly save or meanly lose the last best hope of earth. Other means may succeed; this could not fail. The way is plain, peaceful, generous, just--a way which if followed the world will forever applaud and God must forever bless.[19]

On January 29, 1863, Lincoln appointed Ulysses S. Grant as commander of the Army of the West. On March 30, 1963, President Lincoln issued a historic National Day of Prayer and Fasting. It declared,

> Whereas, the Senate of the United States, devoutly recognizing the Supreme Authority and just Government of Almighty God, in all the affairs of men and of nations, has, by a resolution, requested the President to designate and set apart a day for National prayer and humiliation.
>
> And whereas it is the duty of nations as well as of men, to own their dependence upon the overruling power of God, to confess their sins and transgressions, in humble sorrow, yet with assured hope that genuine repentance will lead to mercy and pardon; and to recognize the sublime truth, announced in the Holy Scriptures and proven by all history, that those nations only are blessed whose God is the Lord.
>
> And, insomuch as we know that, by His divine law, nations like individuals are subjected to punishments and chastisements in this world, may we not justly fear that the awful calamity of civil war, which now desolates the land, may be but a punishment, inflicted upon us, for our presumptuous sins, to the needful end of our national reformation as a whole People? We have been the recipients of the choicest bounties of Heaven. We have been preserved, these many years, in peace and prosperity. We have grown in numbers, wealth and power, as no other nation

has ever grown. But we have forgotten God. We have forgotten the gracious hand which preserved us in peace, and multiplied and enriched and strengthened us; and we have vainly imagined, in the deceitfulness of our hearts, that all these blessings were produced by some superior wisdom and virtue of our own. Intoxicated with unbroken success, we have become too self-sufficient to feel the necessity of redeeming and preserving grace, too proud to pray to the God that made us!

It behooves us then, to humble ourselves before the offended Power, to confess our national sins, and to pray for clemency and forgiveness.

Now, therefore, in compliance with the request, and fully concurring in the views of the Senate, I do, by this my proclamation, designate and set apart Thursday, the 30th day of April, 1863, as a day of national humiliation, fasting and prayer. And I do hereby request all the People to abstain, on that day, from their ordinary secular pursuits, and to unite, at their several places of public worship and their respective homes, in keeping the day holy to the Lord, and devoted to the humble discharge of the religious duties proper to that solemn occasion.

All this being done, in sincerity and truth, let us then rest humbly in the hope authorized by the Divine teachings, that the united cry of the Nation will be heard on high, and answered with blessings, no less than the pardon of our national sins, and the restoration of our now divided and suffering Country, to its former happy condition of unity and peace.[20]

In May of that year, Confederate General Stonewall Jackson died from wounds he accidently received at the hands of his own soldiers. "I have lost my right arm," lamented Robert E. Lee.

Shortly thereafter, in early July, at Gettysburg, Pennsylvania, the tide of the war turned in favor of the Union. Over the three-day battle, over 51,000 (28,000-plus Confederates and 23,000-plus Union soldiers) American men lay dead, wounded, or missing. General Lee began a long slow retreat back into Virginia. The weary Yanks did not pursue, which infuriated Lincoln.

Just a day after the battle at Gettysburg ended, the Union Army of the West, led by General Grant, captured the last remaining Confederate stronghold at Vicksburg, Mississippi. This victory by the Union effectively split the Confederacy in half. The losses at Gettysburg and Vicksburg meant the beginning of the end for the Confederate States of America.

Interestingly, according to the Christian History Institute, in spite of how the war was turning against the South, "A 'Great Revival' occurred among Robert E. Lee's forces in the fall of 1863 and winter of 1864. Some 7,000 soldiers were converted. Revivals also swept the Union Army at that time. Sometimes preaching and praying continued 24 hours a day, and chapels couldn't hold the soldiers who wanted to get inside."[21]

In the midst of such wartime carnage, these revivals justify the fears of C.S. Lewis's fictional demon Screwtape (as I noted earlier), as he explains to his protégé Wormwood that war does not always play into the hands of Satan: "[If] we are not careful, we shall see thousands turning in this tribulation to the Enemy [God], while tens of thousands who do not go so far as that will nevertheless have their attention diverted from themselves to values and causes which they believe to be higher than the self."[22]

On September 2, 1864, General Tecumseh Sherman captured Atlanta. The victory helped to secure Lincoln's re-election as U.S. President. Two days later, Lincoln again corresponded with Eliza Gurney. He wrote,

I have not forgotten—probably never shall forget—the very impressive occasion when yourself and friends visited me on a Sabbath forenoon two years ago. Nor has your kind letter, written nearly a year later, ever been forgotten. In all, it has been your purpose to strengthen my reliance on God. I am much indebted to the good Christian people of the country for their constant prayers and consolations; and to no one of them, more than to yourself. The purposes of the Almighty are perfect, and must prevail, though we erring mortals may fail to accurately perceive them in advance. We hoped for a happy termination of this terrible war long before this; but God knows best, and has ruled otherwise. We shall yet acknowledge His wisdom and our own error therein. Meanwhile we must work earnestly in the best light He gives us, trusting that so working still conduces to the great ends He ordains. Surely He intends some great good to follow this mighty convulsion, which no mortal could make, and no mortal could stay.[23]

On November 8, 1864, Lincoln won 213 of 233 electoral votes and defeated Democrat George B. McClellan to win re-election. Just before Christmas, Sherman reached Savannah, completing his march. On January 31, 1865, the U.S. House passed the Thirteenth Amendment to the U.S. Constitution, which abolished slavery. (The Senate had passed it the previous April.) It would be ratified in December of that year.

In his Second Inaugural Address, on March 4, 1865, President Lincoln's words revealed that he continued to believe in a God who "acts in history." The "sorrowful sermon," as it's described by a modern columnist, is barely 700 words and is widely considered one of Lincoln's best speeches.[24] In the last three paragraphs, Lincoln concludes,

Neither party expected for the war the magnitude or the duration which it has already attained. Neither anticipated that the cause of the conflict might cease with, or even before, the conflict itself should cease. Each looked for an easier triumph, and a result less fundamental and astounding. Both read the same Bible, and pray to the same God; and each invokes his aid against the other. It may seem strange that any men should dare to ask a just God's assistance in wringing their bread from the sweat of other men's faces; but let us judge not, that we be not judged. The prayers of both could not be answered—that of neither has been answered fully.

The Almighty has his own purposes. "Woe unto the world because of offenses! for it must needs be that offenses come; but woe to that man by whom the offense cometh." If we shall suppose that American slavery is one of those offenses which, in the providence of God, must needs come, but which, having continued through his appointed time, he now wills to remove, and that he gives to both North and South this terrible war, as the woe due to those by whom the offense came, shall we discern therein any departure from those divine attributes which the believers in a living God always ascribe to him? Fondly do we hope—fervently do we pray—that this mighty scourge of war may speedily pass away. Yet, if God wills that it continue until all the wealth piled by the bondman's two hundred and fifty years of unrequited toil shall be sunk, and until every drop of blood drawn with the lash shall be paid by another drawn with the sword, as was said three thousand years ago, so still it must be said, "The judgments of the Lord are true and righteous altogether."

With malice toward none; with charity for all;
with firmness in the right, as God gives us to see
the right, let us strive on to finish the work we
are in; to bind up the nation's wounds; to care for
him who shall have borne the battle, and for his
widow, and his orphan—to do all which may
achieve and cherish a just and lasting peace
among ourselves, and with all nations.[25]

Less than a month later, on April 2, the Stars and Stripes was
raised over the Confederate capital in Richmond. A week later,
Robert E. Lee surrendered to Grant at Appomattox Court House in
Virginia. President Lincoln would have less than two weeks to
live. After his assassination at the hands of John Wilkes Booth,
Lincoln was laid to rest on May 4, in his home state of Illinois. By
the end of the month, the remaining Confederate forces
surrendered.

The Southern cause had become the "Lost Cause." However,
according to many religious leaders of the South, though the cause
was lost, it was by no means wrong. To a great extent, the
ministers in the South were very successful in painting a military
defeat into a spiritual victory. Sadly, through the efforts of
Southern clergy and other like-minded public officials, the doctrine
of segregation based on white supremacy soon replaced the
institution of slavery. It would take a century before America
would rid herself of such institutionalized racism.

Nevertheless, the Union of the United States of America was
preserved. A few days after Lincoln's death, in one of the most
memorable sermons of that time, Henry Ward Beecher
summarized well the view of those who believed that it was
nothing less than the Hand of God that preserved the Union.
Beecher preached,

> Republican institutions have been vindicated in
> this experience as they never were before; and
> the whole history of the last four years, rounded
> up by this cruel stroke, seems now in the

> providence of God to have been clothed with an
> illustration, with a sympathy, with an aptness,
> and with a significance, such as we never could
> have expected or imagined. God, I think, has
> said, by the voice of this event to all nations of
> the earth, Republican liberty, based upon true
> Christianity, is firm as the foundation of the
> globe.[26]

Beecher's idea that it was the "providence of God" that kept the U.S. intact was widely held, even among more secular-minded Americans. On April 19, 1865, transcendentalist Ralph Waldo Emerson, in the annual lecture that marked the beginning of the American Revolution, in Concord, Massachusetts elegantly eulogized President Lincoln. In his speech, Emerson asked,

> And what if it should turn out, in the unfolding
> of the web, that he had reached the term; that this
> heroic deliverer could no longer serve us; that
> the rebellion had touched its natural conclusion,
> and what remained to be done required new and
> uncommitted hands,—a new spirit born out of
> the ashes of the war; and that Heaven, wishing to
> show the world a completed benefactor, shall
> make him serve his country even more by his
> death than by his life?[27]

In the next, and last, paragraph, Emerson concluded,

> There is a serene Providence which rules the fate
> of nations, which makes little account of time,
> little of one generation or race, makes no account
> of disasters, conquers alike by what is called
> defeat or by what is called victory, thrusts aside
> enemy and obstruction, crushes everything
> immoral as inhuman, and obtains the ultimate
> triumph of the best race by the sacrifice of

everything which resists the moral laws of the world. It makes its own instruments, creates the man for the time, trains him in poverty, inspires his genius, and arms him for his task. It has given every race its own talent, and ordains that only that race which combines perfectly with the virtues of all shall endure.[28]

# CHAPTER 13

# A New Slavery in America?

By the end of the Civil War, approximately 750,000 American soldiers had died. This total surpassed the number of military deaths in all other American military conflicts combined. Approximately 50,000 Civil War soldiers would return home as amputees. Due to the wide and liberal use of narcotics during the war, hundreds of thousands of American men returned home addicted to morphine or opium. This level of addiction impacted our nation for decades beyond the war.

America paid a steep price for the sin of slavery. The racism that endured in the U.S. beyond the Civil War continues to impact our culture. No longer do we fight the same battles of race in America. Institutionalized racism is virtually extinct in the United States. However, this hasn't stopped many from using the racism of America's past to justify much of the perverse modern liberal agenda.

The cry of "racism" is a frequent and favorite tool of the modern left. Everything from abortion to homosexuality, pornography, same-sex "marriage," Big Government healthcare, education, foolish climate policies, and ironically, an enslaving welfare state, and so on, are very often presented by today's liberals as a matter of "civil rights." Tragically, and again, ironically, these tenets of modern liberalism have decimated the black family in America.

At its despicable peak, the African slave population reached about four million in 1860. Between the years 1880 and 1951, the Tuskegee Institute reports that 3,437 black Americans were lynched in the United States. Approximately six million Jews were murdered in the Holocaust during World War II. A total of about 1.3 million American soldiers have died in all U.S. military conflicts. Each of these figures represents events that are uniquely tragic. However, they pale in comparison to the over 58 million Americans who, as of this writing, have died in the womb since 1973.

Through the specific targeting of the abortion machine, though black women account for only about 11 percent of the U.S. population, they account for 30 percent of abortions in America. Black women are more than five times as likely as white women to have an abortion.[1] Since the infamous Roe v. Wade decision of 1973 which legalized abortion across the U.S., well over 17 million black children have been "lynched" in the womb.

As Dr. Alveda King, the niece of Martin Luther King Jr., put it, "How can the 'Dream' survive if we murder the children? Every aborted baby is like a slave in the womb of his or her mother. The mother decides his or her fate."[2] In the U.S., there are many eerie and tragic parallels between slavery and abortion. Chief among these parallels is the de-humanization both of blacks and the unborn.

On March 21, 1861, in a speech in Savannah, Georgia, the Vice President of the Confederacy, Alexander Stephens said,

> But not to be tedious in enumerating the numerous changes for the better, allow me to allude to one other — though last, not least. The new constitution [the constitution of the Confederacy] has put at rest, forever, all the agitating questions relating to our peculiar institution — African slavery as it exists amongst us — the proper status of the negro in our form of civilization. This was the immediate cause of the late rupture and present revolution. Jefferson in his forecast, had anticipated this, as the 'rock upon which the old Union would split.' He was right. What was conjecture with him, is

now a realized fact. But whether he fully comprehended the great truth upon which that rock stood and stands, may be doubted. The prevailing ideas entertained by him and most of the leading statesmen at the time of the formation of the old constitution, were that the enslavement of the African was in violation of the laws of nature; that it was wrong in principle, socially, morally, and politically. It was an evil they knew not well how to deal with, but the general opinion of the men of that day was that, somehow or other in the order of Providence, the institution would be evanescent and pass away. This idea, though not incorporated in the constitution, was the prevailing idea at that time. The constitution, it is true, secured every essential guarantee to the institution while it should last, and hence no argument can be justly urged against the constitutional guarantees thus secured, because of the common sentiment of the day. Those ideas, however, were fundamentally wrong. They rested upon the assumption of the equality of races. This was an error. It was a sandy foundation, and the government built upon it fell when the 'storm came and the wind blew.'

Our new government is founded upon exactly the opposite idea; its foundations are laid, its corner- stone rests upon the great truth, **that the negro is not equal to the white man; that slavery — subordination to the superior race — is his natural and normal condition.** [Applause.] This, our new government, is the first, in the history of the world, based upon this great physical, philosophical, and moral truth. This truth has been slow in the process of its development, like all other truths in the various departments of science. It has been so even amongst us. Many who hear me, perhaps, can recollect well, that this truth was not generally

163

admitted, even within their day. The errors of the past generation still clung to many as late as twenty years ago. Those at the North, who still cling to these errors, with a zeal above knowledge, we justly denominate fanatics. All fanaticism springs from an aberration of the mind — from a defect in reasoning. It is a species of insanity. One of the most striking characteristics of insanity, in many instances, is forming correct conclusions from fancied or erroneous premises; so with the anti-slavery fanatics; their conclusions are right if their premises were. They assume that the negro is equal, and hence conclude that he is entitled to equal privileges and rights with the white man. If *their premises were correct, their conclusions would be logical and just* — *but their premise being wrong, their whole argument fails.* (Emphasis mine.)[3]

Take note: no less than the vice president of the Confederacy acknowledged that slavery was the chief cause of the Civil War, and he concluded that the "prevailing" thought among our Founding Fathers when it came to slavery was that it was a "violation of the laws of nature."

To justify the slaughter of tens of millions of children in the womb, abortion apologists have regularly employed the same de-humanizing language used by the vice president of the Confederacy. For decades now, modern liberalism has excluded unborn babies "from the universe of moral obligation."[4]

This was on particular display in the 2015 scandal involving abortion giant Planned Parenthood. "These are not 'baby parts,'" insisted Jen Gunter. She preferred that the "tissue specimen" be referred to as "products of conception." The term "baby" doesn't apply until birth, Gunter declared. She concluded, "Calling the tissue 'baby parts' is a calculated attempt to anthropomorphize [humanize] an embryo or fetus [notice that she can't even bring herself to use the word 'human']."[5]

What's more, like their political ancestors of the nineteenth century, who promoted slavery in six consecutive party platforms (from 1840 through 1860)[6], save for one year—1984—where abortion was not mentioned in the party platform, since 1976 the modern Democrat Party has unapologetically stood for the "right" to kill children in the womb.

Along with aiding and abetting the slaughter of millions of black children in the womb, with its unapologetic advancement of the welfare state and its perverse promotion of the sexual agenda, liberalism has been devastating to marriage within America's black community. Even the slave-holders of the Confederate South expressed sorrow for what the institution of slavery had wrought upon the black family.

As author David Chesebrough notes,

> Southern ministers and religious institutions
> were expressing some guilt as to what the South
> had done to black families. Marriage, too, was an
> institution ordained by God, and the slavery
> system had often worked against this divine
> institution. In 1863 a Georgia association of
> Baptists passed a resolution urging that the laws
> of Georgia protect Negro marriages. The Baptists
> noted that the state laws had failed 'to recognize
> and protect this relationship between slaves,' and
> that present laws were 'especially defective, and
> ought to be amended.'[7]

Nevertheless, studies of nineteenth century black families reveal that, just after the Civil War, 75 percent of black families were two-parent. Additionally, "one study of 19th century slave families found that in up to three-fourths of the families, all the children had the same mother and father."[8] Those numbers are quite a contrast to modern CDC statistics which reveal that a shocking 72 percent of black children are born out-of-wedlock. According to Census data, marriage drops the probability of child poverty by 82 percent. Thus, black children in America today are much more likely to be born into poverty than are children born into any other racial group.

In his 1964 State of the Union, U.S. President Lyndon Johnson (D) thundered "This Administration today, here and now, declares unconditional war on poverty in America." Johnson announced that his goals were "not only to relieve the symptom of poverty, but to cure it and, above all, to prevent it," and make "taxpayers out of tax eaters." He further claimed that his anti-poverty programs would bring to an end the "conditions that breed despair and violence." The Johnson administration was particularly concerned with the high rate of black poverty.

After over 50 years, more than 80 means-tested (recipients are required to be below a certain income level) programs that provide, among other things, money, food, housing, and medical care, with over $22 trillion (in 2012 dollars)[9] spent, the overall poverty rate in America has barely budged (from about 19 percent to about 15 percent).[10] Though the poverty rate for black Americans has improved more significantly (42 percent to 27 percent), most of this decline occurred during the 1960s.[11] From 1940 to 1960, poverty among black families in America fell from 87 percent to 47 percent. In other words, the War on Poverty that began in 1964 actually slowed the decline of poverty among black Americans.

Additionally, as a result of the breakdown of the family and the devastating welfare state, black Americans live in some of the most dangerous places in America. As *The New York Times* reported last year, black mortality from homicide is more than seven times that of whites.[12] Additionally, black mortality from AIDS is about five times the rate for whites. Amazingly, black men in the U.S. are half as likely to die if they are in prison than if they are not.[13]

Tragically, and to a great extent thanks to liberalism and the modern Democrat Party, blacks in America have gone from one plantation to another.

# Innovation/Industrial Explosion, Part 1: "Slater the Traitor" and His Textile Mills

Truly the Constitutional republic created in America is unique in the annals of human history. As James Wilson, signer of the Declaration and U.S. Constitution, and who, along with James Madison was considered the most learned political mind involved in drafting the U.S. Constitution, declared, "On the principle…of this Constitution…the supreme power resides in the people…The powers both of the general government and the state governments, under this system, are acknowledged to be so many emanations of power from the people."[1]

A recognition of the "unalienable" rights of individuals and empowering those individuals through the exceptional and brilliant U.S. Constitution presented the young United States with an amazing opportunity. Combining the two aforementioned factors with a people fresh out of revival (who had just experienced the miracles of the Revolution and Constitution), and a wealth of God-given natural resources, and there existed the opportunity for a "magnificent" industrial explosion.

In other words, the United States was ripe for economic growth—growth in almost every sector imaginable. As author George S. White prophetically put it in his 1836 book, *Memoir of Samuel Slater: The Father of American Manufactures*, "The prospect of national greatness is as sure as that of national existence. We are too contracted in our conceptions when we talk of the southern and eastern interests. The rise and progress of empires and nations yet unborn are connected with our prosperity."[2]

By the early 1800s American industry began to take serious hold. In 1790 Samuel Slater built the first factory—a textile mill to produce yarn and cloth—in America. Slater secretly immigrated to America from England at the age of 21 in 1789. In England he worked in the textile industry, serving as a cotton spinner's apprentice. Believing that textiles there had reached their peak, and in hopes of making his fortune abroad, Slater brought his knowledge and industriousness to the vast, new United States of America. Because of such an exit from the UK, the British dubbed him "Slater the Traitor."

Known today as the "Father of the American Industrial Revolution," with funding provided by Rhode Island industrialist Moses Brown, and having memorized the secrets of British textile machinery, Slater built a water-powered cotton spinning mill in Pawtucket, Rhode Island. Slater and Brown's mill was the first water-powered spinning textile mill in America. Also, Slater's wife Hannah invented a new type of cotton sewing thread, and in 1793 she became the first American woman to receive a patent.

Textiles are materials—especially cloth—that are made by interlacing fibers. Textile manufacturing soon exploded and by the early 1800s became the dominant industry in America with hundreds of companies in operation. Mill towns sprang up all along America's east coast. Slater himself would eventually own thirteen spinning mills. Such industry, combined with the liberty present in the U.S., presented opportunities for employment and prosperity on a scale yet unexperienced in early American history.

As White put it in Slater's memoir,

> Employment will be necessary for our immense
> increase of population and the influx of strangers
> from every part of the world, invited to our
> shores by the promise of liberty and plenty, must
> find work to exercise their various abilities and

habits of industry. Many of them are valuable mechanics and artisans, of infinite variety of skill, well adapted to assist in the rapid improvements now commencing, unexampled in ancient or modern history. Who knows but other Slaters may come over to us, and assist in feeding and clothing the population that is forming new states in the vast wilderness, destined to be great empires to exist for many generations—when Rome and Paris and Berlin shall be no more.[3]

Almost 50 years from the birth of the U.S. Constitution, the biographer of one of the most industrious, wealthy, and prominent men in the early nineteenth century United States understood well that it was God who made possible the great opportunities that existed in America. In the introduction to Slater's memoir, White wrote,

Columbus first led the way, and opened a path for the oppressed to find freedom and peace. The old world had become tyrannical and despotic, and the groans of the children of men had come up into the ears of the Lord God of the universe. He inspired his servant with wisdom and courage, and afforded him all necessary means to open a new world to the eyes of astonished millions, to whom it was marvelous and almost miraculous. The wisdom of the wise men was turned backward, their knowledge turned to foolishness. All the maxims of political and spiritual tyranny were turned upside down; and Luther and others exhibiting a mighty spirit of reformation believed there would be deliverance, though they saw not the way. Their faith saved them, and it has happened according to their word. The iron arm has been broken; and the weak and despised have fled for refuge, and have found a quiet habitation.[4]

**White continued,**

> May Americans remember their mercies and
> deep responsibilities! Let us lay aside every
> weight, and the sin that doth so easily beset us;
> and let us run with patient perseverance in every
> good work, and we shall become the praise of
> the whole earth.
>
> Had Columbus been discouraged, and turned
> back, at the mutiny of his crew, or had he then
> hearkened to the timid caution of his friends, we
> never should have reaped the wonderful harvest
> benefits from their disinterested labours that we
> now enjoy...
>
> The strong and prominent trait of character in
> Slater, was his unwavering and steadfast
> perseverance, and his constant application to the
> fulfilment of his object. Had he failed in
> constructing the Arkwright machinery, or had he
> finally failed in his extensive business, the cause
> of manufactures would have been retarded;
> indeed, no one can calculate the evil
> consequences of such an event; but he held on
> his way; he fainted, but yet pursued. And he has
> left us an example, to those engaged in the same
> cause, or in a similar enterprise, to be stedfast,
> unmoveable, and faithful; till America shall
> rival, in the perfection of her manufactures, as
> she does now in the freedom of her institutions
> the nations the earth! We are richly supplied, and
> we possess, in a high and superabundant degree,
> all the natural capabilities for the purpose; all
> that is necessary, is the application of them to the
> proper object. Those philosophers who deny the
> bounties of Providence, in their rich and
> exhaustless abundance, by teaching that this
> globe is unable to support and sustain the natural
> increase of its inhabitants, *[Sounds like the*

*modern global warming crowd!]* have the most contracted and degraded view of the resources of nature, and the arrangement of her laws, not to insist upon the inspiration. They contradict the realities of all ages, by an unbelieving scepticism, fostered by a selfish policy, and a misrepresentation of matters of fact. We have resources for hundreds of millions *[Great foresight!—as we are now a nation of 330+ million]*. He is the true patriot who developes those mines and riches, and who gives employment *[The benefits of capitalism were seen even in the early nineteenth century!]* to the species, to dignify society and ornament the country. We envy not those self-styled patriots, whose thirst for office and distinction allows them to deceive and cajole their fellow citizens, by prejudicing them against the talented and enterprising part of society. *[The "Occupy" crowd operating in the early nineteenth century?!]* Thus teaching them discontent, and prejudicing them against the necessary arrangements to promote the general welfare, making them the tools of their sordid selfish policy; and yet these patriots imagine that their exaltation is essential to the honour and safety of their country. The way of virtue and truth, which only leads to honour and immortality, is too hard for their tender feet. *[Yesterday's "tender feet" are today's liberals.]*… A state of society, not founded the principles of honest industry, must be degraded and low; and like the inhabitants of South America must be wretched miserable. *[South America hasn't changed much in nearly 200 years.]* Mankind must be usefully and honourably employed, in order to be virtuous and happy. *[Amen!]* In proof of this position, compare the condition of South America with the United States, and more especially with that part of the United States manufacturing establishments have come into being and risen eminence. The mighty contrast in the condition and character of the people, is altogether greater than that formed by the hand of nature in the two countries themselves. South America, particularly that part in the neighbourhood of the La Plata, in the hands of New Englanders, would at once become the paradise of world, did they retain their moral and intellectual habits. Without these habits, we can pronounce what they would be, from a resident well acquainted with the country affirms the South Americans are. With governments in distraction, and so enfeebled as to exert no force except by the sword and bayonet, vice, disorder, and confusion everywhere prevail. The finest fields in the world for agriculture are suffered to remain barren and desolate, or to be traveled by wandering herds. Indolence and enfeeble the hands and put out the eyes of the inhabitants. Roaming in poverty, filth, and pollution, *[Again, sounds much like today's South America!]* they are totally blind to their advantages and privileges: they are tossed about by wind of prejudice and passion. Trained to view labour as a degradation, while trampling the most prolific fields *[Occupiers!]* and possessing everything requisite, and of the first qualities, for food and clothing, they would be obliged to go naked and starve, were it not for the industry of other nations. *[And they're still nursing off of the teats of others!]* As it now is, robbers and assassins fill their streets, and thousands are disappearing by the only species of industry for which they have an adaptation, that of destroying each other. The inhabitants of New England, barren and rugged as she is, comparing her with this picture and contrasting it with their own condition will bless that Providence which has placed them as they are, and see at once that an introduction the

172

manufacturing interest has added in no small
degree to their dignity and happiness.

Slater, by the introduction of machinery, and by
his arrangements in the various departments of
the manufacturing establishments, opened the
means of employment, and excavated a mine
more valuable than those of Peru, or than all the
precious metals of the earth; because the human
capabilities are brought into exercise. This gives
to man his full enjoyment, in the pursuit of
happiness. In contrast with South America, it is
pleasing to see the spirit of enterprise and
improvement rising in every part of our country.
This spirit, if not now universal, is rapidly
becoming so. We see it breaking out every
where, in the middle states, in the northern, in
the southern, in the western; and like the
kindling of fire, we see it gathering strength as it
rises and spreads. Who does not see in this rising
spirit, a subject of national felicitation? Perhaps
the greatest this country ever had before;
certainly greater than any other country ever
possessed. Was even the spirit of liberty itself,
which produced the revolution, and gave us our
independence more a subject of national
congratulation? Who can estimate the value of
this new born spirit which now animates our
country, when we consider our great and rapidly
increasing population, their characteristic ardour
in every lucrative pursuit, and the boundless
scope which our country affords for the range of
this spirit? Here we have everything to invite to
enterprise and encourage hope; the great and
growing market afforded by our commerce and
our manufactures is rendering every article of
produce valuable and productive. Thus every
department of wealth aids and unites in
replenishing the boundless resources of our
happy country.[5]

What an amazing account—in the infancy of the United States, no less! It was as if White peeked over the economic and industrious horizons of the U.S. and saw the monstrous economic bull that was looming.

Samuel Slater was not alone in developing and prospering in the textile industry in the late eighteenth and early nineteenth centuries. In 1813, the Boston Manufacturing Company was formed. Frances Cabot Lowell, Nathan Appleton, and Patrick Johnson created the company for the manufacture of cotton textiles. Boston Manufacturing Company was the first integrated textile factory in America that executed every operation necessary to turn cotton lint into finished cloth. Many early New England families obtained their (significant) wealth from textile mills.

As most of us have often heard, "Necessity is the mother of invention." This is certainly the case with the textile industry. As Slater was building his factory in 1790, he sought the services of a well-respected and skilled blacksmith, Oziel Wilkinson, and his son David Wilkinson, a talented machinist and mechanical engineer. Slater needed the Wilkinsons to produce the machinery necessary to run his factory. Samuel and the Wilkinsons would have a lengthy business partnership and grow close. Samuel would marry Oziel's daughter, Hannah.

As David worked to provide the iron forgings and castings for Slater's carding and spinning machines, he also became quite skilled at mass-producing iron nails and screws. In 1794, David invented a screw-cutting lathe. He patented the lathe in 1798. Ten years later, David adapted the design of the lathe to serve as a general-purpose industrial lathe, but he failed to patent this new design. Machinists across the world soon recognized the value of this new lathe and began copying it for use in factories, machine shops, and arsenals.[6]

Wilkinson's lathe would become an indispensable machinist tool. Echoing this sentiment, in 1861, textile machinery manufacturer and scientific writer Zachariah Allen wrote of Wilkinson's lathe, "It has to this day proved the most effective tool placed within the control of mankind for shaping refractory metals and for accomplishing the triumph of mind over matter. The slide engine is employed in the great machine shops of America and Europe."[7]

A growing American population meant an increasing need for clothing, shoes, and the like. This was a significant opportunity for all who were skilled, or who had a desire to be skilled, in the textile industry. An increase in mechanization also meant that there was an excellent opportunity for technological advancements. Men like Eli Whitney took advantage of this opportunity.

Of course, Eli Whitney is most famous for his cotton gin ("gin" is short for engine). Invented in 1793, the cotton gin was instrumental in the industrial and economic growth of the U.S. With this machine the time needed to process raw cotton was greatly reduced. A single gin could produce over 50 pounds of cleaned cotton in a day. Thus, the cotton industry exploded in the south.

**A Model of Eli Whitney's Cotton Gin on Display at the Eli Whitney Museum**

Tragically, an increased need for cotton also helped reinvigorate the slave industry in the American South. Prior to the cotton gin, slavery in the U.S. was on the decline. The Northern textile mills struggled to keep up with the demand for what was now much cheaper cotton textiles. Many people made a lot of money from Whitney's cotton gin—except Eli Whitney. Whitney's machine was relatively simple and thus easy to copy. Counterfeits were abundant, and given the nature of patent law at the time, Whitney could not keep up with the expense of all the lawsuits against those copying his invention. This financial setback put Eli Whitney on quite a different industrial path—one that would prove much more lucrative.

# CHAPTER 15

# Innovation/Industrial Explosion, Part 2: America and the Gun

On the eve of the nineteenth century, with hostilities again brewing in Europe as a result of the French Revolution, the U.S. government felt the need to rearm. Without a factory or workers, and despite having never manufactured a single firearm, in 1798 Whitney obtained a contract from the U.S. government for 10,000 guns. It was the largest of over two dozen firearm contracts awarded that year.[1]

What Whitney lacked in experience and resources, he made up for in ambition and industriousness. Whitney, known as "the father of mass production," was a pioneer in the assembly line method of manufacturing. Furthermore, he helped advance the method of manufacturing using interchangeable parts. Whitney's efforts helped usher in the modern age of mass production and were a boon to the manufacturing industry in general. Production costs were reduced, efficiency increased, and costs to consumers decreased. Whitney's system became known as the "American System" and spread to other industries such as clock-making, sewing machines, farming equipment, watches, and even pistols.[2]

Though it took longer than expected (10 years), Whitney completed his order of 10,000 muskets and, along the way, continued to perfect his method of mass production. After completing the initial order, Whitney soon received another order for 15,000 muskets, which was completed in a fraction of the time of the initial order. Like textiles, the gun industry was on the verge of significant growth. In fact, the gun industry in general was at the forefront of the Industrial Age in the United States.

The gun industry holds special significance for me. I love guns. I grew up with them. My father (an avid and excellent hunter) owned (and still owns) many. One of my most memorable gifts as a young man was a single-shot 410 shotgun. Before I was old enough to own a real gun, my friends and I were quite skilled at using all sorts of scrap wood, duct tape, nails, and so on to manufacture the most magnificent replicas. Back then, if I was not playing with some type of ball, I was in some sort of battle.

**My dad, Edsel Thomas, with four of his grandsons (my two oldest boys, Caleb & Jesse, holding the rabbits, and my sister's twin boys, Matthew & Luke) on a rabbit hunt.**

The story of the gun is a fascinating and riveting look, not only at history, but also at science, business, politics, justice, and morality as well. Throw in a great deal of ingenuity, a lot of heroism, and a small dose of romance, and the story of the gun is the world's greatest tale of human invention, with the young United States helping to lead the way.

The gun's story began with the invention (or discovery) of gunpowder. Gunpowder most likely was invented just prior to 1000 A.D. It became rather prominent around the turn of the twelfth century. Theories abound about who actually invented gunpowder, but no one really knows.

According to noted historian Ian Hogg, "The first positive statement relating to gunpowder appears in a document written in 1242 by Roger Bacon entitled *On the Miraculous Power of Art and Nature.*"[3] Hogg also notes that because "fiery compositions" were considered to be an element of the "Black Arts" during that period, Bacon, a Franciscan friar, concealed his formula in an anagram (which remained unsolved for over 600 years).[4]

Early guns were really cannons. The first illustration of a cannon appears in a 1326 work entitled *On the Duties of Kings* prepared for King Edward III of England. These early cannons fired large stone balls—sometimes weighing up to 200 pounds. However, such stones were still lighter than iron shot of a similar diameter, and due to the relative weakness of early gunpowder, were safer to use.

**A "Hand Cannon" as drawn by German Military Engineer Konrad Kyeser, 1400.**

Such cannons were massive and thus, difficult to move. Smaller calibers that were more mobile were much desired, which led to the development of the "hand-gonne." These were simply miniature iron or bronze cannon barrels attached to the end of a lengthy wooden staff. (A 1475 German manuscript depicts such a device.)

**Yuan Dynasty hand cannon dated to 1288. Photo taken by Yannick Trottier, 2007.**

By the fifteenth century, "arms of fire" with a lock, stock, and a barrel—the same basic look we have today—became somewhat common. The first weapon that could be carried, loaded, and discharged by a single man became known as the matchlock. This was a muzzle-loading gun that was discharged when a hand-lit match was lowered into the flash pan.

**Early 17th century matchlock musket. Photo by Jans Mohr, The Royal Armoury, Stockholm.**

The term "lock" most likely originated from the fact that the gun-lock operated in a similar fashion to the locking mechanisms of the day. American Pilgrims were very familiar with this gun. However, these guns were not very accurate or reliable. They could be quite dangerous to use because the burning wick necessary to ignite the powder in the flash pan was often in close proximity to the stores of powder on the user, and they were virtually useless in wet weather. The matchlock also was not very useful for hunting, as the burning wick alerted most every type of game.

A new lock design for igniting the powder was needed. Thus, around 1500 A.D. the world was introduced to the wheel lock. The wheel lock made use of a centuries-old process for lighting fires: striking stone against steel and catching the sparks. No longer was a cumbersome and dangerous burning cord necessary for discharging a gun. For the first time, a firearm could now be carried loaded, primed, and ready to fire. Again, the actual inventor is unknown, but Leonardo da Vinci had one of the earliest drawings of a wheel lock design.

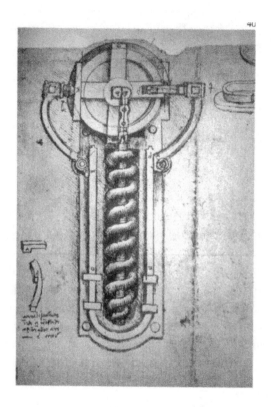

**Wheel lock design of Leonardo da Vinci.**

The wheel lock also led to another advancement in firearms: the pistol. For the first time, a weapon could now be carried concealed. It was at this point that many of the first laws against carrying firearms came into being.

**Wheel-Lock Pistol, 1590-1600**

Like the matchlock, the wheel lock had its short-comings. If the wrench necessary to wind the wheel was lost, the weapon was rendered useless. Also, with over 50 individual parts, the wheel lock was a complicated and intricate design, which made the gun very expensive to own and difficult and expensive to maintain.

Efforts toward a simpler, less expensive, and more reliable gun led to the next significant step in firearms: the flintlock. The first flintlock was designed by the Frenchman Marin le Bourgeoys around 1615. The flintlock was a simpler design, and most of the moving parts were inside the gun, which made it much more weather-proof than its predecessors.

For over 200 years, the flintlock was the standard firearm of European armies. It was used in the greatest battles of the eighteenth century, it helped determine many of the rulers of Europe, and it helped set the borders of many European nations. The flintlock brought to an end the armor-wearing knight and also hastened the end of the Napoleonic wars.

**The first musket manufactured in the U.S. at the Springfield armory, 1795.**

The flintlock was also the customary firearm of the young United States and was instrumental in our battle for independence. In fact, to battle lawlessness, Natives, and to put food on the table, the gun was the most essential and prized tool in early America. As soon as they were old enough properly to hold and fire a flintlock, many young American boys were expected to help feed their families. Thus, generations of boys growing up and using guns from a young age played no small part in America winning her independence. "The Americans [are] the best marksmen in the world," lamented a minister of the Church of England in 1775.

The first original American contribution to firearms was the Kentucky rifle, which was made in Pennsylvania. This gun was superior to most every European contemporary. It was longer, lighter, and used a smaller caliber than other muzzle-loading guns at the time. Most importantly, as the name indicates, the Kentucky gun was "rifled." This process, which involves cutting helical grooves inside the gun barrel, greatly increased accuracy.

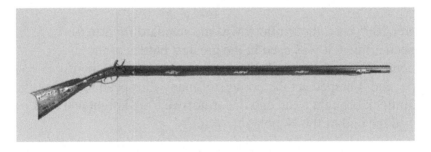

**Early 19th century (circa 1810) Kentucky rifle. Photo by John Spitzer.**

A typical musket fired a lead ball that was smaller in diameter than the barrel. Also, the barrels were smooth. Thus, when the musket was fired, the ball traveled down the gun barrel in a nonlinear path, bouncing off the sides of the barrel. Balls for rifles were made to fit more tightly inside the barrels. Also, a bullet fired from a rifled gun spins and thus helps stabilize any bullet imperfections (which were usually significant in the eighteenth century) that otherwise would distort flight (think bow-and-arrow vs. slingshot, or fastball vs. knuckleball).

In spite of all this, most American revolutionaries still carried smooth-bore muskets. Kentucky rifles took longer to load than smooth-bore muskets, and often the volume of fire was more important than accuracy. General George Washington made significant use of American marksmen armed with Kentucky rifles. These riflemen played major roles (as in picking off British officers) in such conflicts as the Battle of Saratoga.[5]

The birth of a new nation meant the need for a national armory. In 1777, General Washington settled on a strategic location in Springfield, Massachusetts, as the setting for the armory. In addition to being important for our national defense, the Springfield Armory led the world in technological advancements that would change manufacturing forever.

According to the Yale-New Haven Teachers Institute, "Robert Orr, a master armorer also at Springfield, introduced greater standardization of muskets in 1804." Like Eli Whitney's efforts, the manufacture of firearms at Springfield helped mark the beginning of the age of mass production.[6]

An ingenious inventor named Thomas Blanchard, who worked for the Springfield Armory for five years, created a special lathe for the production of wooden gun stocks. Such a lathe allowed for the easy manufacture of objects of irregular shape. This led, for example, to the easy mass production of shoes. Many other technical inventions—such as the typewriter, sewing machine, and the bicycle—were also born out of the gun industry. Factories that produced such products were often located near firearm manufacturers because the firearms industry possessed the most skilled craftsman necessary for creating the complicated parts for such machines.

The Springfield Armory also introduced contemporary business practices to manufacturing. Concepts such as hourly wages and cost accounting practices became customary at Springfield and were important steps in modernizing manufacturing. Again, according to the Yale-New Haven Teachers Institute,

> Roswell Lee, a former employee at the Whitney factory, now superintendent of the governments' Springfield, Massachusetts, Armory, began a factory management system. It included inspection and accounting controls which have become important in the American system of manufacturing.[7]

The next step in firearms development came from a minister. His severe frustration with the delay between trigger pull and gunfire (which too often allowed for the escape of his prized target, wild ducks) from his flintlock motivated the Reverend Alexander Forsyth to invent the percussion cap. Inside the cap was a small amount of impact sensitive explosive (like fulminate of mercury). Thus, muzzle-loading guns now did not have to rely on exposed priming powder to fire, were quicker to fire, and were almost completely weather-proof. However, gun users were still plagued by a centuries-old problem: they were limited to a single shot before reloading. Enter Samuel Colt.

Making use of the percussion cap, in 1836 Colt, with the aid of a mechanic, John Pearson, perfected and patented a revolving handgun. Although little of Colt's design was original, he ingeniously brought together existing features of previous guns and fashioned them into a mechanically elegant and reliable revolver. Along with being an inventor, Colt was a shrewd and capable businessman. His genius was not only in his gun design, but in the techniques used to manufacture it. His guns were made using interchangeable parts (made by machine and assembled by hand).

In 1847, with an order of 1,000 pistols from the U.S. Army and no factory to build them, Colt looked to noted gun-maker Eli Whitney Blake, the nephew of Eli Whitney, to help fill the order. It was the production of guns, and men such as Whitney, Blake, and Colt, that led the way in the pioneering and perfecting of the assembly line. Colt's sidearm soon became the preferred weapon of civilians and military personnel alike.

In 1850, heroes of the Texas Revolution, General Sam Houston and General Thomas Jefferson Rusk lobbied government officials to adopt Colt's revolvers as the standard-issue sidearm for the U.S. Army. Rusk testified that "Colt's Repeating Arms are the most efficient weapons in the world and the only weapon which has enabled the frontiersman to defeat the mounted Indian in his own peculiar mode of warfare." Lt. Bedley McDonald added that, while fighting in Mexico, 30 Texas Rangers used Colt's revolvers to keep 500 Mexicans in check.[8] Colt's 1851 Navy Revolver became the standard sidearm of U.S. military officers.

**Samuel Colt's 1851 Navy Revolver.**

When Colt's American patent expired in 1857, there were many who stood ready to take the next step in firearms, none more so than a pair of men who had spent much of their time perfecting ammunition, Horace Smith and Daniel Wesson. In 1856, just in time to take advantage of Colt's expiring patent, their partnership produced the world's first revolver that fired a fully self-contained cartridge. This cartridge was a "rimfire" variety that Smith and Wesson patented in 1854.

As handgun technology was progressing, long arms were beginning to catch up, and another American icon enters our history, a wealthy shirt maker named Oliver Winchester. Winchester took over a fledgling arms company in 1855 and in 1857 hired a gunsmith named Tyler Henry to turn it around.

By 1860, Henry had created a breech-loading lever-action repeating rifle, firing 16 rounds. The Henry Repeating Rifle was a tremendously popular, useful, and reliable gun. It was this weapon that began to make the single-shot muzzle-loading rifle obsolete.

*Civil War Henry Rifle*

**Henry Model 1860**

In 1866, Winchester improved on the Henry rifle and produced a model named after himself. The Winchester model 1866 fired 18 rounds, had a wooden forearm to make it less hot to handle, and contained the now-familiar side-loading port.

It was in 1873 that the two most legendary guns of the Old West were produced—the Winchester model 1873, which was a larger caliber than the 1866 model, and the Colt model 1873 (or Colt Single Action Army), otherwise known as "The Peacemaker." Carrying on with the savvy business sense of its founder, the Colt Company built this model to hold the exact same ammunition as the Winchester model 1873. The Peacemaker is officially known as "The Gun That Won the West."

**Winchester Model 1873**

**Colt Single Action Army ("Peacemaker")**

Integral to the success of Winchester Arms was the greatest gunsmith in the history of America, and maybe the world, John Browning. Over a 19-year relationship, Winchester manufactured 44 firearms designed and built by Browning. A devout Mormon, Browning held 128 gun patents and sold designs not only to Winchester, but also to Colt, Remington, Savage, and Fabrique Nationale.

Browning had his hand in almost every type of firearm design. Everything from single-shots and lever-actions to rifles and shotguns bore the influence of John Browning. Browning's guns, along with those by Colt, Winchester, and others put more fire-power in the hands of an individual than ever before. However, they paled in comparison to what was next. With virtually every step in gun advancement, there were many attempts toward the same goal. This was no different for the "machine gun."

Certainly the most famous of the early versions of the machine gun was the Gatling Gun. Mounted on a central axis with six rotating barrels, the Gatling Gun was fired by hand turning a rotating crank mounted on the side. Although not a true automatic, the Gatling could achieve several hundred rounds per minute.

The most successful and famous of the early fully automatic guns was the Maxim gun. Invented by an American-born Brit, Sir Hiram Stevens Maxim, this gun was introduced in 1884. The Maxim was completely automatic in the sense that it was "self-powered." In other words, using the tremendous amount of energy that was released when the gun was fired, it was now unnecessary for a discharged cartridge to be manually ejected and the next cartridge to be manually loaded. With the Maxim gun, this action continued with a single trigger pull. Maxim's gun could fire 10 rounds per second.

**Maxim with his 1884 machine gun.**

Maxim spent several years studying how to put the recoil energy of a gun to good use. He patented virtually every possible way of automatically operating a gun—so much so that, as Ian Hogg put it, "he could have probably quoted [only] one of his many patents and stifled machine gun development for the next 21 years, since almost every successful machine gun design can be foreseen in a Maxim patent."[9]

Men like Browning, Baron Von Odkolek, John Thompson, Mikhail Kalashnikov, and several others built off of Maxim's success, and machine guns became smaller and lighter. Browning was perhaps most famous for his automatic designs. By the 1890s Browning had designs that were vastly superior to the Gatling guns used by the U.S. military at the time.

Enter the twentieth century where fully automatic weapons that could be carried and operated by a single man were common place and necessary for any successful army. When the U.S. entered WWI, our soldiers were armed with rifles that were significantly inferior to those of our enemies and allies. In 1918, Browning equipped the U.S. military with his .30 caliber Browning Automatic Rifle (BAR). Though it was highly successful, the BAR did not become standard issue for the U.S. military until 1938. Toward the end of WWI, the tank was introduced to the battlefield. To serve as an anti-tank weapon, Browning upgraded his .30 caliber design to a .50 caliber. This machine gun was officially designated as the Browning M2, but was affectionately referred to as "Ma Deuce."

Though improving tank armor made it ineffective as an anti-tank weapon, the M2 became standard equipment for many U.S. vehicles, including planes and ships. Still in use today, and with nearly 100 years of service, the M2 is the longest-serving fully automatic weapon in the U.S. arsenal.

From before the founding of this great nation, firearms have been essential to the preservation of life, the enforcement of law and justice, and the establishment and protection of liberty. Our Founding Fathers understood well how important the gun was to the founding and maintaining of liberty in the U.S. and recognized the need for, "A well regulated militia, being necessary to the security of a free state…" And just what is the "militia?" No less than the co-author of the Second Amendment, George Mason, told us: "I ask, sir, what is the militia? It is the whole people ... To disarm the people is the best and most effectual way to enslave them." Even Jesus Christ Himself understood the significance of an armed man. In Luke He states, "When a strong man, fully armed, guards his own house, his possessions are safe."

A constitutional, unrestricted, universal right to keep and bear arms, such as the U.S. Constitution's Second Amendment secures, is unique. No other nation the world over allows for such access to firearms.[10] There can be little doubt that such access to guns has contributed to the unique and long-lasting liberty enjoyed by Americans.

Moreover, the technology that drove the progression of firearms and the improved manufacturing and business practices adopted at gun factories propelled the U.S. into the Industrial Age. With men like Whitney, Colt, Smith, Wesson, Henry, Winchester, and Browning leading the way, American gun manufacturing was at the forefront not only of the U.S. becoming an industrial world leader, but also a military leader as well.

# Innovation/Industrial Explosion, Part 3: Trains, Tocqueville, and the Telegraph

Textiles and firearms are only the beginning of the mighty Industrial Revolution in America. Around the same time as the biographer of Samuel Slater wrote Slater's memoir, Alexis De Tocqueville was touring the young United States. Tocqueville had been sent by the French to study the U.S. prison system. He used this opportunity to study American society in general, publishing his results in the classic *Democracy in America* in two volumes, the first, in 1835, the second, in 1840. Upon arriving in America, what first struck Tocqueville was the "religious atmosphere," which would be pivotal for America's economic success.

Writing on the influence of religion in America, Tocqueville concluded that religion is "considered as a political institution which powerfully supports the maintenance of a democratic republic among Americans." Tocqueville also took time to demonstrate "the direct act of religion on politics in the United States." He wrote that, though there was a wide variety of religious sects in the United States, offering differing forms of worship to the Creator, "they all agree about the duties that men owe to each other."[1]

Tocqueville added that, "Each sect adores God in its own particular way but all sects preach the same morality in the name of God…Moreover, all the sects in the United States unite in the

body of Christendom whose morality is everywhere the same."
This unity of morality led Tocqueville to note that,

> in the United States, the sovereign authority is
> religious...[and America is] the country in the
> world where the Christian religion has retained
> the greatest real power over people's souls and
> nothing shows better how useful and natural
> religion is to man, since the country where it
> exerts the greatest sway is also the most
> enlightened and free...Americans so completely
> identify the spirit of Christianity with freedom in
> their minds that it is almost impossible to get
> them to conceive one without the
> other...Tyranny may be able to do without faith,
> but freedom cannot.[2]

When reflecting upon the "philosophic method" that drove
democracy in America, Tocqueville concluded that,

> It is religion which has given birth to Anglo-
> American societies: one must never lose sight of
> that; in the United States, religion is thus
> intimately linked to all national habits and all the
> emotions which one's native country arouses;
> that gives it a particular strength...Christianity
> has therefore maintained a strong sway over the
> American mind and—something I wish to note
> above all—it rules not only like a philosophy
> taken up after evaluation but like a religion
> believed without discussion.[3]

The young French philosopher credited women, particularly wives,
as the "protectors of morals" in America. Religion "reigns supreme
in the souls of women," Tocqueville concluded. He added that,

> America is certainly the country where the bonds
> of marriage are most respected and where the
> concept of conjugal bliss has its highest and
> truest expression…Whereas the European seeks
> to escape from his domestic troubles by
> disturbing society, the American draws the love
> of order from his home which he then carries
> over into his affairs of state.[4]

The "conjugal bliss" enjoyed by many Americans, along with the fervent faith prevalent in the United States, contributed significantly to what Tocqueville would describe as an unusual degree of "tranquility of the people," along with the "stability of the institutions they have adopted."[5] Such faith, tranquility, and stability laid an excellent foundation for innovation and prosperity. Tocqueville would also conclude that if Americans were "free of all shackles, one would soon encounter among them the boldest innovators and the most relentless logicians in the world."[6] As the world would soon discover, the liberty enjoyed in America did indeed allow for an abundance of "bold innovators" and "relentless logicians."

In volume two of *Democracy in America*, Tocqueville took notice of the burgeoning industrial growth in the U.S:

> It is only fifty years since the United States
> emerged from the colonial dependence in which
> Britain held it. The number of great fortunes is
> very small and capital is still scarce. Yet no
> nation of the earth has made such swift progress
> in trade and industry as the Americans. Today
> they are the second maritime nation of the world
> and although their goods have to struggle against
> almost insurmountable obstacles, they do not fail
> to make fresh advances daily.

> In the United States, the greatest industrial
> projects are completed without trouble because
> the entire population is engaged in industry and

because the poorest and the richest citizens are
ready to unite their efforts for this purpose. It is
thus a daily surprise to see the huge works
achieved without difficulty by a nation which
has, so to speak, no wealthy people. The
Americans arrived but yesterday upon the
ground they inhabit, but already have turned the
natural order inside out, to their financial
advantage. They have joined the Hudson and
Mississippi rivers and linked the Atlantic to the
Gulf of Mexico across a continent of more than
twelve hundred miles separating the two seas.
The longest railroads ever constructed up until
the present are in America.[7]

As Tocqueville implied, improved transportation was vital to the
Industrial Revolution in the U.S. In addition to the massive U.S.
railroads, ambitious construction projects such as the Erie Canal
were undertaken in the early nineteenth century. Begun in 1817,
the Erie Canal was a civil engineering marvel. Opening in 1825,
with a length of over 360 miles, the canal was far longer than any
other canal previously built in America or Europe.

The success of the Erie Canal set off a canal frenzy in the U.S.
Such infrastructure, combined with the development of the
steamboat, resulted in an impressive water transportation network
that allowed for much easier transportation of people and goods.
Combined with railroads, this innovative transportation network
led not only to improved development in the east, but also to
expansion to the west as well.

Though the steam engine was largely a British development, the
steamboat was pioneered in the U.S. In 1787, in the presence of
delegates of the Constitutional Convention, John Fitch made the
first successful trial of a steamboat. The next year Fitch would
begin a commercial operation of a passenger steamboat that
operated between Philadelphia, Pennsylvania, and Burlington,
New Jersey, along the Delaware River. However, Fitch's operation
would not be a commercial success until 1811.

Success would fall to Robert Fulton, partnering with Robert Livingston, a lawyer from New York who served in the Continental Congress. In August of 1807, Fulton's boat, the *Clermont*, would make the 150-mile trip from New York City to Albany in 32 hours. Fulton's steamboat success brought him much notoriety and respect, leading the Governor of New York to appoint Fulton to the Erie Canal Commission.

In 1819, the American-built *Savannah* was the first steam ship to cross the Atlantic, though only a small portion of the trip was made under steam power. However, the *Savannah* made the trip in just over 29 days, which was 11 days shorter than the average sailing ship's time of 38 days. Steamboats improved not only travel, but also trade as well. The development of the steamboat was just in time to turn the mighty Mississippi River into a major thoroughfare of commerce in the United States. Just five years prior to the *Clermont's* maiden voyage, the American government purchased the Louisiana Territory from France. This purchase approximately doubled the size of the U.S., giving the opportunity for vast expansion to the West. It also gave free and total access to the Mississippi River, as well as the port of New Orleans.

No one took more advantage of the new shipping technology and network of waterways in the U.S. than did Cornelius Vanderbilt. After purchasing his first ferryboat at the age of 16 with a loan of $100, the Vanderbilt name soon became synonymous with shipping. With a fleet of ships delivering goods and passengers to virtually every part of the U.S., within the span of about four decades, "The Commodore," as Vanderbilt was known, built the largest shipping empire in the world.

However, just prior to the Civil War, Vanderbilt saw that the future of transportation was not in shipping. During the war, he liquidated his vast shipping assets and invested exclusively in railroads.

After the invention of the steam locomotive, it wasn't long before railroads were competing with steamboats. Colonel John Stevens was the earliest pioneer of railroading in the U.S. Stevens, a wealthy New Jersey lawyer, engineer, and business man, is considered the father of American railroads. Not long after Fulton launched the *Clermont*, Stevens built his own steamboat. Canal building, and boat or ship building, in addition to needing large bodies of water, were extremely expensive undertakings. Early steamboats were also quite dangerous, as boiler explosions were not uncommon. Thus, railroads were seen as a more practical means of transportation.

**Replica of John Stevens' steam carriage.**

On his estate in Hoboken, New Jersey, in 1825 Col. Stevens built a steam locomotive capable of pulling several passenger cars. In 1826 Stevens built the first railroad in the U.S. It was also on his estate in Hoboken and was a circular 630-foot wooden track. Before long, iron rails would replace wooden ones, which allowed for larger and faster locomotives. Initially, while not very comfortable or practical for passengers, trains soon became instrumental in transporting American commodities and products, such as cotton from the South which was sent via train to the textile mills of the North.

The first long-distance railroad in America was built in the South. It ran a distance of 136 miles and connected the town of Hamburg, South Carolina, to the port city of Charleston. At the time of its opening, the South Carolina Railroad was the longest railroad in the world.

"A railroad is like a lie"—wrote American icon Mark Twain— "you have to keep building it to make it stand." "Keep building" is exactly what Americans did. By 1840, there were over 300 railway companies in the U.S. By 1850, about 9,000 miles of railroad track had been laid in the U.S. In 1851, according to *Scientific American*,[8] "No country in the world could equal ours for the number of railroads." By the end of the Civil War, in 1865, over 30,000 miles of railroad track covered America. Every major eastern and mid-western city was connected by rail. By 1900, there were over 200,000 miles of track in the U.S.—more than Europe, Asia, and Africa combined.[9]

The real boom in the railroad industry began in 1862 when President Lincoln signed the Pacific Railway Act. The act provided for the construction of a transcontinental railroad. To encourage the construction, two railroad companies, Union Pacific and Central Pacific, were given land along the right-of-way of the track. Central Pacific began laying track eastward from Sacramento, California, in January of 1863. After the Civil War ended, Union Pacific began westward construction from Omaha, Nebraska, in 1865. The two lines were joined with the placement of a ceremonial golden spike in the final section of track at Promontory Summit in the Utah Territory on May 10, 1869.

The construction of the transcontinental railroad was the beginning of the consolidation of the hundreds of disconnected rail lines that ran throughout the East. Men such as Cornelius Vanderbilt were behind these consolidation efforts. The joining of railway lines was significant for the wider transport of commodities across the U.S. With the development of more comfortable passenger cars, trains also made it easier for people to move about what was becoming an ever more vast United States.

Railroads became the first real example of big business in the U.S., and Cornelius Vanderbilt was king of this business. At the height of his empire, he owned more rail lines than anyone in the world. One of the consolidations by Cornelius Vanderbilt resulted in the New York Central and Hudson River Railroad, which was one of the first giant corporations in American history. The Central, the Hudson, and the Harlem railroads were joined in the heart of New York at the Grand Central Depot. The Grand Central building was the largest building in New York at the time, and Grand Central Station was the largest train station in the U.S.

According to Richard Sylla and Robert E. Wright, in 1856, transportation enterprises, mostly railroads, made up 341 of the top 500 (68 percent) U.S. companies.[10] Furthermore, of the 25 largest companies in 1856, 17 were railroads, with an additional two being railroad-bank hybrids. The three largest companies were all newly formed railroads. By 1860, railroads were the first billion dollar industry in America. America was on the verge of leading the world economically, and railroads were paving the way.

Running a railroad, especially a large one, was a massive undertaking. As author Stanley Buder points out, "Daily decision-making operations involved people, stations, offices, warehouses, car barns, trains, tracks, and telegraph lines."[11] Additionally, a schedule of train movements had to be established. Thus, new business practices had to be tried and tested. Much like the gun industry decades earlier, the railroad industry was instrumental in pioneering modern business practices.

Also, much like the gun and textile industries, the railroad industry was a home for invention, innovation, and skilled craftsmen. Again, as Buder points out,

> The railroads provided a workshop for American industry, training several generations of engineers. American mechanics learned to work with precise measurements to high standards of reliability for the sake of safety. An ancient respect for leisurely craftsmanship surrendered to

a need for quick servicing and repairs as well as knowledge of the right parts and tools: what impressed English observers about American mechanics was 'the application of special tools to minute purposes.' A nascent machine-tool industry for the textile industry had sprung up in the 1820s in Windsor, Vermont, and Providence, Rhode Island. 'Yankee tinkers' became celebrated for their versatility in devising the light, accurate, machine tools needed to manufacture tiny clock parts, gun components, and pieces for the newly invented sewing machine. Now machine shops for the railroads took their places alongside the older tool shops. The railroad industry spurred the development of machine-tool factories to build milling machines, engine parts, boilers, frames, axles, and wheels as well. Other shops manufactured the specially developed tools and machines necessary to make these parts. By 1860, Britain's long-enjoyed lead over the United States in machine tools had been reversed.[12]

Newly organized railroads required specialized departments such as finance, purchasing, traffic, sales, real estate, engineering, and law.[13] Railroads were the first in the modern era of business to require regular use of speedy logistics. Lives literally depended on it. Telegraph lines were essential in coordinating the complex movements of passenger trains as well as freight trains.

A network of telegraph was developed throughout the 1830s and 1840s both in Europe and America. After the growth of the railroads and passenger trains, widespread fear grew among the public that two trains on the same track travelling in opposite directions would collide. To allay such fears, engineers and scientists started stringing up wires for an electrical communications system alongside the track that enabled the signalmen at various positions along the rail line to communicate. Soon, electronic telegraphy, or simply "the telegraph," was born.

Synonymous with the telegraph in the U.S. is painter and inventor Samuel Morse. In the 1830s, along with Leonard Gale and Alfred Vail, Morse developed a single-wire electronic telegraph that was capable of transmitting messages over many miles. Of course, Morse is best known for the "Morse code"—a method of using sounds or light to transmit textual information—that he and Vail also developed.

In 1843, Morse and Vail received funding from the U.S. Congress to run their telegraph line between Baltimore, Maryland, and Washington, D.C. Upon completion, on May 24, 1844, giving credit and glory to the One who is the Creator of all things, Morse sent Vail the historic message: "What hath God wrought!" Soon telegraph lines ran along railroad tracks throughout America. Communications that once took days or weeks now only took a few seconds or minutes.

Just as the railroad and steamboats changed the way we moved people and goods across this great land and laid the foundation for transportation innovation, the telegraph—the forerunner to the telephone, fax machine, and the internet—forever changed the way we communicate and share information, and again, just as with railroads and steamships, America was at the forefront of this innovation.

In 1855, Morse, together with Peter Cooper, Abram Hewitt, Moses Taylor, and Cyrus Field formed the American Telegraph Company. They bought up other companies and, like the railroad companies, consolidated lines. They linked Maine with the Gulf Coast, and lines were extending further and further to the West. The era of instant communication was born.

However, communication across the oceans still took a matter of weeks. Cyrus Field was determined to change that. The wealthy son of a Congregationalist minister, Field had achieved a great deal of business success by the time he was in his mid-thirties. The Fields were an amazing family. Cyrus had several siblings who were just as successful professionally as he was. One brother was an engineer, another a judge, two others were successful merchants. It was Cyrus' brother, Matthew Field, the engineer, who came to him with the idea of laying telegraph cable along the bottom of the sea.

Such a venture required large amounts of capital, much beyond that which Field himself possessed. Peter Cooper, one of the wealthiest men in America at the time, was the most significant financial partner in the laying of the first transatlantic telegraph cable. Cooper, who designed and built the first steam locomotive in the U.S., the Tom Thumb, and who made money in everything from glue to paint to iron-works, helped supervise the laying of the cable across the Atlantic in 1858.

Cooper, like Field, was a man of faith and saw his wealth as a means to improve the world. The Transatlantic cable, though certainly a project in which all investors hoped to see a financial return, was also seen as much more than a money-making opportunity. It was not lost on men such as Field and Cooper that significant good was possible through shrinking the world by connecting two continents with a cable.

Though several attempts had to be made before it was successful, Europe was connected with North America by undersea telegraphic cable on August 5, 1858. On August 16, 1858, the first official message was sent and received. As was the case with Samuel Morse's message across his D.C. telegraph lines, God was given the glory. The message read, "Europe and America are united by telegraphy. Glory to God in the highest; on earth, peace and good will toward men."

Queen Victoria sent a telegram of congratulations to U.S. President James Buchanan that expressed a hope that the cable would provide "an additional link between the nations whose friendship is founded on their common interest and reciprocal esteem." President Buchanan replied that,

> [I]t is a triumph more glorious, because far more useful to mankind, than was ever won by conqueror on the field of battle. May the Atlantic telegraph, under the blessing of Heaven, prove to

> be a bond of perpetual peace and friendship
> between the kindred nations, and an instrument
> destined by Divine Providence to diffuse
> religion, civilization, liberty, and law throughout
> the world.[14]

News quickly spread across America, and jubilant celebrations were not uncommon. New York City was filled with fireworks and parades. Tens of thousands marched up Broadway. Cyrus Field received a message from his brother: "Cyrus, your father danced like a boy and all over town bells are being rung. The joyful news has nearly overwhelmed your wife and family."

Cyrus, however, was not celebrating. It was clear from the beginning to those with technical knowledge of the system that the cable was not operating as it should. The Queen's message took hours to transmit, and signals were continuously getting weaker. The problem was that the voltage used to create the signals was too high, and the cable was inoperable within a matter of about three weeks. Celebration soon turned to derision, and some wondered if the whole matter wasn't a hoax.

Field went from being the toast of the town to a laughingstock. However, he remained undeterred. It was his Christian faith that sustained him during these trying times. In a sermon delivered to students at the chapel of Ohio State University in the early twentieth century entitled, *Is Faith Rational*, Dr. W.O. Thompson noted,

> Do you know that Cyrus Field ruined himself
> financially and a lot of his friends and that they
> abused him and cursed him and that the
> newspapers were full of the names of the victims
> of Cyrus Field? The talk all over the country was
> what a foolish man he was to ruin himself
> financially and lose his fortune and that of his
> friends in a false notion he could tie the
> continents together with a cable. Cyrus Field
> lived long enough to hear the first message sent

across the ocean by means of the cable. It was
the undying spirit of faith that gave him the
vision and power to do these things. Today you
and I enjoy the victory of his faith because his
faith was the factor my young friends.[15]

Dr. Thompson added,

> Do you suppose in the days of the darkest hours
> of this republic when Abraham Lincoln was
> walking his floor by night and by day when that
> sad faced statesman looking across those hills
> and valleys feeling that the pressure of a great
> republic was upon him and that the greatest issue
> of modern history was being enacted when he
> did not know what the next day would bring
> forth; do you suppose that great man in those
> hours ever lost his faith in the integrity of the
> American people or ever lost his faith that this
> ought to be a long continued republic?...It was
> because of his undying faith that Abraham
> Lincoln stood secure in his place. The great
> victories of this world have been the victories of
> men of faith.[16]

The Civil War in the U.S. hindered attempts at laying new cable
and gave Field time to seek out new investors and better scientists.
The next attempt was in 1865, another attempt which failed when
the cable snapped. The broken cable was retrieved and spliced
together with new cable in 1866. During this retrieval, a second
cable was laid as well. Each cable was a vast improvement over
the 1858 one. Along with being more durable, the new ones were
nearly 100 times faster.

These two cables worked to carry messages from the U.S. to Great
Britain until 1872 and 1877, respectively.[17] By then, four new
cables had been laid. Since 1866, direct communication between
America and England has never been broken. By 1890 there were

well over 100,000 miles of undersea cable, connecting all parts of the world. Even into the twenty-first century, most communication between the U.S. and Europe was still carried by transatlantic cable.[18]

By 1861, the first transcontinental telegraph lines were strung. The Pacific Telegraph Company constructed a line westward starting from Omaha, Nebraska, while the Overland Telegraph Company built eastward from Carson City, Nevada. The two lines met in Salt Lake City in October of 1861. Thus, with the completion of the transcontinental railroad in 1869, it was now possible to send a message or a package from one coast of America to the other with relative ease and significant speed.

As Buder would summarize,

> In 1866 the first transatlantic telegraph cable was laid; three years later the first transcontinental railroad opened for business. Soon the nation's rapidly evolving railroad system serviced a continent-wide market; the size of this national marker created an explosive demand for goods and services, offering incentives for technological advance. In the ten years between 1865 and 1875, the nation's industrial output rose 75 percent. The escalating breakneck pace of change in the next several decades signifies the advent of a technology of mass production based on steam power and steel—the Machine Age. The immense fortunes of the final third of the century, the fabled wealth of men such as John D. Rockefeller and Andrew Carnegie, came from industry, not commerce or real estate. Industrial America had arrived.[19]

# CHAPTER 17

# Innovation/Industrial Explosion, Part 4: Let There Be Light!

Like the railroad industry, the telegraph industry was also home to innovation and innovators. By far the most significant innovator to get his start in telegraphy was "the most ingenious inventor" of the nineteenth century, and perhaps of all time, Thomas Edison. Edison held over a thousand patents, and the impact of his inventions was widespread. The electrical, transportation, communication, photographic, recording, and sound industries were especially impacted.

Along with the first practical incandescent light, Edison invented the electrographic vote recorder, the automatic telegraph, and the phonograph.

See sketches of Edison's inventions on the following pages:

Edison's phonograph or "Speaking Machine:"

T A. EDISON.
Phonograph or Speaking Machine.
No. 200,521.          Patented Feb. 19, 1878.

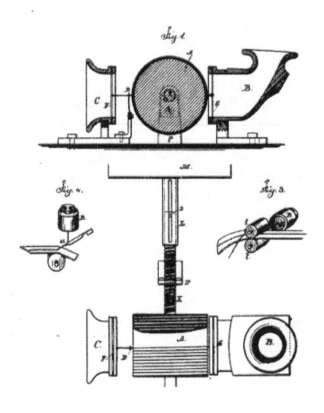

Edison's electric motor:

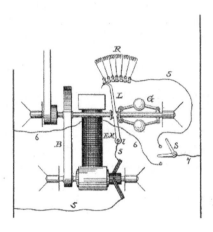

and the alkaline battery:

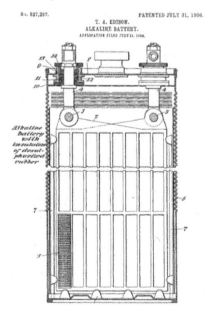

Edison also made improvements to the telephone and the electric lighting system.

Almost every one of these inventions was born out of what may have been Edison's most significant contribution to science and industry: Menlo Park, which has been called the world's first research and development laboratory. Menlo Park was opened in the spring of 1876. It was here that Edison first started experimenting with the idea of recording the human voice, and by late 1877, the phonograph was born. The phonograph brought Edison great fame and fortune. He was soon after dubbed "The Wizard of Menlo Park."[1]

Not only was Edison a prolific inventor; he was a savvy businessman as well. Edison used the funds from the phonograph, not to live extravagantly, but to fund further research and invention. As evidence of his financial shrewdness, Edison, always aware of the need for publicity and marketing, in the influential magazine the *North American Review*, detailed how the phonograph could be used:

> Among the many uses to which the phonograph will be applied are the following:
>
> 1) Letter writing and all kinds of dictation without the aid of a stenographer;
>
> 2) Phonographic books which will speak to blind people without effort on their part;
>
> 3) The teaching of elocution;
>
> 4) The reproduction of music;
>
> 5) The Family Record (a registry of saying, reminiscence, etc., by members of a family in their own voices, and the last words of dying persons;
>
> 6) Music boxes and toys;
>
> 7) Clocks that should announce inarticulate speech the time for going home, time for meals, etc.;

8) The preservation of languages by exact reproduction of the manner of pronouncing;

9) Educational purposes, such as preserving the explanations made by a teacher so that the pupil can refer to them at any moment; and spelling or other lessons placed upon the phonograph for convenience in committing to memory;

10) Connection with the telephone so as to make that instrument an auxiliary in the transmission of permanent and invaluable records, instead of being the recipient of momentary and fleeting communication.[2]

With his new capital, Edison expanded Menlo Park, hired more engineers, and began work on what would be his most memorable invention, the incandescent light. Around this time, Edison also made improvements to Alexander Graham Bell's telephone.

Bell, a Scottish-born American, patented the telephone in 1876. He conducted what historian Thomas Costain dubbed "the three great tests of the telephone," including the world's first true long distance call (58 miles) in the summer of 1876. In September of that year, *Scientific American,* in an article entitled "The Human Voice Transmitted by Telegraph," described Bell's tests.

Edison had been pursuing a "speaking telegraph" at the same time as Bell and others. Although Bell won the race, Edison saw serious flaws in Bell's work and set out to correct them. By 1877, Edison had a significant improvement to Bell's transmitter (microphone). According to Robert Silverberg in *Light for the World: Edison and the Power Industry*, in a test in March of 1878, Edison's carbon grain transmitter successfully carried messages loudly and clearly over a distance of 107 miles along a line between New York and Philadelphia.[3]

Edison's transmitter patent was sold to Bell in 1879. The telephone was soon a significant commercial success the world over. Again, the U.S. led the way. As author Lee Wyatt III notes in *The Industrial Revolution*, by 1883, in New York City, there was one telephone for every 500 persons. This compared to one per 1,000 in Paris, one per 3,000 in London and Berlin, and one per 4,000 in St. Petersburg.[4]

By the time Edison abandoned his efforts with the telephone, along with his efforts to improve the phonograph, he became captivated with the idea of the incandescent light. Edison had long been intrigued by the work of Michael Faraday. As Silverberg put it,

> In Faraday he felt he had found a kindred spirit, a man who probed the mysteries of the universe not by scratching calculations on a sheet of paper, but by building machines and making them work. The night he brought the Faraday books home, Edison began reading at four o'clock in the morning and continued well into the day. The clear prose, the revelation of exciting possibilities, the sense of dedicated questing—these things drew Edison's deepest sympathies. "His explanations were simple," Edison later wrote. "He used no mathematics. He was the master experimenter."[5]

One of the most significant scientists of the nineteenth century, Faraday invented the first modern "dynamo." A dynamo is essentially an electrical generator that produces direct current. These were the first generators used in industry. Faraday's model was only a crude prototype and not practical for commercial use. Faraday simply didn't have Edison's acumen for business, and it was left to later men to perfect the dynamo. Men like Pixii (French), Saxton (American), Nollet (French), Holmes (English), Hjorth (Danish), Siemens (German), Pacinotti (Italian), Gramme (Belgian), Alteneck (German), Wheatstone (English), and Brush (American) improved the dynamo to the point that it was capable of producing power for industry.

Early applications for dynamos focused on lighting instead of power. By the late 1870s the dynamo was frequently used to power arc lights, a forerunner of the incandescent light. As more and more people became exposed to electrical lighting, the race was on for a better light. In an attempt to light the world, many others prior to Edison had done great work in the field. However, a solution that would widely bring light into homes, churches, schools, factories, offices, stores, and so on, was elusive.

After a restful sabbatical, Edison immersed himself in the problem. As he put it,

> When I want to discover something, I begin by reading up everything that has been done along that line in the past—that's what all these books in the library are for. I see what has been accomplished at great labor and expense in the past. I gather the data of many thousands of experiments as a starting point, and then I make thousands more.[6]

Edison envisioned far more than a bulb that would glow as electrical current flowed through it. He had the idea for a whole system of lighting where electricity would be generated and distributed to homes, churches, schools, factories, offices, and stores. "A general system of distribution" was how Edison put it, which was the "only possible means of economical illumination."[7]

Such a system was magnificently complex. Everything from the generation of electricity, to the logistics of the poles and the wires to carry it, to the sockets, fuses, and switches necessary to receive it properly, to the meters necessary to measure how much was being used, to the devices that would run on the current, all had to be conceived first, and then solved and manufactured. It was just the type of problem on which Edison thrived. Edison patented his system for the distribution of electricity in 1880.

Edison's system was as expensive as it was complex. The power plants alone were massive expenditures. Serious capital was needed to create and deliver the electricity that would be demanded by homes, businesses, and the like. Thus, Edison turned to Wall Street.[8] Advised to do so by his corporate attorney, Grosvenor Lowrey, in late 1878 Edison began a self-promotion campaign. Using veiled telegrams and disguised quotes to reporters, Edison shrewdly teased the media and potential investors with talk of what was the cornerstone of his electrical system: the incandescent light.

Edison left the details of the financial negotiations with Lowrey. Lowrey secured the backing of railroad tycoon W.H. Vanderbilt and America's most powerful banker, J.P. Morgan, among others. By the middle of October, 1878, the Edison Electric Light Company was formed.

Edison's big talk and open optimism led to the notion that he was only a few weeks away from mastering the electric light. However, this was far from the case, and as weeks turned into months, his investors became very nervous. Even the press began to question openly Edison's progress with the electric light. Edison was doggedly undeterred.

Such persistence was one of the biggest reasons behind Edison's legend. As he would note in 1890,

> Just consider this. We have an almost infinitesimal filament heated to a degree which it is difficult to comprehend, and it is in a vacuum under conditions of which we are wholly ignorant. You cannot use your eyes to help you, and you really know nothing of what is going on in that tiny bulb. I speak without exaggeration when I say that I have constructed 3,000 different theories in connection with the electric light, each of them reasonable and apparently likely to be true. Yet in two cases only did my experiments prove the truth of my theories.[9]

Thus, we can see the motivation for the famous Edison quote: "Genius is one percent inspiration and 99 percent perspiration."

On November 4, 1879, Edison submitted a patent application for his carbon filament lamp. "Fifteen Months Of Toil," as the *New York Herald* put it, finally bore fruit.[10] The lighting business was off to a strong start. However, as usual, Edison saw room for improvement. The carbonized paper filament was far too fragile and difficult to make. In addition, others had patented a paper filament, and litigation was inevitable. The search for a better filament was on again.

In 1880 Edison found bamboo to be preferable to paper. With thousands of species of bamboo, the search was on again for the best replacement for the paper filament. By this time, a share of stock in Edison Electric Light was worth nearly $3,000. Edison's financiers were very willing to fund the search. Carbonized bamboo was soon used to light Edison's bulbs.

In 1881, in order to help sell the concept of electrical lights, J.P. Morgan had Edison install his lighting system throughout Morgan's Fifth Avenue home in New York City. The Morgan home became a laboratory for Edison's lighting experiments. Using a steam engine and a dynamo, Edison installed a small power plant in a backyard shed on Morgan's property. Edison ran 4,000 feet of wiring through the walls and ceilings of Morgan's mansion and installed nearly 400 electric light bulbs. After several months of toil and experimentation, Morgan and Edison were ready for the home to be displayed. Morgan's home was the world's first private residence to be lit by electricity.

As Edison worked tirelessly on his light, he simultaneously gave attention to every aspect of his electrical system. The Edison Illuminating Company, today ConEdison, built the world's first commercial power plant at Pearl Street in Manhattan, New York. It started generating electricity on September 4, 1882. According to author Dan Rottenberg, the Pearl Street plant was "a huge complex of boilers, steam engines, and dynamos."[11] The dynamos heated water to the point of steam inside a boiler. The steam would build up pressure and flow through a turbine rotating the turbine blades. The rotating blades would induce an electrical current inside a generator attached to the turbine. The electricity then went from the generators to the power lines.

By the middle of 1883, Edison set out to build power plants all over the U.S. However, far more than power plants needed to be manufactured to light up America. The bulbs had to be manufactured, thus the Edison Lamp Company was formed. To produce the dynamos and other heavy equipment necessary to run the power plants, Edison Machine Works was formed. The Thomas A. Edison Construction Department was organized to sell and build the power plants.[12] In 1889, with the aid of J.P. Morgan, Edison's companies, including Edison Electric Light, in which Edison was no longer the majority stock holder, were merged into one corporation: Edison General Electric Company, which would soon become the renowned General Electric.

Edison was known the world over. His factories and research facility drew some of the best minds in the world. One such mind belonged to Nikola Tesla. A Serbian-born engineer and physicist, Tesla was an electrical genius. Some view Tesla's electrical ability and expertise beyond that of Edison. However, Tesla was socially awkward, and his ability to woo investors and win the public was sorely lacking. In addition, Tesla had a difficult time putting his brilliant ideas into practice.

Tesla came to New York in 1884 at the age of 28. He went to work two days later at Edison Machine Works. Tesla was given the job of fixing the problems with Edison's dynamos (DC generators). According to Tesla, Edison offered him $50,000 if he could complete the task. In a few months, Tesla was done. When he inquired about the pay, Edison told Tesla that it was only a joke, and that he didn't understand American humor. Tesla would soon depart Edison's company.

Tesla, partnering with others who were willing to finance him, soon formed his own companies and filed his own patents. The Tesla Electric Light Company failed. However, Tesla caught the attention of George Westinghouse. Soon the "Battle of the Currents" was on.

Alternating current (AC) had been around as long as direct current (DC). Originally, Edison's preference for direct current seemed to be simply a matter of convenience. The dynamos that existed when

Edison built his plants were almost exclusively of the DC variety, so that's what he used. Before long, though, Edison made a final decision and was irreversibly wed in favor of DC current for his electrical system.[13]

It was not so much the current that mattered to Edison, but the voltage. His system was based on the idea that customers would receive their power at about 110 volts, approximately the same voltage at which it left the plant, and at a low amperage. The main concern was safety. An unsuspecting customer who came in contact with an exposed line or wire with this type of current would receive only a mild shock. The risk of fire with Edison's system was also low.

However, direct current at 110 volts could be transmitted only a relatively short distance (one to two miles from the power plant) before the drop in voltage was too large to provide sufficient light to customers' lamps. Thus, a large number of expensive power plants would be necessary to provide a large number of customers with satisfactory power. None of this was the case with alternating current.

Edison's chief rival in the current wars was another titan of early American industry: George Westinghouse. Westinghouse made his initial fortune with his 1869 invention of a railroad braking system that made use of compressed air. The Westinghouse Air Brake Company was formed in the early 1870s, and this new braking system was nearly universally adopted across the railroad industry. Given the vastness of the railroad industry in America at this time, Westinghouse's fortune was soon made. The braking system on modern trains is based on the Westinghouse design.

By the 1880s, Westinghouse saw the opportunities in the electrical industry and was eager to get into the business. To be a true rival to Edison, Westinghouse wanted to explore the opportunities offered by alternating current (AC). To do this, he needed two things: a practical industrial AC generator and a workable transformer.

Unlike DC current, AC current could be generated at very high voltages, and then, with the use of a transformer, stepped down as it reached the customer. Westinghouse purchased the rights (an opportunity Edison turned down) to a European transformer (Z.B.D. transformer) in order to create an AC lighting system.

Like Edison, Westinghouse was also a magnet for some of the best engineers in the U.S. as well as the world. When Tesla left Edison, it wasn't long until he was working for Westinghouse. Tesla was a proponent of AC current, which also put him at odds with Edison. Tesla built and patented the first AC motor and developed the technology for AC generation and transmission. In 1888, Westinghouse purchased Tesla's patents and hired him as a consultant. By the 1890s, the future for widespread household and industrial use of electricity lay with alternating current. Eventually, even the executives at Edison General Electric were won over.

"Between 1890 and 1905, the amount of electric power available in the United States increased hundred-fold."[14] By the time of Edison's death in 1931, the electrical industry in the U.S. was serving over 86 million Americans—about 70 percent of the population. Over 3,800 power plants provided electricity to nearly 25 million American structures.[15]

This system of producing and delivering electricity is the quintessential symbol for the beginning of the modern age. The harnessing of electricity spawned countless inventions that revolutionized the way the world lived. Again, it was Americans who led the way. In 1902, in order to cool production at a printing company in Brooklyn, New York, American research engineer Willis Carrier invented the world's first electrical air conditioning system.[16] In 1908, American James Spangler patented the first commercially successful vacuum cleaner. (He soon sold his patents to fellow American William Hoover.)[17] Though there is dispute about who is the actual inventor, Americans such as Chicago engineer Alva Fisher developed the world's first electric clothes washing machines. Patented in 1910, Fisher's "Thor washing machine" was the first electric clothes washer sold commercially.[18]

The "Edison System" is widely considered the greatest invention of a great—if not the greatest—inventor. This amazing innovation would forever change the world. Edison's main focus was the lighting of homes. Through his efforts a young boy could now read *Treasure Island* in the comfort of his home, in the middle of the darkest night, without having to light a fire. However, as virtually all who live in twenty-first century America well know, a modern home is not much of a home without TVs, computers, refrigerators, ovens, air conditioning, washers, dryers—and of course, lights. Thirty minutes without electricity is usually enough to remind all of us how important electricity is to our lives. In addition, without electricity, today's schools, hospitals, factories, and so on, shut down.

As the use of electricity grew, by the late nineteenth century, the standard of living in the U.S. was the envy of the world. In addition, Edison's system of electricity changed the manufacture of nearly everything. With the industrial advantages already possessed by the U.S., American manufacturing also became the envy of the world. What's more, the U.S. was now on the doorstep of becoming the world's leading economic power.

# CHAPTER 18

# Innovation/Industrial Explosion, Part 5: Fossil Fuels

The best, most efficient fuel to create the necessary steam for power plants was coal. By this time in American history, coal was already a significant source of fuel in industry across America. Of course, steam engines required fires, and thus a plentiful source of fuel was necessary to power the trains and the ships that ran on steam. Initially wood was used as the main fuel source for steam engines. By about 1870 wood was replaced by coal. Power plants only increased the use and need for coal. At this point, fossil fuels became indispensable to American industry and the U.S. economy.

By the mid-1800s the use of coal to power U.S. factories was significant. Along with the manufacture of arms and ammunition, the American Civil War expanded the use of coal as fuel for the growing industrialization taking place in the U.S. The growth of the railroad and gun industries gave birth to the modern steel industry. By the late 1850s, William Kelly of Pittsburgh, Pennsylvania, and in Britain, Henry Bessemer, simultaneously developed a process for converting pig iron into steel. (Kelly implied that Bessemer learned of the process from Europeans who had been to Kelly's mill.) Pig iron could now be converted into steel in a matter of minutes. According to Dan Rottenberg,

> When the Cambria Iron Works produced
> America's first two and a half tons of steel rails
> in 1867, the Pittsburgh Courier declared that the
> steel would last twenty years, compared to the

> three-year life of the iron rails it would replace.
> 'The day of iron is past!' declared Andrew
> Carnegie before launching his steel works at
> Braddock, twelve miles from Pittsburgh in 1873.
> 'Steel is king!'[added Carnegie][1]

Carnegie's steel mill was the first in the U.S. Like many of the other prominent industrialists of the nineteenth century, Carnegie was quite adept at perfecting mass-production in the steel industry. His efforts were so profitable that he and his associates quickly bought out other steel mills, and in 1892 Carnegie Steel Company was formed. It was headquartered in Pittsburgh, Pennsylvania.

Bessemer's attempts to solve the problems in the manufacture of steel were the result of his efforts in trying to improve production of guns. Moreover, the massive amounts of steel produced in the U.S. literally allowed for a new framework for industry and industrial products. As Wyatt notes in *The Industrial Revolution*, "[P]erhaps no industry represented the new age dawning in the United States more than that of steel production. In 1865 the nation produced 16,000 tons of steel. Sixty years later the annual production was 56 million tons."[2] By the turn of the twentieth century, the U.S. was the world's largest producer of steel, with production more than doubling that of the second-place nation, Great Britain.[3] Additionally, steel made everything from railroad rails to gun barrels and generators more reliable.

As it was for the railroad industry, coal was the fuel for the steel industry. And as is still the case today, coal was plentiful in the United States. By the latter half of the nineteenth century, trains, ships, steel mills, power plants, textile factories and the like were using vast quantities of coal. Thus, by the 1890s the U.S. was the largest coal producer in the world, which certainly was a significant reason for the explosion in the steel industry. Not coincidentally, around this time America surpassed Britain as the world's leading industrial nation. There's no doubt that coal literally fueled the early industrial revolution in America, and for the most part, the world over.

Though coal was the fuel for industry, prior to Edison's system of electricity, it was kerosene, refined from oil, that powered homes. To make money, railroads needed to fill their trains with goods and/or passengers. The burgeoning new industry of oil soon drew the attention of the railroads. In 1863, at 24 years old, John D. Rockefeller invested all of his financial resources in his first oil refinery. In 1870, along with his brother William and four others, John formed Standard Oil. For the most part, the oil was refined into a safe, stable form of kerosene which was used for heating and lighting in homes. By the end of the decade, Standard Oil was refining over 90 percent of American oil.

In search of cargo for his trains, Cornelius Vanderbilt called on Rockefeller. In late December of 1867 they were to meet in New York to discuss transport rates. On the morning of December 18, 1867, Rockefeller was uncharacteristically running late. He had decided to take the opportunity to make a holiday visit to family and friends in New York. Along with his personal attire and effects, he packed many Christmas gifts. He sent the bags ahead of him to the train. Rockefeller pulled into Cleveland's Union Station a few minutes late. His bags made it aboard, but Rockefeller missed the train. His tardiness would save his life.

About 3 p.m., the last two cars of the Lake Shore Express jumped the track while passing over a high bridge in Angola, New York. The cars plummeted about 50 feet into a gorge and burst into flames. Nearly 50 people died. Rockefeller would have been in the last car. Only three people in that car survived. His luggage was destroyed in the crash. Traveling on a later train, Rockefeller came upon the wreckage and was a personal witness to the carnage. In a letter he would write to his wife describing the wreck, Rockefeller acknowledged (with literally underlining emphasis) that "I do (and did when I learned that the first train left) regard the thing as the *Providence of God*."[4]

The tragic event changed Rockefeller's life. He believed now more than ever that he was a man with an important divine destiny. Rockefeller's negotiations with Vanderbilt were affected. Rockefeller obtained the significant shipping discount of $1.65 per barrel. In return, he promised to fill Vanderbilt's trains with oil.

Though this meant that he needed to increase his production, Rockefeller was aware that his Cleveland refineries sat atop vast reserves of oil—the "Middle East of its time." He recognized this amazing natural resource as one of the "gifts of the great Creator." Though the Angola disaster changed him spiritually, Rockefeller had long operated from a biblical worldview. According to *John D. Rockefeller: Anointed With Oil,*

> At Erie Street Church, he gave money to support preachers, poor congregants, missionaries, and a school for the poor. His gifts rose from about 6 percent of his pay the first year to 10 percent four years later. (It has seemed as if I was favored and got increases,) he would tell his biographer, (because the Lord knew that I was going to turn around and give it back.)[5]

Also, Rockefeller was known as a "fatherly boss" who paid his workers more than the industry average. In one instance he offered a partner more than a year of paid sick time. In another instance Rockefeller instructed a railroad lawyer to restore permission for an elderly Standard employee to tricycle to work along the train tracks. Additionally, "He forgave a swindler, kept him on staff, and eventually spent $1,000 on the worker's funeral. He spread shoe-shining kits about the office. He discouraged liquor, tobacco, divorces, and lavish living."[6]

Rockefeller was also involved in the abolition movement. He helped to purchase the freedom of slaves. He was a lifelong member of the Republican Party and cast his first presidential vote for Abraham Lincoln. In 1868, after moving to Euclid Avenue in downtown Cleveland, Rockefeller moved his church to the same street. From that point on, the church was known as Euclid Avenue Baptist Church. "He often shook hands with needy worshipers there and slipped them envelopes of money. For decades, even when living out of town, he superintended the Sunday school and Laura (his wife) superintended its infant classes. The couple also taught briefly at a poorer church."[7]

Along with her duties as a wife and mother, Laura Rockefeller helped to found the national Woman's Christian Temperance Union, which waged war on liquor. John sometimes joined his wife in kneeling on tavern floors and praying for the drinkers. "He also helped to build an alcohol-free shelter that can be considered Cleveland's first settlement house, a kind of center for social and other services springing up in the nation's cities to help poor and working-class families." Over his lifetime, John Rockefeller would spend more than a half-million dollars fighting the scourge of alcohol.[8]

By 1870, Standard Oil would become the world's most famous business brand. By 1872, Rockefeller's oil accounted for 40 percent of rail cargo in the U.S. In 1872, Rockefeller bought out nearly all of his competition (22 out of 26) among the Cleveland refineries. He would go on to do the same in Pittsburg, Philadelphia, Baltimore, and New York. Even though many considered his buyouts fair, and even generous, such monopolizing turned many Americans against him and his company.

After Standard's precipitous rise, the railroads attempted to force higher transport costs on Standard Oil. Rockefeller responded by building a 4,000-mile-long network of pipeline from Ohio to Pennsylvania. This ended his dependence on the railroads and gave Standard Oil even more power. By 1877, Rockefeller controlled about 90 percent of America's refineries and pipelines.

By 1885, Standard Oil was the world's largest and most profitable corporation. Rockefeller owned not only the oil market in the U.S., but the world over. In addition to oil refined into kerosene,

Standard also developed more than 300 by-products. It made tar and asphalt for America's growing network of roads, and lubricants for America's rapidly multiplying machines and trains, strengthening its grip on the railroads. It made ingredients for candles, matches, paint, paint remover, and a Cleveland novelty called chewing gum. It took over production of

> Vaseline and made it a household staple. (We
> had vision,) Rockefeller would tell his
> biographer. (We saw the vast possibilities of the
> oil industry, started at the center of it, and
> brought our knowledge and imagination and
> business experience to bear in a dozen, in 20, in
> 30 directions.)[9]

Rockefeller's use of pipelines for transporting Standard Oil
significantly hurt American railroads. The decline of the railroad
industry in turn put a dent into the steel industry that was
dominated by Andrew Carnegie. If railroads weren't being built,
steel rails were not needed. However, by this time in American
history, large numbers of Americans in search of work were
moving into U.S. cities. As the population of the cities increased,
the construction industry also grew. Carnegie brilliantly saw an
opportunity. Soon, the production of structural steel for the
building of skyscrapers, hotels, apartment buildings and so on,
replaced the losses of the steel industry as a result of the decline of
the railroads.

The first skyscraper in the world, the Home Insurance Building,
was built with Carnegie steel in 1884 in the city of Chicago. It was
10 stories tall, or 138 feet high. It was the tallest building in the
world until 1889. Steel was now the product of choice for large
construction projects. By 1889, the U.S. passed Britain as the
world leader in steel production. Between 1890 and 1900, steel
output in the U.S. tripled.

In 1901, through the efforts of J.P. Morgan and others, Carnegie
Steel Company merged with Elbert Gary's Federal Steel Company
and William Henry Moore's National Steel Company to form U.S.
Steel. It was capitalized at $1.4 billion, making it the largest
corporation in the world, along with the first billion dollar
corporation in the world.

Fossil fuels literally fueled the building of modern America. (The
U.S. is far from alone in this regard.) The fossil fuel industry is still
king when it comes to powering America, and the world.

Currently, 87 percent of the energy consumed in the world comes from fossil fuels. The United States contains the world's largest reserves of recoverable coal. Today, about 50 percent of U.S. electricity is generated from coal.

Since 2009, the U.S. has been the world's largest producer of natural gas. About one-fourth of the energy consumed in the U.S. is from natural gas. As a result of the process of hydraulic fracturing—or "fracking"— developed and perfected in the U.S., as of 2014, for the third year running, the U.S. produced more crude oil and natural gas than any other nation in the world.[10]

The pioneering efforts in the oil and coal industries—which led to great expansion of the electrical, steel, and other such industries— led to the United States becoming home to the world's largest corporations. Of course, fossil fuels were integral to the U.S. becoming, and remaining, the world's largest economy. With new technologies and developments in the fossil fuel industry, along with our abundance of God-given natural resources, and as long as fossil fuels are not foolishly abandoned for inferior alternatives, the United States is poised to remain a giant in energy production.

# CHAPTER 19

# Innovation/Industrial Explosion, Part 6: The Engine that Moved America

Edison's light bulb and electrical system changed how homes, churches, schools, factories, offices, stores, and so on were powered and lighted. Of course, the replacement of kerosene with electricity had a tremendously negative impact on Standard Oil. However, as the twentieth century approached, a once unwanted byproduct of refining oil, gasoline, would figure prominently in the energy consumption of the U.S. The age of the internal combustion engine made gasoline as indispensable as coal for fueling American industry.

For decades in Europe and the U.S., men had attempted to marry the steam engine with the wagon. The excessive weight of steam engines, combined with the crude and rough roads that were typical in the nineteenth century, meant that if people needed to travel where rails (steam-powered or electric) or water couldn't take them, they had to walk, peddle their way with the relatively new invention called the bicycle—which also was not very useful over long distances and rough terrain—or use a horse or similar animal.

As was the case with the steam engine, the telegraph, and the electrical generator (dynamo), experiments with various forms of the internal combustion engine were being done throughout Europe and in the U.S. As early as the second decade of the nineteenth century, patents on such an engine were being applied for and approved. In 1823, British engineer Samuel Brown patented the first internal combustion engine that was used in industry. Just three years later, Samuel Morey patented his "vapor engine," the first internal combustion engine in the U.S. In the mid-1850s, Italians Eugenio Barsanti and Felice Matteucci patented what some consider to be the first four-cycle engine. Working in France, Belgian mechanic and inventor Jean Joseph Etienne Lenoir created an internal combustion engine that greatly resembled a steam engine in design and operation. Lenoir's engine also offered a major new innovation: the ignition of the fuel was due to an electric spark provided by a plug that was wired to a battery. Lenoir's engine was the first one to be significantly mass produced.

In 1866, German Nicholas Otto patented an internal combustion engine that was much more efficient than Lenoir's. In addition, Otto's engine was a gasoline engine. After gaining the necessary financing, Otto soon began manufacturing and selling his engine. In 1872, Otto's company became the Deutz Gas Motor Factory. Soon, a skilled engineer named Gottlieb Daimler was hired to run the factory.

In the same year that the Deutz Gas Motor Factory was born, an American mechanical engineer and inventor in Boston named George Brayton patented an internal combustion engine that ran on gasoline vapors. Brayton's engine was a commercial success, but it was too heavy for road vehicles. It was in Europe—especially France and Germany—that automobile manufacturing first took off. Men like Daimler, Benz, and Peugeot led the way.

The first automobile boom, which amounted to only a few hundred cars, began in 1895. At this time, almost all of the cars in the world were made by three companies: Benz in Germany, along with P &L and Peugeot in France. By 1900, the French were producing nearly 5,000 cars annually, which was over five times more than Germany, and 25 times the production of the British. However, by 1900, the U.S. nearly matched the French production of automobiles. By 1905, U.S. production overtook that of France. By 1907, at 44,000, the U.S. production of automobiles easily surpassed that of any other single nation, and nearly surpassed that of the rest of the world combined. In other words, as it did with guns, trains, communications, steel, and electricity, the U.S. again led the nations in an industry that had the attention of the whole world.

*The Automobile Revolution: The Impact of an Industry*, noted that, "Among the earliest automobile manufacturers, those who wagered on gasoline as an energy source would win out over those who favored steam or electricity. The French were the first to develop this industry, and they set the pattern."[1] Early efforts at large-scale automobile manufacturing in the U.S. focused on electric cars, but that soon gave way to cars powered by gasoline.

The Ransom E. Olds Company produced a world-record 3,000 Oldsmobiles in 1903, the same year that the Ford Motor Company was organized. In 1907, Ford sold a world record 8,423 units of its model "N" car. However, over the next several years the Buick Motor Car Company would overtake Ford in production. In 1908 Ford came out with its low-priced four cylinder model "T." By 1927, over 15 million had been sold.

**1910 Model T**

Also in 1908, Buick, Olds, Cadillac, and others merged to form General Motors. By this point, American manufacturing of automobiles was primed for explosive growth. Again, according to *The Automobile Revolution: The Impact of an Industry,*

> In 1913 production reached 485,000 cars and trucks, more than ten times that of the leading European country, France, and more than three-fourths of world output. As production rose to these massive proportions, two basic characteristics emerged in the American automobile industry: the establishment of very large business organizations, and the perfecting of manufacturing techniques to make and assemble huge numbers of identical parts without using an enormous work force, especially of highly skilled workmen.[2]

Though the U.S. was already the world's largest economy, the automobile industry would drastically set the United States apart from the rest of the world—economically and otherwise—like no other industry in American history. The mass production techniques perfected in America—branch assembly plants; the use of presses, dies, lathes, milling machines, grinders, drills, and the like; the development of special steel alloys; the use of interchangeable parts; and the moving assembly line introduced by Henry Ford—were unmatched by any other nation. It was Ford's assembly line, where all of these production advancements were brought together, that was the most significant step in the mass production of automobiles.

The advantage that the U.S. had already achieved in older industries, such as in the manufacture of firearms, sewing machines, bicycles, and so on, meant that American machine tool firms were better equipped to meet the needs of the new automobile industry. The U.S. advantage in machine tools was so significant that many early European car makers used American-made machine tools. It wasn't long until Europeans were adopting the mass production techniques of the Americans as well.

American automobile manufacturers were huge consumers of electricity. The assembly line method of manufacturing cars, which was soon adopted by other industries as well, only increased the need for electrical power. The massive factories being built across the U.S. presented a tremendous opportunity for growth for G.E. and other suppliers of electricity.

By the early 1920s, American car makers were so successful that they began seriously looking to markets outside of the U.S. Canada was the first target. By 1929, U.S. capital controlled over 80 percent of the Canadian automobile industry, and Canada became the world's second leading automobile manufacturer. Unlike their parent companies in the U.S., over 40 percent of Canadian-made cars were exported.

The 1920s also saw the large U.S. car makers build assembly plants in Europe. Ford was Britain's largest automobile manufacturer until 1924. In 1926, Ford, G.M., and Chrysler each built assembly plants in Berlin. Around this time the Soviet Union was beginning to enter the automobile market. Initially, nearly half of their tractors, trucks, and parts were supplied by the Americans. In 1928, the Soviets began negotiations with several American auto makers to build a factory in the Soviet Union that was capable of producing 100,000 cars per year. Ford was chosen. The factory would produce trucks and Model A cars. A deal was struck in which the Soviets agreed to purchase $33 million in Ford cars and parts up to 1933.

U.S. domination of the automobile market spread to other parts of the world as well, including Latin America, the Far East, and Australia. By 1930, 80 percent of the world's automobiles were American. In addition, more than half of American families owned a car. As was the case with the railroad and electrical industries, the automobile industry brought with it wide-ranging effects to America's corporations, the economy, and the culture in general.

By 1925, the automobile industry was the largest industry in the U.S. It consumed 80 percent of the rubber industry's production, 75 percent of glass, 25 percent of machine tools, and 20 percent of steel.[3] In addition, the automobile industry was a boon to the construction industry, the real estate industry, the housing industry, and so on.

Relatively new industries such as commercial advertising became a regular part of American culture. Between 1920 and 1927 the advertising budgets of American car makers tripled. Travelers Insurance added automobile insurance to its company product line in 1897. Aetna added it in 1907. Of course, the automobile industry led to a massive increase in the building of highways. During the decade of the 1920s, the number of paved roads doubled, including bridges, multiple lane parkways, and a national system of highways.

It was now much easier to travel to see a doctor, get to school, and receive mail delivery. People were able to work further from home and to travel further for vacations and recreation. With gasoline-powered farming equipment, more land could now be used to grow crops and raise livestock. By 1930, U.S. farmers owned nearly one million trucks. America was suddenly a much smaller place, and it was about to get even smaller.

In the early twentieth century, along with the automobile, the invention and development of the airplane would help propel the U.S. to world leadership. Octave Chanute, a renowned American civil engineer, was the most successful early pioneer of the "heavier-than-air flying machine." After his death in November of 1910, *Popular Mechanics* hailed Chanute as the "father of aviation."

Retiring from a railroad career in 1883, Chanute devoted his time to the new science of aviation. After over a decade of studies, experiments, and correspondence with other early aviators, in 1894 Chanute wrote the classic and influential *Progress in Flying Machines*. The book offered an insightful and up-to-date survey of all the work in aviation. At the time, it was the world's most comprehensive work on heavier-than-air flying machines.

Though he was too old to fly, Chanute built several gliders. Orville and Wilbur Wright based their glider designs on Chanute's biplane design that made use of the Platt truss. However, gliders were a long way from successful powered flight that included a pilot who could control the airplane.

In April of 1898, the U.S. declared war on Spain. The Spanish-American war lasted only about three-and-a-half months, but it was long enough for President William McKinley to become interested in the possible military applications of flight. The United States Army Signal Corps had established a War Balloon Company in 1893. The balloon dubbed the *Santiago* saw limited combat during the conflict. However, in December of 1898, Samuel Langley, the director of the Smithsonian Institution in Washington, received a $50,000 grant from the War Department to build a "man-carrying airplane."[4]

Two-and-a-half years before, Langley had conducted successful flight experiments (witnessed by the likes of Alexander Graham Bell) with his steam powered "aerodrome." The aerodrome weighed about 30 pounds and had a wingspan of 14 feet. It was powered by a lightweight steam engine. According to Langley's own account,

> The signal was given and the aerodrome sprang into the air. I watched it from the shore with hardly a hope that the long series of accidents had come to a close. And yet it had.
>
> For the first time, the aerodrome swept continuously through the air like a living thing. Second after second passed on the face of the stopwatch until a minute had gone by. And it still flew on.
>
> As I heard the cheering of the few spectators, I felt that something had been accomplished at last. For never in any part of the world or in any period had any machine of man's construction sustained itself in the air for even half of this brief time.[5]

On its first flight, the aerodrome flew over 3,000 feet. A later model flew about one mile. However, placing a human being in the air at the helm of a flying machine "of man's construction" is a much more complicated task than getting a relatively small model airborne, and ultimately Langley was unsuccessful at piloted flight. By 1899, it was the Wright brothers' turn. After immersing themselves in all the available literature of the time, Wilbur wrote, "there was no flying art in the proper sense of the word, but only a flying problem." He declared that so-called flying machines, "were guilty of almost everything except flying." Wilbur added that the existing literature was "mere speculations and probably ninety percent was false. Consequently, those who tried to study the science of aerodynamics knew not what to believe and what not to believe."[6]

Regarding what to believe and what not to believe, up until the twentieth century, most aviation inventors had "conceived of flying machines as wing-flapping ornithopters (which attempted to mimic the flight of birds). The Wrights saw them as bicycles with wings. This point of view proved to be completely correct…"[7]

Orville and Wilbur Wright were the sons of Milton and Susan Wright. Milton was the descendant of Samuel Wright, a Puritan who immigrated to Massachusetts in 1636. The Wrights had a long history as faithful Christians. Milton's father was Dan Wright. Dan became a devoted Christian in 1830.

> He embraced abstinence; in a community where most men drank corn liquor routinely, he did not allow alcohol to pass his lips. He grew corn but refused to sell it to the local distillers, even though they were often ready to buy at the highest prices. Young Milton became a sincere believer as well.
>
> Milton's mother shared his father's strong convictions. When he was eight years old and under her influence, Milton began to pray regularly and to attend church, where he listened attentively to the preaching. Then in 1843, at age fourteen, he was working in the family cornfield when he found himself called by God. He later wrote of 'an impression that spoke to the soul powerfully and abidingly,' bringing 'a sweet peace and joy never known before.' He went on to pursue a career in the church, and he was not alone. All three of his brothers made similar commitments to the ministry.[8]

Additionally, Dan Wright was a strong opponent of slavery. Milton shared his father's hatred of slavery. Milton's career life was broad and fulfilling. Along with preaching, he taught, farmed, and was a landlord. He also was the editor of his church's weekly newspaper, *The Religious Telescope*. Milton and Susan Wright had seven children, five of whom survived early childhood. (Twins born in 1870 died within a month.)

Each of the boys was given a strong Christian name. Wilbur, the older of the famous Wright brothers (and the third child), was named for a minister whom his father admired. Orville was also named for an admired clergyman.

Wilbur and Orville's mother Susan was a talented and unique woman. She was very well educated, which was quite unusual during her day. She attended Hartsville College where she studied literature, in addition to having courses in mathematics, Latin, and Greek. Because she took an interest in her father's work as a carriage maker, Susan developed skills as a carpenter. Interestingly, as Wilbur and Orville grew into curious tinkerers, they often went to their mother when they had mechanical questions.

With their hard-working hands and bright minds, Milton and Susan earned a fairly comfortable living. To educate their children properly, the Wrights were devoted homeschoolers. With their education, travels (to preach the Gospel in various parts of the U.S), talents, and financial resources, the Wrights offered their children a rich and well-rounded education.

> All children grow up with something from the mother, something from the father, and something that is all their own. Milton and Susan entered their marriage with significant strengths that in time were to influence Orville and Wilbur, as well as their other children. At the outset, their pervading religious faith carried overtones of personal strength and seriousness of purpose, of making commitments and holding to them. This gave the young Wrights a good underpinning when they set out to accomplish difficult tasks.[9]

This "good underpinning" was often tested when it came to the invention of the airplane. After years of toiling and experiments with gliders, in December of 1903, the Wright brothers succeeded in flying the first piloted flight of a power-driven, heavier than air plane.

The first flight, shown in the famous photograph above with Orville as the pilot and Wilbur looking on, was on December 17, 1903. The plane was aloft for about 12 seconds—an estimate because in the excitement of the moment, Wilbur had forgotten to start his stopwatch—and traveled 120 feet at an altitude of about 10 feet. The next two flights, taking place on the same day, were just slightly longer. However, the fourth and final flight of the day Wilbur remained in the air for 59 seconds and traveled 852 feet.

The excited brothers sent a telegram to their father and wanted him to inform the press. It read, "Success four flights Thursday morning all against twenty-one-mile wind started from level with engine power alone average speed through air thirty-one miles longest 59 seconds inform press home Christmas. Orville Wright."[10] Nevertheless, because they deemed the flights too short to be important, the *Dayton Journal* (Dayton, Ohio) refused to publish an account of the flights.

However, without the Wrights' permission, the telegraph operator in Kitty Hawk leaked news of the flights to a reporter at the *Virginian Pilot*. The *Pilot* attempted to contact the Wrights, but the brothers were nowhere to be found. Much like the modern media, this did not stop the *Pilot* from running its own version of the facts. On December 18, in large bold type, the headlines of the Pilot read,

FLYING MACHINE SOARS 3 MILES IN TEETH OF HIGH
WIND OVER SAND HILLS AND WAVES
AT KITTY HAWK ON CAROLINA COAST NO BALLOON
ATTACHED TO AID IT
Three Years of Hard, Secret Work by
Two Ohio Brothers Crowned with Success
ACCOMPLISHED WHAT LANGLEY FAILED AT
With Man as Passenger Huge Machine
Flew Like Bird Under Perfect Control
BOX KITE PRINCIPLE WITH TWO PROPELLERS[11]

The story rightly concluded that, "The problem of aerial navigation without the use of a balloon has been solved at last." It continued:

> Over the sand hills of the North Carolina coast
> yesterday, near Kitty Hawk, two Ohio men
> proved that they could soar through the air in a
> flying machine of their own construction, with
> the power to steer it and speed it at will.
>
> Like a monster bird the invention hovered above
> the breakers and circled over the rolling sand
> hills at the command of the navigator and, after
> soaring for three miles, it gracefully descended
> to earth again and rested lightly upon the spot
> selected by the man in the car as a suitable
> landing place.
>
> While the United States government has been
> spending thousands of dollars in an effort to
> make practicable the ideas of Professor Langley,
> of the Smithsonian Institute, Wilbur and Orville

Wright, two brothers, natives of Dayton, O.,
have quietly, even secretly, perfected their
invention, and put it to a successful test. [At least
they got this part correct.]

They are not yet ready that the world should
know the methods they have adopted in
conquering the air, but the Virginian Pilot is able
to state authentically the nature of their
invention, its principle and its chief
dimensions.[12]

The erroneous news began to spread. In order to correct matters,
on January 5, 1904, the brothers sent a news release to the
Associated Press. It began,

It had not been our intention to make any
detailed public statement concerning the private
trials of our power 'Flyer' on the 17th of
December last; but since the contents of a private
telegram, announcing to our folks at home the
success of our trials, was dishonestly
communicated to the newspapermen at the
Norfolk office, and led to the imposition upon
the public, by persons who never saw the 'Flyer'
or its flights, of a fictitious story incorrect in
almost every detail, and since this story together
with several pretended interviews or statements,
which were fakes pure and simple, have been
very widely disseminated, we feel impelled to
make some correction.[13]

Their report gave accurate details of their flights, and ended with,
"From the beginning we have employed entirely new principles of
control; and as all the experiments have been conducted at our own
expense without assistance from any individual or institution, we
do not feel ready at present to give out any pictures or detailed
descriptions of the machine."[14] The AP reported the news, but in

order to protect their cohorts in the press, deleted the opening paragraph.

In order to guard their work, the Wrights spent the next few months and years operating under as much secrecy as possible. Though they had indeed invented a flying machine, there was still much to do to build an airplane.

By 1905, at a secluded field near Dayton, Ohio called Huffman Prairie, instead of seconds, the flights were being measured in minutes. In September they had flights of 17, 18, and 20 minutes. October saw flights of 26, 33, and 38 minutes. By the end of 1905, by all practical measures, the Wrights had a functioning airplane.

The brothers made no flights at all in 1906 and 1907. This time was spent attempting to obtain patents and sell planes. In April of 1906, the Wrights obtained U.S. patent No. 821,393. Interestingly, the patent avoided all reference to powered flight and instead focused on the methods of controlling a flying machine, whether it was powered or not. Specifically, the patent made mention of ways to maintain lateral control, the ability to make coordinated turns, and the means by which a flying machine could ascend and descend.

> [T]he Wright patent showed brilliant originality.
> Though framed in an era when literally no one
> else properly understood the control of a heavier-
> than-air machine, it embraced technical advances
> that the brothers had not initially contemplated.
> Indeed, it covered many aspects of flight control
> that are familiar to designers to this day.[15]

The patent granted to the Wrights represented a significant achievement; however it did not put money in their pockets. The actual production and sale of airplanes was a far different matter. Always leery of their competition, the Wrights were unwilling to put on public displays of their plane, even in the case of the U.S. military, and the military was not interested in a flying machine they could not see in action.

The Wrights were willing to show photographs of their Flyer (as their plane was dubbed) in the air, but only after a contract was signed and money was in hand would they put on a flying display of their plane. After all,

> They were sons of Bishop Milton Wright; they had no doubt either as to their own honesty or to their reputation for probity, at least in Dayton. Moreover, their religious background encouraged them to view the wide world as a nest of sin and corruption. It did not readily occur to them that the sinners with whom they hoped to negotiate might take the view that skillful liars and professional con artists were far more common than men who could invent a successful airplane.[16]

The U.S. military would not budge, however, and the Wright brothers turned to Europe to sell their airplane. The threat of war in Europe made interest in flying machines a bit more pressing than was the case in the U.S. In 1905, the Germans were threatening French control of Morocco. (This is widely considered one of the leading causes of World War I.) If there was to be fighting in the African desert, the French had the idea of using airplanes to scout their enemies and deliver crucial wartime messages and plans. Also, with the Wrights having done many flying experiments on the beaches of Kitty Hawk, they were quite adept at constructing an airplane that would land safely on desert sands.

Ferdinand Ferber, a French Army officer who had a strong interest in aviation—he had attempted unsuccessfully to build his own aircraft—contacted the Wright brothers on behalf of France. In October of 1905, the brothers responded to the French request for the purchase of a powered airplane. They quoted the French a price of $200,000. French emissaries visited the Wrights shortly after Christmas. Although Wilbur and Orville still refused to perform flight demonstrations, based on photographic and eye witness evidence, the French were convinced that the Wrights could indeed provide what they claimed to be selling.

In February of 1906, France provided $5,000 in earnest money to the brothers. If the French were to proceed with a purchase, the rest of the $200,000 would be placed in escrow while the Wrights would travel to France for actual flight tests. In the early spring of 1906, as a result of the Algeciras Conference, the threat of war in Europe dissipated. As a result, France backed out of the deal with the Wrights for the purchase of an airplane. However, the Wrights kept the $5,000 in earnest money. This was the first money the brothers made from their invention.

At the end of 1906, a deal with the British fell through as well. 1906 ended without the Wrights even attempting a flight, much less actually selling an airplane. However, there was renewed interest in airplane production in the U.S. Also, a favorable article in *Scientific American* gave further hope to the Wrights' prospects of making money from their invention. It read, "In all the history of invention there is probably no parallel to the unostentatious manner in which the Wright brothers, of Dayton, Ohio, ushered into the world their epoch-making invention of the first successful aeroplane flying machine."[17]

In 1907 the U.S. Army again showed interest in a deal with the Wrights. By late December, 1907, the Army and the Wrights worked out a deal for $25,000 that called for a "Heavier-Than-Air Flying Machine" that was to be "supported entirely by the dynamic reaction of the atmosphere and having no gas bag." The plane was to have a range of 125 miles along with "a speed of at least forty miles per hour in still air." It also was to be "quickly and easily assembled and taken apart and packed for transportation in army wagons" while being able to operate "in any country which may be encountered in field service."[18]

While the Wrights were trying to drum up business, with their plane grounded, French aviators were trying to catch up. By 1907, men like Leon Delagrange and Henri Farman were measuring their flights in kilometers. By 1908, Delagrange and Farman had flights whose time and distance were approaching the records held by the Wrights. Still, the French knew that the Wrights' plane was the standard. In 1908, wealthy French investors offered Wilbur and Orville 500,000 francs (about $100,000) for delivery of a single airplane, and 20,000 francs each for four additional Flyers. Of course, this meant a flying demonstration in France.

On August 8, 1908, at the Le Mans racetrack, in what was the first real public display of their airplane, Wilbur Wright set out to show the French what their Flyer could really do. Using wing-warping and his rudder, Wright executed flight control, including sweeping banked turns, unlike anything the French had ever seen. Though the flight was less than two minutes in length, onlookers were amazed.

The French press was captivated. Paris newspapers expressed amazement and offered high praise. Two days after his initial French flight, Wilbur took to the skies again. Attendance at Le Mans swelled significantly, and onlookers were not disappointed. Wright flew longer and higher than before, reaching an unprecedented altitude of 100 feet, and for the first time ever in Europe, Wilbur Wright flew a plane in a figure eight pattern. Delangrange excitedly and humbly declared, "Well, we are beaten! We just don't exist!"

Again America and Americans were at the forefront of new technology and innovation that forever changed the world. As historian Fred Culick put it,

> [W]hen the Wrights first flew publicly, no one else yet understood the need for lateral control, much less the function of the vertical tail. Therefore no one else could execute proper turns. No one else knew how to make propellers correctly. Above all, no one else had pursued a comparable program: doing the necessary research, constructing his own aircraft and doing his own flying, so that he understood the entire problem.[19]

With the use of the internal combustion engine, the Wright brothers had indeed solved the problem of powered human flight. Nearly everything that followed in aviation was built upon what the Wrights accomplished.

Nevertheless, the French took the early lead in the mass production of airplanes. By the outbreak of World War I in 1914, French manufacturers had built more than 2,000 aircraft, while American companies had built less than 100.

> During the 1920s, aircraft assumed their modern shape. Monoplanes superceded (sic) biplanes, stressed-skin cantilevered wings replaced externally braced wings, radial air-cooled engines turned variable pitch propellers, and enclosed fuselages and cowlings gave aircraft their sleek aerodynamic shape. By the mid-1930s, metal replaced wood as the material of choice in aircraft construction so new types of component suppliers fed the aircraft manufacturers.[20]

In the U.S., during the 1920s, the airmail industry took off—literally—with The Kelly Air Mail Act of 1925. This law gave airmail business to hundreds of small pilot-owned firms. Eventually, these operations were consolidated into larger airlines.[21] As airmail business in the U.S. grew, advancements in airplane design accelerated.

In the 1920s monoplanes (fixed-wing or single-wing airplanes) replaced multi-wing planes, especially biplanes, and aircraft began to take on their modern, more aerodynamic look. By the mid-1930s metal—especially aluminum—replaced wood as the preferred material of choice for airplane construction. Also, during the 1930s airline companies began seriously to challenge the railroads for customers in the commercial travel industry. With its growing population and wide-open spaces, this was especially the case in the U.S.

As people began to fly commercially, many advancements in airplane comfort, efficiency, and safety took place. With the onset of World War II, and with the concept of mass-production already near-perfected in other manufacturing industries, the United States was soon leading the world in airplane production. From 1940 to

1945, American manufacturers built over 300,000 military aircraft, including over 95,000 in 1944 alone. In the previous six-year period, American firms built only about 20,000 planes. With over 1.3 million employees, by 1943, the aviation industry was America's largest producer and employer.[22]

By the end of World War II, and as it still does to this day, the United States reigned supreme in the air. Today, four of the world's top five airline companies are American. (Delta is #1, followed by Southwest, China Southern, United, and American.)[23] Also, the United States has more military aircraft than the rest of the world combined.[24]

Powered by the internal combustion engine, and fueled by fossil fuels, the airplane and the automobile literally propelled the United States into the twentieth century. These amazing machines revolutionized, not only travel, but manufacturing and production practices, the transport of goods and mail, military operations, national defense strategies, and the like. What's more—and again with the United States of America leading the way—once mankind took to the airways, our sights were soon set even higher.

# CHAPTER 20

# Innovation/Industrial Explosion, Part 7: Science Fiction Becomes Science Fact

In 1865, when French author Jules Verne wrote *From Earth to the Moon*, the idea of powered human flight was already well imagined. Verne took the concept to an extreme that few of his time dared to imagine. In Verne's classic tale, through the use of an enormous cannon—the Columbiad Space Gun—three men were launched to the moon in a bullet-shaped capsule. Verne's novel, along with H.G. Wells' 1901 novel, *The First Men in the Moon*, inspired the first science fiction movie—*A Trip to the Moon*.

Verne's writing also inspired real rocket science. One of the earliest astronautic pioneers, the renowned Russian rocket scientist Konstantin Tsiolkovsky, actually took the time and effort to prove that Verne's space cannon was an impossibility. Tsiolkovsky is considered to be one of the founding fathers of rocketry. In the 1920s he mathematically developed the technique for how a vehicle, powered by staged rockets, could reach the velocity necessary to escape the gravitational pull of the earth. Tsiolkovsky's mathematics required the use of liquid rocket fuel, another concept he helped to develop. The Russians were significantly involved in early rocketry.

In Moscow in 1927, the Interplanetary Section of the Association of Inventors held the world's first exhibition of "interplanetary vehicles." Space enthusiasts from all over the world, including America, were in attendance. By 1927, Robert Goddard—an

American physicist, engineer, and inventor—was already famous worldwide for his contributions to rocketry. In 1920, less than two decades after the Wright brothers astounded the world by flying for 12 seconds at an altitude of 10 feet, the Smithsonian Institution published Goddard's groundbreaking paper, "A Method of Reaching Extreme Altitudes."

Called "The father of the Space Age," Goddard was the first scientist to give serious scientific treatment to the idea that space travel was possible. U.S. newspapers widely reported on Goddard's work, and for the first time, Americans began to believe that men really could travel to the moon. Inspired by the science fiction of H.G. Wells and a climb into a tall cherry tree when he was 17 years old, Goddard became fixated on the idea of humans traveling in space. By the end of his distinguished career, Goddard obtained 214 patents, including a multi-stage rocket and a liquid-fuel rocket. (He had discovered that rockets powered by traditional powder fuel converted only 2% of the fuel into thrust.)

More than a decade prior to 1927, Goddard was successfully building rockets, rocket engines, and making rocket fuel. A staunch patriot, and with the goal of producing rockets that would assist in the war effort, in 1917 Goddard went to work for the U.S. Army. He was able to develop rockets with launchers that could be fired from trenches. He also developed hand-held launchers similar to what would later be known as the bazooka. However, Goddard's struggle with tuberculosis slowed production, and he was only able to provide the Army with a successful demonstration of his weapons just days prior to the armistice that ended World War I.

Goddard was the first to build a rocket engine that used liquid fuel. Fifteen years later the Nazis would use the same type of engine in their V-2 rocket weapons. With funding from the Guggenheim Fund for the Promotion of Aeronautics, in 1935 Goddard became the first to launch a liquid-fueled rocket faster than the speed of sound. In addition to fuels and engines, in his pursuit of getting rockets into space, Goddard also invented many of the components necessary for space travel. Thus, again, America was leading the world into new frontiers. "According to historian Frank H. Winter, prior to Goddard, the rocket was a small 'pasteboard amusement device' with limited use elsewhere. 'Now, astonishingly and suddenly, it was transformed into a revolutionary way to penetrate space.'"[1]

By the late 1930s, as the world stood at the brink of war, Goddard's failing health and a lack of significant interest by the U.S. military in using rockets in warfare slowed his work. The Germans, on the other hand, were highly motivated when it came to the development of new weapons. During World War II, with the benefit of massive state funding and slave labor, the Germans improved on Goddard's work.

In the fall of 1932, just prior to the Nazis coming to power in Germany, Wernher von Braun began working for the German army. With the Nazi focus on rebuilding Germany's military, significant resources for rocket research were made available. Work was done, not only with ballistic missiles, but also "rocket-planes." Von Braun's efforts were mostly limited to his work with the missile program, while the Luftwaffe performed its own research with jet aircraft.

On June 13, 1942, with the Nazis' new armaments minister Albert Speer looking on, the first V-2 launch took place. The rocket traveled faster than the speed of sound but broke up in mid-flight. A second launch in August was no more successful. On October 3, a third launch was a complete success. The rocket traveled 50 miles high and splashed down in the ocean about 120 miles away from the launch site. General Walter Dornberger, the head of Nazi Germany's V-2 rocket program, boldly declared "the spaceship has been born!"[2]

In September of 1944, the first fully operational V-2s were launched on Paris. By the end of the war, over 3,200 V-2s were fired against Allied targets. London and Antwerp—which contained a significant port used by the Allies—were the main targets. After the defeat of the Nazis, the U.S., Great Britain, and the Soviet Union rushed to get their hands on German rocket technology. Von Braun and over 100 other V-2 personnel surrendered to the U.S. forces. A V-2 engineer famously said: "We despise the French; we were mortally afraid of the Soviets; we do not believe the British can afford us, so that leaves the Americans."[3]

In the spring of 1945, just a few months prior to von Braun and his colleagues surrendering to U.S. forces in the German Alps, Robert Goddard got his first look at a German V-2. After his inspection of the rocket, Goddard was convinced that the Germans had stolen his work. In 1963, von Braun admitted that Goddard's rockets "... may have been rather crude by present-day standards, but they blazed the trail and incorporated many features used in our most modern rockets and space vehicles." He also concluded that "Goddard's experiments in liquid fuel saved us years of work, and enabled us to perfect the V-2 years before it would have been possible."[4]

The V-2 was indeed a weapon ahead of its time. It was built prior to the availability of nuclear warheads and before the digital guidance systems that made later rockets much more accurate and deadly. The technical innovations that made the V-2 work as a rocket not only laid the foundation for a new generation of weapons, but also jump-started space exploration programs around the world.[5]

In August of 1945, President Truman authorized the Office of Strategic Services (OSS—the predecessor of the CIA) to begin Operation Overcast (later Operation Paperclip). Created in order to keep German rocket technology out of the hands of other nations—especially the Soviets—Operation Overcast was a program in which hundreds of German engineers and scientists were brought to the U.S. By 1946, V-2s were being launched from American soil.

As a result of these efforts, the United States achieved many of the world's firsts in space travel. On October 24, 1946, a 35-mm motion picture camera placed aboard a V-2 took the first ever photo from space. It was a simple and quite grainy black-and-white image of a small portion of the earth.

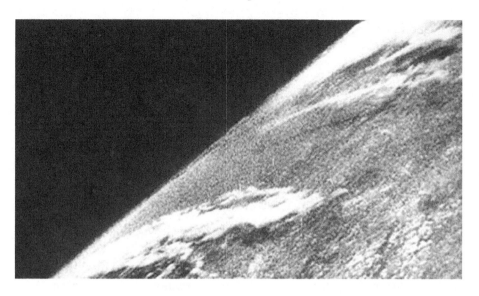

**View of Earth from a camera on V-2 #13, launched October 24, 1946.
(White Sands Missile Range/Applied Physics Laboratory**

The U.S. was the first to put animals into space. On February 20,
1947, in order to study radiation exposure at high altitudes, fruit
flies were launched aboard a V-2 and reached an altitude of 68
miles, just over the "Karman line," the imaginary line where the
earth's atmosphere meets outer space. On June 14, 1949, the U.S.
put the first mammal in space. Albert II, a Rhesus monkey, reached
an altitude of 83 miles. Albert II survived his time in space and
died upon re-entry impact. Also, multiple V-2 rockets flew
"experiment packages" in the nose cones. Such packages
performed various measurements in the upper regions of the
earth's atmosphere as well as in the lower regions of space.

Given the limited supply and the expense of the relatively large V-
2, U.S. rocket scientists developed the sleeker and much less
expensive Aerobee rocket. The Aerobee was a two-stage rocket. It
greatly reduced the cost of rocket research missions.

As the U.S. was sending more and more rockets and live animals
into space, the idea of manned space flight drew closer and closer
to a reality. In addition to the effects of high altitudes and low
gravity on the human body, the impact of extremely high speed

was another necessary and significant area of research by rocket scientists.

On August 27, 1939, just days prior to Hitler's invasion of Poland (which marked the official beginning of World War II), the world's first jet airplane took off in Germany. The world's first operational jetfighter flew in 1942, but not until the war was nearly lost, in 1944, were the Germans able to deploy jetfighters in combat. Before the war ended, both the British and the Americans had operational jetfighters.

Although these jetfighters were significantly slower than the rockets being fired into space, jet planes offered an opportunity to study how much force the human body could withstand in high-speed aircraft. Also, higher speeds meant greater forces acting on the aircraft itself. Thus, the design of the jet planes was always a matter of research and development, and men with the "need for speed," who were the pioneering rocket pilots, got their start in jets.

The earliest significant speed challenge for man and machine was the sound barrier. On October 14, 1947, in the rocket-powered Bell Aircraft X-1, at an altitude of about 45,000 feet, traveling at Mach 1.07, Air Force test pilot Chuck Yeager became the first human to travel faster than the speed of sound. Supersonic flight soon became a regular occurrence. By the 1950s, Edwards Air Force Base (named for Captain Glenn E. Edwards, a test pilot who died in 1948 when his Northrop YB-49 Flying Wing—an early forerunner of the stealth planes perfected in the 1980s—crashed) was *the* destination for pilots thought to have "the right stuff."

Edwards Air Force Base, along with the United States Naval Test Pilot School in Patuxent River, Maryland, soon became the home of legendary American pilots. "On their way to the stars, the first generation of Americans who would fly into space passed first through Edwards or Pax River."[6]

In spite of all the technological, industrial, and human resource advantages held by the United States, with the launch of the first artificial Earth satellite, Sputnik (Russian for "satellite") 1, on

October 4, 1957, the Russians, not the Americans, ushered in the space age. The news shocked the world. With Sputnik passing over the United States multiple times a day, Americans, most of whom had little to no idea what a satellite was, were quite unnerved that our cold war enemies had beaten us into orbit. The idea of western technological superiority was shattered.

When Sputnik 2, with the dog Laika aboard, was launched on November 3, 1957, Americans were demanding answers. A media riot ensued. Legendary science editor John Campbell declared, "There is nothing like a good, hard kick in the pants to wake up somebody who's going to sleep on the job." Congress held hearings. In order to train scientists and engineers, Representative Earl Wilson (R-Indiana) called for a "West Point for the Sciences." Representative Kenneth Keating (R-N.Y.) said that America needed a "Manhattan Project of international dimensions to coordinate and bring to perfection the satellite missile projects of all the North Atlantic Treaty Organization nations."[7]

Senator Lyndon Johnson declared,

> The Roman Empire controlled the world because it could build roads. Later—when men moved to the sea—the British Empire was dominant because it had ships. In the air age, we were powerful because we had airplanes. Now the Communists have established a foothold in outer space. It is not very reassuring to be told that next year we will put a better satellite into the air. Perhaps it will also have chrome trim and automatic wind-shield wipers.[8]

In order to assure Americans that there had been a significant American effort to get into space, four days after the launch of Sputnik 2, President Eisenhower began a series of televised speeches from the Oval Office on the subject of "Science and National Security."

Since at least the early 1950s several U.S. organizations and agencies, both private and government—American Rocket Society, National Science Foundation, United States Naval Research Laboratory, Army Ballistic Missile Agency, Jet Propulsion laboratory—at one time or another, had the goal of placing an artificial satellite in orbit around the earth.

On July 29, 1955, White House press secretary, James C. Hagerty, announced official U.S. plans for launching satellites into space. By September of that year, the U.S. Navy's Vanguard satellite program became the official satellite program of the United States. Feeling pressure as the result of the successful launch of Sputnik, on December 6, 1957, Vanguard TV3 was the first attempt by the U.S. to put a satellite into space. The picture below reveals the sad result of the launch:

With millions of Americans anxiously watching on TV, two seconds after launch, and a mere four feet in the air, Vanguard TV3 lost thrust, fell back to the earth, and exploded. It was a sweeping humiliation for the U.S. Newspapers ran headlines using words like "Flopnik," "Kaputnik," "Stayputnik," and "Dudnik" to describe the launch failure. Vanguard soon became a byword for failure.

However, only a few weeks later, on January 31, 1958, America joined the Soviets in space. Launched aboard the Juno I rocket, the Explorer 1 was the first satellite of the United States. 1958 saw multiple efforts by both the Soviets and the Americans to put additional satellites into orbit. There were successes and failures on both sides. However, through the next several years the Soviets achieved a number of other notable firsts in the space race.

On January 4, 1959, the Soviets' Luna 1 became the first satellite to reach the vicinity of the Moon and was the first satellite to reach heliocentric orbit (orbit around the Sun). On September 13, 1959, Luna 2 became the first man-made object to land on a celestial body, the Moon. Luna 3 was the first to photograph the far side of the Moon. In August of 1960, Sputnik 5 was the first spaceflight to carry animals into orbit and return them safely to earth. On April 12, 1961, Soviet cosmonaut Yuri Gagarin became the first human in outer space.

In addition to leading the world into space, the Soviets developed the world's first intercontinental ballistic missile (ICBM), the R-7. Because of its operational shortcomings—extremely large, lengthy launch preparation time, cryogenic fuel—the R-7 was never much of a military threat. However, Sputnik 1 was carried into space by an R-7 rocket, and the R-7 became the basis for a long line of Soviet space launch vehicles.

With the Soviets having exploded their first thermonuclear bomb in 1953, when Sputnik 1 was launched into space, military leaders in America rightly feared the idea that the Russians now had a significant first-strike nuclear advantage. Thus, the space race was also quite literally a "rocket race." Though the U.S. had been working on an intercontinental ballistic missile since just after the end of WWII, the first successful launch of an American ICBM, the Atlas, did not occur until November 28, 1958, more than a year after the first successful launch of the R-7.

However, the Soviets failed to build on their lead in ICBM technology, and by the early 1960s the United States took and maintained an advantage in strategic missile technology. By the time John Kennedy took office as U.S. President in 1961, the U.S.

had nearly 200 ICBMs and was quickly building more. On the other hand, in 1961 the Soviets had only four ICBMs.[9]

Additionally, the U.S. had a massive advantage over the Soviets in the total number of nuclear warheads—27,000 to 3,600. This distinct military advantage by the U.S. led to the Cuban Missile Crisis. In order to compensate for the Soviet disadvantage in long-range missiles, and as a response to U.S. missiles recently installed in Turkey in 1962, Soviet leader Nikita Khrushchev came up with the idea of installing Russian missiles with nuclear warheads in Cuba.

The U.S. missile advantage was due in part to the creation of NASA. On July 29, 1958, President Eisenhower signed the National Aeronautics and Space Act. NASA absorbed the 46-year-old NACA (National Advisory Committee for Aeronautics) and the Jet Propulsion Laboratory. NASA also incorporated elements of the Army Ballistic Missile Agency and the Naval Research Laboratory. It would be NASA that would take America to the moon.

In addition to improving American rocket technology, by 1961 NASA planners had firmly set their resolve on the goal of placing a man on the moon. On May 5, 1961, aboard the space capsule *Freedom 7*, Alan Shepard became the first American to travel into space. About three weeks later on May 25, President Kennedy announced the goal of a lunar landing by the end of the decade. Toward the end of 1961, the Soviets announced the moon as a target as well.

The failing health of the leader of the Soviet space program, the brilliant Sergei Korolev, and his eventual untimely death in 1966, kept the Russians behind the Americans in the race to the moon. On July 20, 1969, American Neil Armstrong became the first human to set foot on the Moon. About 19 minutes after Armstrong first set foot on the Moon, fellow *Apollo 11* astronaut Buzz Aldrin joined him.

*Apollo 12*, *Apollo 14*, *Apollo 15*, *Apollo 16*, and *Apollo 17* all sent American men to the surface of the Moon. Twelve men, all

Americans, have walked on the surface of the moon. Chronologically, they are Neil Armstrong, Buzz Aldrin, Pete Conrad, Alan Bean, Alan Shepard, Edgar Mitchell, David Scott, James Irwin, John Young, Charles Duke, Eugene Cernan, and Harrison Schmitt.

Soon after the success of *Apollo 11*, the Soviets abandoned their efforts at a manned lunar landing. Just prior to the end of the Apollo program in early 1972, U.S. President Nixon announced the start of a Space Shuttle program. With 135 missions flown, this manned space-launch vehicle program was and remains unparalleled, though it is no longer in operation.

The space race not only resulted in improved missile technologies, orbiting satellites, and men on the moon. Space exploration also has resulted in a wide array of products and technologies that have improved the lives of hundreds of millions of people the world over. Everything from artificial limbs and infrared ear thermometers, to memory foam and the "Jaws of Life" are the result of space exploration, and of course, the U.S. leads the world in these technologies.[10]

# CHAPTER 21

# Innovation/Industrial Explosion, Part 8: The Digital Age

Perhaps the most significant technological result of the space race was the advancement in computer technologies. As Daniel Lockney, an editor of *Spinoff*, a NASA publication since 1976, noted in 2009, "The first integrated circuit—the forefather of the modern microchip—was built by Texas Instruments but funded by the Apollo program and the Air Force's Minuteman Missile Project. They developed it, but the customer was NASA."[1] However, significant progress in computers began prior to the space race and NASA.

British mathematician, engineer, and philosopher Charles Babbage is widely considered to be the "father of the computer." Babbage was born in 1791. In 1810 he began his study of mathematics at Trinity College of Cambridge University. He soon found himself to be more knowledgeable than his instructors. In 1819 Babbage began traveling to Paris. There Babbage learned of the ambitious table-making project undertaken by the French. Begun in 1791 and finished about a decade later, the tables (mostly logarithmic and trigonometric) were an effort to bring uniformity to standards and measurements across France.

The project was led by Baron Gaspard de Prony. It was the largest table-making project the world had ever known. Inspired by the division of labor advocated in Adam Smith's *Wealth of Nations* (more on this fabulous work later), de Prony divided up the work into a table-making "factory." The largest section was made up of several dozen human "computers" who did the final calculations, usually only involving simple arithmetic, that went into the tables.

Babbage first saw the tables in the library of the French Scientific Academy. He knew firsthand of the difficulties of table-making because he had been involved in making star tables for the Astronomical Society. He found the process to be extremely tedious and filled with errors. However, he found inspiration in de Prony's organization and process. With the industrial revolution underway and with factories in Europe and America replacing human workers with machines, Babbage decided that de Prony's table-making factory should be replaced by a table-making machine.

Because his machine used the same method of differences in table-making employed by de Prony, Babbage called his steam-powered device a "Difference Engine." (Historically, "divided differences" is an algorithmic method of calculating tables of logarithms and trigonometric functions that employs the process of recursive division.) Babbage designed his engine not only to perform the table-making calculations, but also to set the type for printing. Babbage was able to build only a small prototype of his Difference Engine. After nearly two decades of effort, in 1842 the British government, which was funding Babbage's production of his Difference Engine, decided that Babbage's machine was too expensive and too technically intricate to be feasible.

By this time Babbage had already conceived of a device that would do everything the Difference Engine would do, and far more. Babbage called his new concept the "Analytical Engine." According to computer historians, in virtually all the important details, Babbage's machine had the same logical design as the modern computer.[2] The Analytical Engine was based on the Jacquard loom.

Joseph-Marie Jacquard had invented a loom that would weave by following a pattern that was determined by a series of large paper punched cards (see photo below). Jacquard's loom allowed for the production of weaves of complicated patterns such as flowers or leaves.

**Jacquard loom in the National Museum of Scotland. © Ad Meskens / Wikimedia Commons**

Babbage's Analytical Engine would be driven by two sets of punched cards, "one to direct the operation to be performed, and the other for the variables of the problem."[3] Instead of weaving thread, as Babbage's assistant, Ada King, explained, the Analytic Engine "weaves algebraic patterns." Also, unlike the Difference Engine, the Analytical Engine could "remember." In other words, it could store information.

Most importantly, the Analytical Engine possessed a key feature that distinguishes computers from mere calculators: "if-then," or conditional statements. (Conditional statements are a common feature of modern computer programming language.) According to Babbage himself, the Analytical Engine could reach a point in its calculations, read the value, and then continue its calculations, in one direction or another, based on the measure of the value.

The Analytical Engine became Babbage's complete focus, which contributed to the undoing of his Difference Engine. Neither the Difference Engine nor the Analytical Engine would be built. In 1842, Ada Lovelace (Babbage's assistant, previously Ada King) would publish an important and detailed account of the Analytical Engine, *Sketch of the Analytical Engine*. Though almost all of the technical content revealed in *Sketch* was the result of Babbage's work, King's publication was so well written and widely read that some pronounced her the world's first programmer. (She even had a programming language, *Ada*, named after her.)

Babbage's work was not limited to mathematics and computer science; he was a devout Christian, and in 1837 he wrote the *Ninth Bridgewater Treatise*. This work was in response to the eight Bridgewater Treatises. The Bridgewater Treatises were a work of "Natural Theology" which explored "the Power, Wisdom, and Goodness of God, as manifested in the Creation." The treatises were commissioned by Francis Henry Egerton, Earl of Bridgewater, and were written by various nineteenth century naturalists. Babbage's treatise was a separate work of theology where he drew upon his experience as a mathematician and programmer.

In the *Ninth Bridgewater Treatise,* Babbage presented God as a sort-of "divine programmer." On the issue of science and religion, which are often erroneously presented as being in irreconcilable conflict,[4] Babbage declared that "there exists no fatal collision between the words of Scripture and the facts of nature."[5] Near the end of his life, in 1864, Babbage published his autobiography *Passages from the Life of a Philosopher*. He devoted one chapter to "Miracles" and one to "Religion." In the Religion chapter, Babbage concluded,

> There remains a third source from which we arrive at the knowledge of the existence of a supreme Creator, namely, from an examination of his works. Unlike transmitted testimony, which is weakened at every stage, this evidence derives confirmation from the progress of the

individual as well as from the advancement of the knowledge of the race.

Almost all thinking men who have studied the laws which govern the animate and the inanimate world around us, agree that the belief in the existence of one Supreme Creator, possessed of infinite wisdom and power, is open to far less difficulties than the supposition of the absence of any cause, or of the existence of a plurality of causes.[6]

Babbage died in 1871 at the age of 79. He was a man whose thinking was literally decades ahead of his time. Few of his contemporaries were able to comprehend what he was working toward. Thus, scientists and engineers of the nineteenth century failed to pick up where he left off. Instead, a non-digital path, what we now call analog computing, was pursued. A century passed before Babbage's amazing vision would be realized.

In an effort to expedite the processing of census data, American Herman Hollerith would take the next step in bringing Babbage's vision to reality. With the U.S. population just over 50 million in 1880, the census took almost eight years to count. Nearly 1,500 clerks were employed to process the census data. Using the traditional method of counting by hand, the Census Bureau feared the next count would go beyond 10 years and thus render the census useless.

Hollerith obtained his undergraduate degree at Columbia University in 1879. While he was a student at Columbia, one of Hollerith's professors was an advisor to the Census Bureau. This professor asked the recently-graduated Hollerith to assist him in his census work. There, Hollerith witnessed first-hand the extreme tediousness and the extraordinary scale that went into tabulating the census data. In 1882, Hollerith began teaching at the Massachusetts Institute of Technology. Inspired by observing a train conductor punch paper tickets that revealed the hair color, eye color, and other details, of the ticket holder, Hollerith began conducting tabulating experiments using punched cards.

In 1884, Hollerith submitted a patent entitled "The Art of Compiling Statistics." His patent described a system that would electromechanically read and record data stored on punched cards, later known as "Hollerith cards." Along with the cards which stored the information, Hollerith's system contained a tabulating machine. Hollerith's tabulator contained 288 retractable pins. As a pin passed through a hole in one of the punched cards, it completed an electrical circuit. The electricity then activated a counter. The circuit could also open compartments that would send the card along to the next stage of tabulation. For the first time, an "intelligent" machine was driven by electricity.

Hollerith's system was used in the 1890 census. It was the largest census effort the world had ever seen. About 100 of Hollerith's machines were used in the effort. The complete census was done in a fraction of the time of the last one—about two-and-a-half years—and saved the U.S. government about one-third of the cost (approximately $5 million). The age of "data processing" and "information technology" was born.

Hollerith's census success led him to start his own business. In 1896 he formed The Tabulating Machine Company. Census bureaus around the world—England, Italy, Germany, Russia, Austria, Canada, France, Norway, Puerto Rico, Cuba, and the Philippines—used Hollerith's machines. By the turn of the twentieth century, with the explosion of industry already well underway in the U.S., the desire for office machines began to grow significantly.

The United States was the first nation in the world to make large-scale use of office machinery. This head start allowed the U.S. to become the world's leading producer of information technology products, a position it still holds today. Also, the U.S. dominated the typewriter, record-keeping, adding machine, and accounting machine industries for most of their histories; it established the computer industry, and it dominates this industry today.[7]

In 1911, The Tabulating Machine Company was the most significant of four companies that consolidated to form International Business Machines, better known today as IBM. By

1928, the world's top four office-machine supply companies were all American. Remington Rand, known mostly for its typewriters, led the way with annual sales of $60 million. Next was National Cash Register (NCR) at $50 million, Burroughs Adding Machine Company at $32 million, and IBM at $20 million.[8]

Each of these companies began their manufacturing in the late nineteenth century. At this time, typewriters, adding machines, and the like (with some containing thousands of small parts) were some of the most complicated, if not the most complicated, equipment to manufacture. Thus, these companies developed some of the best manufacturing techniques and practices in the world. Also, the art of selling a piece of office equipment was pioneered and perfected at these companies.

Still, for the first several decades of the twentieth century, the science of machine computing was almost exclusively limited to analog machines. (A common example to illustrate the difference in computing machines: a watch with hands that sweep over a circular display of numbers is analog; a watch with an electronic display of numbers is digital.) The expanding electrical power system in the U.S. was one of the most significant customers of analog computing machines in the early twentieth century.

In the early years of the U.S. electrical grid, the mathematics of electricity and electrical networks was very challenging and poorly understood. The differential equations that described the electrical currents were elaborate and very difficult to solve. Thus small analog models were built. (A model is an "analogy" of the real thing. The word "analog" is derived from "analogy.") The word "small" is very relative, for some of the network models that were built filled entire rooms. One of the most elaborate of these "network analyzers" was the AC Network Calculator, built at MIT in 1930.

At this time, MIT was the world's leading research center for analog "computing machines." From 1928 to 1931, Vannevar Bush, a member of the Department of Electrical Engineering at MIT, led a team that built a "Differential Analyzer." The Differential Analyzer was an analog computer that was originally designed to model power networks. It was an elaborate network of wires, shafts, wheels, pulleys, and about 1,000 gears. It could solve differential equations with as many as 18 independent variables. Bush soon discovered its value as a general-purpose analog computer.

**Women operating the Differential Analyzer in the basement of the Moore School of Electrical Engineering.**

Bush's Differential Analyzer wasn't a general-purpose computer in the modern sense. It could solve only differential equations. However, this ability made it widely useful in science and engineering. Several copies of the Differential Analyzer were made and put to use at companies such as General Electric and at several universities, most significantly at the University of Pennsylvania.

Still, as our knowledge of the world around us was expanding at a magnificent rate—again, with America leading the way—everything from electrical grids to airplanes, automobiles, skyscrapers, telephones, and the like were becoming commonplace. The need for large-scale digital computations was growing, but the only way of doing such mathematics continued to be with the use of human "computers."

One of the earliest successful efforts at a digital calculator came as the result of research done at Bell Telephone Laboratories. For years, Bell Labs had been working on the science of turning the numbers dialed into a telephone, along with the sound that needed to be transmitted, into an electrical signal that could be carried along a wire. In the mid-1930s, while working on electromechanical relays (a relay is an electrically operated switch) in order to create circuits that would transmit information, George Stibitz, a research mathematician working at Bell, realized that such circuits were perfectly suited to perform the binary arithmetic he had learned in algebra class. He then realized that he could build an electrical calculator.

In November of 1939, the Complex Number Calculator (or Complex Number Generator, or Complex Number Computer) was complete. This was the world's first electrical digital computer.[9]

Inspired by Babbage's Difference Engine, American physicist Howard Aiken approached IBM's chief engineer James Bryce about funding the building of a general purpose electro-mechanical computer. Aiken was a researcher at Harvard. His goal was to build an electro-magnetic version of Hollerith's punch card machine. Aiken's proposal convinced Bryce of the feasibility of his idea. Bryce then convinced chairman and CEO of IBM, Thomas J. Watson, personally to approve the project.

Once approved, Aiken's role was mostly that of consultant. Trusted IBM engineers oversaw the actual design and building of the computer. Built by IBM at their Endicott plant, the Harvard Mark I was shipped to Harvard University in February of 1944. It was a massive machine weighing five tons. It was driven by a 50-foot shaft and had approximately 750,000 moving parts.

According to IBM archives,

> The Automatic Sequence Controlled Calculator
> (Harvard Mark I) was the first operating machine
> that could execute long computations
> automatically...A steel frame 51 feet (16 m) long
> and eight feet high held the calculator, which
> consisted of an interlocking panel of small gears,
> counters, switches and control circuits, all only a
> few inches in depth. The ASCC used 500 miles
> (800 km) of wire with three million connections,
> 3,500 multipole relays with 35,000 contacts,
> 2,225 counters, 1,464 tenpole switches and tiers
> of 72 adding machines, each with 23 significant
> numbers. It was the industry's largest
> electromechanical calculator.[10]

One of the first programs run on the Mark I involved the
Manhattan Project, the top-secret American project to create a
nuclear bomb. In order to study the type of detonation needed (gun
design vs. implosion) for a plutonium atomic bomb, in August of
1944, American physicist John von Neumann arrived at Harvard
with two mathematicians in order to run calculations on the Mark
I. The calculations confirmed von Neumann's belief that the
implosion design was necessary for the plutonium bomb. The
implosion-type design was used successfully in the "Fat Man"
bomb that was detonated over Nagasaki, Japan.

The onset of World War II was a boon for the emerging field of
computer science. The Office of Scientific Research and
Development (OSRD), headed by Vannevar Bush, led the
scientific war effort in the United States. The mathematics and
computer applications to things such as radar and ballistics were
given particular attention. The OSRD superseded and continued
the work of the National Defense Research Committee (NDRC).
Both were created by Executive Order, and both were led by Bush.

One of the significant achievements of the NDRC, which was
continued by the OSRD, was that the efforts of hundreds of

civilian research groups were combined with those of the U.S. War Department. One example of this occurred at the Moore School of Electrical Engineering, part of the University of Pennsylvania. The Moore School had a Bush Differential Analyzer, and the U.S. Army's Ballistics Research Laboratory (BRL) used it for ballistics calculations. By the early 1940s, physicist Dr. John Mauchly was teaching at the Moore School. In order to complete the lengthy firing tables required by the BRL more efficiently, in 1942 Mauchly proposed the building of an electronic calculating machine. What's more, he was far from alone.

Due to the war effort, several other scientists in the U.S. and Europe (especially in England and Germany) were working toward the same goal. Beginning in 1937 at Iowa State University, Professor John Atanasoff and graduate student Clifford Berry began work on an electronic computing device. By 1941, they had completed the machine—the Atanasoff-Berry Computer (ABC). It was the world's first fully automatic electronic digital computer. Atanasoff, described by his biographer as the "forgotten father of the computer," was visited by Mauchly the year the ABC was completed. Mauchly spent several days studying the machine.

Mauchly returned to the Moore School, this time as a student. By the middle of 1941 the war in Europe was nearly two years old, and many people in the U.S. were beginning to make preparations in case America was drawn into the war. In order to train scientists in the new field of electronics, the U.S. War Department asked the Moore School to offer a 10-week course called Engineering, Science, Management War Training (ESMWT).

Mauchly was the oldest student in the class. The lab for the course was run by John Presper (Pres) Eckert, who was without question the best electronic engineer in the Moore School.[11] Mauchly and Eckert quickly developed a strong rapport. The fascination that each shared with electricity and wiring led to many long discussions about computing machines. Inspired somewhat by the ABC, they shared a vision of replacing the wheels and gears of a conventional computing machine (i.e., the Differential Analyzer) with vacuum tubes, relays, resistors, capacitors, and the other necessary components.

The vision of Mauchly and the engineering of Eckert resulted in the *Electronic Numerical Integrator And Computer*, or simply ENIAC. Built between 1943 and 1945, ENIAC was the first electronic general-purpose computer.[12] Unlike the ABC, ENIAC was programmable, though the programming was lengthy and laborious. Nevertheless, it was 1,000 times faster than the Harvard Mark I. By the time ENIAC was completed, World War II was over, but for nearly a decade following the war, ENIAC served as the primary computing engine of the U.S. Army. Some computer historians have proposed that during its 1945 to 1955 run, ENIAC did more calculations than the previous combined efforts of all of mankind.

Around the same period of time, computer scientists in Europe, especially in Great Britain, also made great strides in electronic computing. Almost all of the early computer science efforts of the British were to assist in their cryptography efforts. Brit Alan Turing, who worked for the Government Code and Cypher School at the renowned Bletchley Park, is widely considered the father of theoretical computer science.

In 1940, Turing built an electromechanical computer, dubbed a "bombe," to help decipher the German Enigma-machine. The bombe was followed by Colossus. Colossus was actually a series of electronic computers used by the British in their codebreaking. Following World War II, the British and the United States were the only nations with enough infrastructure and resources to pursue computer science seriously.

In 1948, the British became the first to create a computer—the "Baby"—that could execute a program from memory. Storing instructions in a computer's memory in order to tell it what to do was a groundbreaking achievement. Every computer since has operated under this principle. Software was born.

The United States built the world's first practical stored-program computer. John von Neumann joined Mauchly and Eckert at the Moore School as a consultant. Though a disgruntled Mauchly and Eckert would leave the project, the results of their collaboration yielded *Electronic Discrete Variable Automatic Computer*, or

EDVAC. Though EDVAC was an improvement over ENIAC, it did not begin operation until 1951, about two years after it was delivered to the Army's BRL, and then with only a limited use.

By the late 1940s and early 1950s, commercial uses of the computer were starting to be explored. By the early 1950s, about 30 U.S. companies had entered the commercial computer business. The only other nation in the world to come close to this was Great Britain, where about 10 companies started making computers to sell. In the U.S., after departing the EDVAC project, Mauchly and Eckert founded what is probably the first company devoted solely to creating, manufacturing, and selling computers. The Eckert–Mauchly Computer Corporation (EMCC) was founded in 1946 and incorporated in December of 1947. In 1947, EMCC began design work on the UNIVAC (Universal Automatic Computer), the first commercial computer created in the United States. UNIVAC was completed in 1951 after EMCC was acquired by Remington Rand.

Instead of punched cards, data input into UNIVAC was through the ingenious magnetic tape system designed by Eckert. UNIVAC I, as it was later designated after subsequent UNIVACs were manufactured, was delivered to the Census Bureau in 1951. In order to create interest in UNIVAC, Remington Rand executives approached CBS about using the new computer to analyze the 1952 presidential returns and help predict the winner.

In the name of entertainment, Walter Cronkite agreed. While Pres Eckert sat in the CBS studios with Cronkite, programmers at EMCC in Philadelphia, using a program devised by Mauchly and a statistician from the University of Pennsylvania, took sample returns from eight states: New York, Pennsylvania, Massachusetts, Ohio, Illinois, Minnesota, Texas, and California. The data were placed onto computer tape and loaded onto UNIVAC. Using voting patterns from the 1944 and 1948 presidential elections that were programmed in, the results from UNIVAC showed a landslide victory for Eisenhower over Stevenson, 438 electoral votes to 93. This result contradicted virtually all of the political polls of the day, including Gallup's.

In order to protect CBS and Remington Rand from perhaps significant embarrassment, these results from UNIVAC were kept quiet. The actual electoral tally in the 1952 U.S. Presidential election: Eisenhower 442, Stevenson 89. UNIVAC, it turns out, was nearly exactly correct. CBS explained its doubt in the computer to its viewers. Once the accuracy of UNIVAC was revealed to the public, the computer became an instant celebrity, and sales reflected this.[13]

Along with several orders from the U.S. military, including the Air Force and the Navy, U.S. corporate giants such as General Electric, Westinghouse Electric, U.S. Steel, and Metropolitan Life soon owned UNIVACs. IBM took notice. Big Blue had been a bit slow in recognizing the computer as something beyond a mathematical tool. By 1954, General Electric had created the first successful payroll application for UNIVAC. By 1956, Westinghouse was using UNIVAC to calculate payroll, sales records, sales forecasts, and the like. The wide use of a computer as a data-processing machine was underway.[14]

IBM's vast resources soon had it building computers that were faster and more reliable than UNIVAC. By 1956, IBM computers were out-selling UNIVACs. However, these early computers were huge compared to modern standards and very expensive—priced anywhere from about $250,000 to $1 million dollars each. Only large companies and governments were able to afford them, thus sales were measured by the dozen, but by the end of the 1950s, though the commercial computer industry was still in its infancy, it was becoming clear to all astute observers that the computer was soon to be an indispensable tool for business.

By 1965, IBM had 65 percent of the computer market. The next seven largest companies combined for a 34 percent market share, with Sperry Rand, a company formed when the Sperry Corporation bought Remington Rand in 1955, being the largest of these with a 12 percent share. IBM would dominate the computer industry for decades. By the 1970s, as computers started shrinking in size, IBM's domination began to wane.

Two American inventions are most responsible for significant reduction in the size of the computer: the transistor and the integrated circuit (or microchip). Without these, the digital age as we know it and, for the most part, love it, would not exist. In 1947, working at Bell Labs, American physicists John Bardeen, Walter Brattain, and William Shockley invented the transistor, an achievement which won them the Nobel Prize in Physics in 1956. Some researchers and analysts consider the transistor "the single most important invention of the 20th century."[15]

Everything from our electronic tablets to digital toasters contains transistors. The transistor is the building block for the modern microprocessor. It is the key component in all modern electronics. Generally, transistors act as a switch or an amplifier. The early transistors were essentially switches, and they replaced vacuum tubes. However, in spite of the advantages transistors provided, scientists and engineers of the 1950s soon found that as circuits grew larger and more complex—like those in a computer—the vast number of transistors, wires, and other components that were necessary to create such circuits were impractical to build. (This dilemma became known as the "tyranny of numbers.")

Jack Kilby, an engineer at Texas Instruments, provided the solution to this "tyranny of numbers." On February 6, 1959, Kilby filed for a patent on a device he described as "a body of semiconductor material…wherein all the components of the electronic circuit are completely integrated." Thus, the integrated circuit, or microchip, was born. Others, especially Robert Noyce, an engineer at Fairchild Semiconductor, and later co-founder of Intel, are also credited with advancing the concept of integrated circuits.

Texas Instruments (TI) was having difficulty convincing its clients of the reliability of integrated circuits.[16] Without customers to buy integrated circuits, TI was not going to be able to continue the research into this new field of technology. Since Kilby had developed a good working relationship with Richard D. Alberts, head of the Air Force Electronic Components Laboratory, the Air Force funded a small TI integrated circuit research program. Soon, U.S. defense equipment, including the Minuteman missile, incorporated integrated circuits. Thus, U.S. missiles became the world's most accurate and deadly. The first computer to make use of integrated circuits was the Apollo Guidance Computer.[17] Between 1961 and 1965, NASA was the world's largest consumer of integrated circuits. The computers necessary to send men to the moon had to get smaller, and integrated circuits—the microchip—made this possible.

In order to place a product that incorporated the use of microchips in the hands of American citizens, and thus commercialize microchips, TI challenged Kilby to create a hand-held calculator. In April of 1971, *Pocketronic* was launched.

*Pocketronic* could perform only the four basic arithmetic functions, yet it cost $150. LED technology was not yet available, so the results of calculations printed out on a thin strip of paper.

From vacuum tubes, relays, resistors, and capacitors, to transistors and microchips, in a span of two decades, computer hardware in the U.S. made great strides. The same could be said for programming languages, as well as computer software. A programming language communicates instructions to a computer, often directing it to perform certain tasks. Virtually all early widely used computer programming languages—such as FORTRAN, COBOL, BASIC, and C—were created in the U.S.

Computer software is a widely used phrase that typically describes a set of instructions, a program, that enables a computer user to interact with a machine to perform certain tasks. Popular types of software include word processing, web browsing, email, gaming, and databases. By the mid-1960s there were dozens of software contractors in the United States, employing hundreds of programmers. Total software sales for these American companies was in the tens of millions of dollars. Again, no one else in the world was close.

As computers got smaller, they got much less expensive. By 1970, for $20,000 a business could purchase a "minicomputer" that had the same power of a 1965 mainframe that had cost ten times as much.[18] By the mid-1970s the cost of a hand-held calculator had dropped below $10. In 1971, Intel announced the first available microprocessor. An ad in *Electronics News* read, "Announcing a new era of integrated electronics: A microprogrammable computer on a chip."[19]

In January of 1975, on the cover of *Popular Electronics*, the world's first personal computer was announced. The Altair 8800 was also the first microprocessor-based computer. It cost just under $400 and was sold as a mail-order kit that the customer had to assemble. There was no monitor, no keyboard, and only 256 bytes of memory. It could be programmed only by the user entering pure binary code. Only the most dedicated computer hobbyists were able to appreciate the machine.

Nevertheless, the Altair 8800 spawned the personal computer industry. Most early personal computing companies were made up of a handful of people working out of their homes, garages, or apartments. The components to make a computer a "personal" device—monitors, keyboards, disk drives, and printers—already existed. Some of these small companies also provided software.

In 1976, making use of new microprocessor technology, Steve Wozniak and Steve Jobs assembled the Apple I in Jobs' garage. The Apple I not only lacked a keyboard and a monitor, but also lacked a case and a power supply. Nevertheless, they sold about 200 machines that first year. In the late 1970s, along with Apple, companies such as Commodore and Tandy were also making their mark in the personal computing world.

By 1980, when IBM came calling, a small 32-person company was ready to make its mark in the personal computing world. Microsoft was founded in 1975 by Bill Gates and Paul Allen. When IBM decided to get into the PC business, it was looking for a software company to design an operating system. Microsoft was unable to produce a product in the timeframe IBM required. Thus, Gates purchased software from a local Seattle software company, Seattle Computer Products, for $30,000 and made the necessary improvements. This resulted in MS-DOS, the operating system that ran virtually every IBM PC. By 1983, the IBM PC was the industry standard. Soon, the software industry at large had produced thousands of programs to run on the IBM PC. The software industry soon became as big as the computer industry itself.

In 1980, with over 80 percent of worldwide revenues, the U.S. dominated the computer industry. By 1990, the U.S. still had over 60 percent worldwide market share in the computer industry. Also, in 1990, there were over 50 million personal computers in the United States alone. This was more than three times the per capita computer power of Japan.[20]

Today, with well over 300 million personal computers in use, nearly one for every citizen, there is more computing power in the United States than the next two nations (China and Japan) combined.[21] In addition, technology companies are the world's largest businesses. The world's most valuable company, with $740 billion in market capitalization, is Apple. The world's second largest company is Google. Eight of the world's top ten technology companies (Apple, Microsoft, Google, IBM, Intel, Cisco, Oracle, and HP) are American companies.[22]

The internet was born in the United States, as was e-mail. As with the invention of trains and the railroad, the telegraph and the Transatlantic cable, the automobile and the airplane, American technology again made the world a much smaller place.

# A Super Power is Born, Part 1: America's Economic Might— Christianity Creates Capitalism

The Industrial Revolution and the amazing economic growth that accompanied it continued well into the twentieth century for the United States. By the mid to late nineteenth century—just decades after its birth—the United States was a world leader in textiles, transportation, communication, education, farming, firearms, machine tools, the production of steel and other metals, the production and use of electricity, and the discovery and development of fossil fuels. By the early twentieth century, in virtually every one of these sectors, the U.S. was *the* world leader. With barely five percent of the world's population and approximately the same ratio of total land area, in about 120 years the U.S. became the world's leading economic super-power. As the twentieth century advanced, with the manufacture of automobiles, the invention and manufacture of the airplane, the discovery and harnessing of nuclear power, the development of rockets and space flight, the invention and manufacture of computers, and all of the technological advancements that went hand-in-hand with each of these sectors, America cemented its standing as the world's leading industrial, technological, and economic power. The twentieth century, as Henry Luce aptly noted in 1941, was indeed "The American Century."[1]

As was noted earlier, the U.S. was the world's largest economy prior to the invention of the automobile. In 1900, just prior to the automobile explosion in the U.S., American gross domestic product (GDP) was nearly twice that of the UK, China, and Germany, and nearly three times that of France. From 1900—just after the introduction of the automobile in America—to 1910, the U.S. economy grew one-and-a-half times as fast as the German economy, more than three times as fast as the British economy, and more than 10 times as fast as the French economy. After the U.S., and along with India and China, whose economic growth during this period was also much slower than American growth, the German, British, and French economies were the world's largest.

By 1912, with the addition of Oklahoma, New Mexico, and Arizona to the Union, the continental U.S. was complete. The mainland of the United States exceeded three million square miles. Overseas territories, which extended halfway around the world, covered another 125,000 square miles. In 1900, the population of the U.S. was just over 76 million. By 1920, it was just over 106 million. Early in the twentieth century, per capita income in the U.S. was the highest in the world. A nice balance of trade led to a dramatic increase in foreign investments, from $700 million in 1897, to $3.5 billion in 1914. With wise foresight, international observers were predicting that New York would soon become the center of world finance. "London and Berlin are standing in perfectly abject terror," observed novelist Henry James in 1901, "watching Pierpont Morgan's nose flaming over the waves, and approaching horribly nearer their bank vaults."[2]

The prospect for even further U.S. economic advancement was aided by the devastation that World War I brought to Europe. With tens of millions of Europeans and Russians dead, farming and manufacturing production fell off dramatically. Contrastingly,

The United States was the world's largest agricultural and manufacturing producer and during the 1920s, remarkably, produced more industrial output than the next six powers

combined. The war solidified the nation's
position as a creditor. (Following World War I,
the U.S. became the world's leading creditor.) It
was the world's leading financial power and had
a large supply of gold. Its productivity, wealth,
and standard of living were the envy of people
across the globe.[3]

With American products such as automobiles, tires, petroleum
products, cash registers, radios, typewriters, sewing machines,
household appliances, agricultural equipment, and so on in high
demand, by 1929, the U.S. was the world's leading exporter.
Driven (pun intended) largely by the automotive industry, this
accelerated economic growth in America continued until the Great
Depression. In 1929, even with the onset of the Great Depression,
the goods and services produced in the United States "exceeded
that in any country during any previous year of world history."[4] Of
course, 1929 saw great changes in the financial landscape the
world over.

As the result of the Great Depression, unemployment in the U.S.
exploded to nearly 25 percent. Between 1929 and 1932, the
American gross national product fell 50 percent. Manufacturing
fell by 25 percent, construction by 78 percent, and investors in the
U.S. almost completely closed their wallets, as American investing
dropped by a shocking 98 percent.

During the World War II era—from the beginning of 1939 until
the end of 1945—the U.S. economy grew at an unprecedented rate.
The gross domestic product more than doubled. While the U.S.
economy boomed, World War II caused most of the rest of the
world's large economies to contract significantly. The spread of
Soviet communism that followed the war caused further
widespread economic strife. For decades, millions of people the
world over suffered under the wicked schemes of communism and
socialism, and for decades the United States led the fight—both
hot, cold and fiscal—against such oppressive ideologies.

In 1990 International Dollars, according to British economist
Angus Maddison (*Contours of the World Economy, 1–2030 AD*),

by 1950, the U.S. GDP was about $1.5 trillion. This was more than one-quarter of the world's total GDP, more than all of Western Europe combined, three times all of Latin America combined, and three times the GDP of the Soviet Union. By 1973, at $3.5 trillion, U.S. GDP had dropped to about 22 percent of world GDP, but still far outpaced any other single nation, more than double that of the Soviet Union, and more than triple that of Japan.[5]

In 2003, U.S. GDP was $8.5 trillion, or 20.5 percent of world GDP. China was close with $6.2 trillion, while the total for Western Europe was $7.9 trillion. As of 2014, at $17.4 trillion, U.S. GDP still led the world. China was second at $10.4 trillion, and Japan third at $4.6 trillion.[6] According to the Wall Street Journal, an American today earns, on average, $130 per day. Of course, this leads the world and is nearly five times the world average of $33 per day. In China the average is $20 a day. In India, it's $10 a day.[7]

In spite of the many rumors of America's economic demise, which may yet come, for well over a century now, the United States has been the dominant economic power in the world. And there are no real serious challengers. As *Forbes* magazine noted in 2013,

> [T]he United States is the world leader and likely to remain there for decades. It has the greatest soft power in the world by far. The United States still receives far more immigrants each year (1 million) than any other country in the world. The United States leads the world in high technology (Silicon Valley), finance and business (Wall Street), the movies (Hollywood) and higher education (17 of the top 20 universities in the world in Shanghai's Jaotong University survey). The United States has a First World trade profile (massive exports of consumer and technology goods and imports of natural resources).
>
> It is still the world's leader for FDI at 180 billion dollars, almost twice its nearest competitor. The United States, spending 560 billion dollars a

year, has the most powerful military in the
world. Its GDP (16 trillion dollars) is more than
twice the size of China's GDP. As the first new
nation, it has the world's longest functioning
democracy in a world filled with semi-
democratic or non-democratic countries. Its
stock market, at an all-time high, still reflects
American leadership of the global economy.[8]

Even the most lax of students examining history and economics
would ask: How and why? How exactly did the United States
come to lead the world so dominantly in terms of its economy, and
why did this happen? The answer (implied at the end of chapter 4
and the beginning of chapter 14) to these questions is that, in the
United States of America, for the first time in human history, we
see the near-perfect combination of Christianity, constitution, and a
wealth of human and natural resources. This should come as little
surprise. Remember that in the 1830s, with his commentary on
Puritanism, Tocqueville concluded the same.

Ask most Americans to name the most important document
produced in 1776, and almost no one would answer with Adam
Smith's *An Inquiry into the Nature and Causes of the Wealth of
Nations*, more commonly known as *The Wealth of Nations*. Some
would argue that Smith's work had more of a global impact than
even the Declaration of Independence.[9] The first edition of *The
Wealth of Nations* sold out in six months. It would have an almost
immediate impact on government financial policy and is
considered by many to be the most important treatise on economics
ever written. Adam Smith is often called the "Founding Father" of
capitalism.

American founders soon recognized the importance of *The Wealth
of Nations* as it applied to economics and sound fiscal policy.
Writing to John Norvell in 1807, Thomas Jefferson said that on
"the subjects of money & commerce, Smith's *Wealth of Nations* is
the best book to be read."[10] *The Wealth of Nations* is a collection of
five books and is widely considered the world's earliest, most
comprehensive defense of a free-market economy.

Author W. Cleon Skousen concludes that Smith's doctrines of free-market economics "fit into the thinking and experiences of the Founders like a hand in a glove."[11] As Skousen also points outs, the U.S. was the first nation on earth of any size or consequence "to undertake the structuring of a whole national economy on the basis of natural law and the free-market concept described by Adam Smith."[12]

Natural Law, or "[The] Law of Nature," wrote English philosopher John Locke (who profoundly influenced our founders), "stands as an eternal rule to all men, legislators as well as others. The rules that they make for other men's actions must…be conformable to the Law of Nature, i.e. to the will of God…"

"True law," as Cicero called it, is the "one eternal and unchangeable law [that] will be valid for all nations and all times, and there will be one master and ruler, that is God, over us all, for he is the author of this law…"

Blackstone declared in his presuppositional basis for law that, "These laws laid down by God are the eternal immutable laws of good and evil…This law of nature dictated by God himself, is of course superior in obligation to any other. It is binding over all the globe, in all countries, and at all times: no human laws are of any validity if contrary to this…"[13]

C.S. Lewis concluded that, "Natural Law or Traditional Morality…is not one among a series of possible systems of value. It is the sole source of all value judgments. If it is rejected, all value is rejected. If any value is retained, it is retained."[14]

Throughout the early colonies, the incorporation of Natural (or "Divine") Law was prevalent. The *Fundamental Orders of Connecticut* (the first constitution written in America), as well as similar documents in Rhode Island and New Haven, specifically mentioned that their civil law rested upon "the rule of the word of God," or "all those perfect and most absolute laws of His."

References to, not vague religious babble, but specific biblical texts, such as the Ten Commandments, can be found in the civil law of every original U.S. colony.[15] It is a fact of history that throughout our pre-Colonial, Colonial, Revolutionary period and beyond, America's lawmakers and laws were steeped in Natural Law.

When Jefferson wrote of the "Laws of Nature and Nature's God" he was borrowing from Lord Bolingbroke, of whom Jefferson was a student. In a famous letter to Alexander Pope, Bolingbroke wrote, "You will find that it is the modest, not the presumptuous enquirer, who makes a real, and safe progress in the discovery of divine truths. One follows nature, and nature's God; that is, he follows God in his works, and in his word."[16]

Belief and acceptance of Natural Law, as understood by America's founders, is exactly in line with what Scripture reveals. As Paul wrote in Romans,

> The wrath of God is being revealed from heaven against all the godlessness and wickedness of people, who suppress the truth by their wickedness, since what may be known about God is plain to them, because God has made it plain to them. For since the creation of the world God's invisible qualities—his eternal power and divine nature—have been clearly seen, being understood from what has been made, so that people are without excuse (Rom. 1:18-20).

Since the creation of the world, the "natural" state of mankind has been "clearly seen." As the Garden of Eden revealed, Natural Law begat liberty. In other words, our natural state is to be free. We were created that way. With God's laws as the foundation for government, with God's law written on the hearts of so many Americans, and with a thirst for liberty, a free-market capitalistic society was simply the logical and right direction for the United States of America. In *How Christianity Created Capitalism*, philosopher Michael Novak wrote,

> It was the church more than any other agency,
> writes historian Randall Collins, that put in place
> what Weber called the preconditions of
> capitalism: the rule of law and a bureaucracy for
> resolving disputes permanence that allows for
> transgenerational investment and sustained
> intellectual and physical efforts, together with
> the accumulation of long-term capital; and a zest
> for discovery, enterprise, wealth creation, and
> new undertakings.[17]

In other words, America did not become—and for well over a
century now—remain the most prosperous nation on earth merely
by the blind forces of unfettered capitalism. And neither did the
U.S. become the world's most prosperous nation through an
immoral and undisciplined form of liberty. In opposing the godless
and bloody French Revolution, on liberty, Edmund Burke, the
father of modern conservatism, concluded that,

> I should therefore suspend my congratulations on
> the new liberty of France, until I was informed
> how it had been combined with government;
> with public force; with the discipline and
> obedience of armies;…with morality and
> religion;…with peace and order; with civil and
> social manners. All these (in their way) are good
> things too; and, without them, liberty is not a
> benefit whilst it lasts, and is not likely to
> continue long. The effect of liberty to individuals
> is, that they may do what they please: We ought
> to see what it will please them to do, before we
> risk congratulations.[18]

Led by the so-called "philosophers of the Enlightenment," whom
Burke referred to as "a 'literary cabal' committed to the destruction
of Christianity by any and every available means,"[19] what the
French were "pleased to do" was execute over 40,000 of its
citizens, close churches, ban crosses, destroy religious monuments,

and outlaw public and private worship and education.[20] On the other hand, it was the Christianity practiced by millions of Americans, along with the Christian principles that formed the foundation of our laws and government that produced a free, moral (but not perfect), capitalistic, and prosperous society unlike anything the world has ever known.

This capitalism gave birth to the monstrous industrial revolution in America. It did not take long until Americans were enjoying the highest standard of living in the world. Millions rose out of poverty or poverty-like conditions. The United States experienced a prosperity like the world has never seen. We were soon being described as a "superpower."

# CHAPTER 23

# A Super Power is Born, Part 2: The Birth of the Modern American Military

There are several factors that go into defining a nation as a "superpower." Certainly the industrial and economic power achieved by the United States in the nineteenth and twentieth centuries significantly set us apart from the rest of the world. *The Stanford Journal of International Relations* defines a "superpower" as "[A] country that has the capacity to project dominating power and influence anywhere in the world, and sometimes, in more than one region of the globe at a time, and so may plausibly attain the status of global hegemon."[1]

In addition, "The basic components of superpower stature may be measured along four axes of power: military, economic, political, and cultural."[2] Thus, it could be argued that the United States was not a complete superpower until after the massive military expansion in the U.S. that occurred during World War II. Our military dominance was, and perhaps still is, so overwhelming that it could also be argued that nothing defines the role of the United States as a superpower as does the strength of the U.S. military.

In the late nineteenth century, as the United States began to emerge as a world power, with westward expansion, and as American overseas trade interests also expanded, U.S. political leaders realized that more investment in the military, especially the navy, was necessary. In 1873, the Unites States Naval Institute was founded as a non-profit, private organization. It served two purposes: to lobby on behalf of naval issues, and to modernize the American navy. This organization, along with the Office of Naval Intelligence (created in 1882), and the Naval War College (founded in 1885), provided the philosophical foundations and directions for changing U.S. naval policy.[3]

Admiral David Dixon Porter, Captain Stephen B. Luce, later a U.S. Navy admiral, and Commodore Foxhall A. Parker, among others, were credited with founding the Naval Institute. Rear Admiral John L. Worden, the former commander of the USS Monitor—the first ironclad warship commissioned by the Union Navy—served as the first president. Luce was also the founder and the first president of the Naval War College.

Luce served as president of the Naval War College from 1884 to 1886. His vision was to teach naval officers the art and science of naval warfare. Luce attributed this vision to conversations he had with Union General William T. Sherman. Luce claimed Sherman taught him that there were "certain fundamental principles underlying military operation; principles of general application whether the operation were conducted on land or at sea." And that there was "such a thing as a military problem, and there was a way of solving it; or what was equally important, a way of determining whether or not it was susceptible of solution."[4]

One of the first teachers Luce brought to the War College was the renowned Alfred Thayer Mahan. Mahan was a U.S. Navy admiral and a respected historian. (Ironically, as a young sailor, he hated sea duty.) When Luce asked Mahan to teach at the War College, he also asked him to prepare a series of lectures on naval history. This series of lectures would become *The Influence of Sea Power on History 1660-1783*. Published in 1890, Mahan's history of naval warfare is widely considered the world's most influential book on naval strategy.

More than any other single individual, Mahan was responsible for the development of sea power and strategy worldwide. Mahan contended that Britain becoming the world's greatest power—economic, military, and otherwise—was the result of the British controlling the seas. *The Influence of Sea Power on History 1660-*

*1783* became an international best seller. Along with the U.S., nations such as Great Britain, France, Germany, and Japan adopted Mahan's naval theories. Mahan would become the second president of the Naval War College.

For the first time in its history, the notion that even in times of peace, a nation must prepare for war, began to prevail in America. By 1900, the U.S. had the world's third most powerful navy. After the turn of the twentieth century the U.S. began to take a much more active role in world affairs.

Much like the efforts of Alfred Mahan with the Navy just before the turn of the twentieth century, Elihu Root, Secretary of War for President Theodore Roosevelt (who would also serve as Secretary of State), sought to reform the army. Root is widely recognized as the father of the modern U.S. Army. He modernized and organized the Army, restructured the National Guard, and created the Army War College. Root was also a strong proponent of the use of diplomacy and international law to resolve conflicts between nations. He helped design the Permanent Court of International Justice. Root won the Nobel Peace Prize in 1912.

In addition to investments in the Army and Navy, by the time Theodore Roosevelt took office in 1901, the United States was on the verge of one of the most ambitious engineering undertakings in the history of humanity. In 1898, the Spanish-American War convinced many in the U.S. government that a more efficient route for moving warships between the American East and West coasts was necessary. President Roosevelt strongly believed that American control of a canal across Central America was vital to U.S. strategic and economic interests.

After the successful completion of the Suez Canal in 1869, the French believed the same kind of access could be accomplished through Panama. However, the rocks, rivers, and jungles of Panama proved to be a much greater challenge than the sands of Egypt. Unfortunately, the landscape of Panama was not the greatest challenge. Tropical diseases, particularly malaria and yellow fever, devastated the French efforts. From 1881, when the construction in Panama began, until 1889 when work was suspended, the death toll for canal workers was over 22,000.[5]

Given the French failure in Panama and the fact that Nicaragua was closer to the U.S., had a more favorable climate, and posed fewer engineering challenges than Panama—all of which made it a better financial alternative—in late 1901, a private commission recommended that the canal be built across Nicaragua. As the result of the loss of well over $200 million, French investors lobbied heavily for the U.S. to purchase the French-held land in Panama and continue the canal efforts there. After the French company that owned the rights to a canal through Panama significantly dropped its price (from $109 million to $40 million) for the rights to the canal property, the U.S. Canal Commission now recommended the Panama route. The Spooner Act of 1902 authorized the purchase. Americans began work on the canal on May 4, 1904. After 10 years and over $320 million spent, the canal officially opened on August 15, 1914.

Strikes, landslides, and World War I held canal traffic down significantly in its first few years of operation. It did not open to civilian traffic until July of 1920. The Panama Canal was, and remains, the largest construction project in U.S. history. Upon completion, the canal was another major step in establishing the United States as an economic and military world power.

Woodrow Wilson was President of the United States (1913-1921) as the Panama Canal was completed. Just two-and-a-half weeks prior to the completion of the canal, World War I broke out. Wilson was determined to keep the U.S. out of the European conflict. When the Germans sank the British ocean liner *Lusitania*, over 1,100 people died, including 128 Americans. Wilson warned the Germans against future attacks that cost American lives. Campaigning on the slogan, "He kept us out of war," with a narrow electoral margin of 277-254, Wilson won a second term as U.S. President.

However, in 1917, barely into Wilson's second term, the Germans renewed their unrestricted submarine warfare, including targeting American ships. Knowing that this action would almost certainly bring the U.S. into the war, on January 11, 1917, the Foreign Secretary of the German Empire, Arthur Zimmerman, sent a coded telegram to Heinrich von Eckardt, the German Ambassador in Mexico. Decoded by British intelligence, the message instructed Eckardt that if the United States should enter the war against Germany, the Ambassador was to approach the Mexican government with proposed military alliance. The telegram read:

> We intend to begin on the first of February unrestricted submarine warfare. We shall endeavor in spite of this to keep the United States of America neutral. In the event of this not succeeding, we make Mexico a proposal of alliance on the following basis: make war together, make peace together, generous financial support and an understanding on our part that Mexico is to reconquer the lost territory in Texas, New Mexico, and Arizona. The settlement in detail is left to you. You will inform the President of the above most secretly as soon as the outbreak of war with the United States of America is certain and add the suggestion that he should, on his own initiative, invite Japan to immediate adherence and at the same time mediate between Japan and ourselves. Please call the President's attention to the fact that the ruthless employment of our submarines now offers the prospect of compelling England in a few months to make peace.[6]

The British intercepted the message, and their cryptographers decoded it. On February 19, 1917, the contents of the message were revealed to U.S. Secretary of State Edward Bell. He had to be convinced of its authenticity, but once that was the case—which Zimmerman himself later confirmed to an American journalist, and to the Reichstag in a speech—America's entrance into World War I was virtually assured. On April 6, 1917, Congress voted to declare war on Germany.

Entrance into World War I would cement America's role as a world power. After World War I ended, U.S. President Woodrow Wilson boldly declared, "We saved the world, and I don't intend to let those Europeans forget it."[7] The United States emerged from "The Great War" as the world's leading industrial power. Wartime preparation and manufacturing further enhanced America's skill at mass production. As of 1918, no other nation in the world could match the mass production capabilities of the U.S. German sociologist Max Weber prophesied that American global dominance was now "inevitable."[8]

Additionally, the victorious European nations owed the U.S. around $10 billion. British economist John Maynard Keynes described the "new world order:" "The American armies were at the height of their numbers, discipline, and equipment. Europe was in complete dependence on the food supplies of the United States; and financially she was even more absolutely at their mercy. Europe ... already owed the United States more than she could pay."[9]

After the war, the U.S. scaled back its military, though, America came out of World War I with the world's largest navy. However, as Harvard scholar Joseph Nye points out, during the 1920s, America's "soft power"—the "global influence deriving from its economic might, technological superiority, and cultural sway"— was far more important than our military strength. "At the end of the war, the United States stood above the rest of the world, youthful, dynamic, and prosperous, the city upon a hill Puritan leader John Winthrop had spoken of three hundred years earlier."[10] Winthrop's prophecy of American Exceptionalism seemed to be taking hold as never before. However, in 1929, when the Great Depression hit, many Americans were not feeling very exceptional.

The chaos—economic, social, and otherwise—produced by the Great Depression created an extremely tense political environment the world over. Desperate to pull themselves out of the financial muck, and still reeling from World War I, nations tended to isolate themselves and focus on domestic policies, which was certainly the case with the United States. As potential European conflicts continued to brew, Americans were nearly united in their desire to stay out of another war. By the mid-1930s, when Hitler announced that Nazi Germany would ignore the Versailles Treaty and re-arm, and as Italy invaded Abyssinia (now Ethiopia), American politicians took legislative measures to try to remain neutral.

On September 1, 1939, Germany invaded Poland. On September 3, Franklin D. Roosevelt, in one of his "fireside chats" addressed the American people. He began,

> Until four-thirty this morning I had hoped against hope that some miracle would prevent a devastating war in Europe and bring to an end the invasion of Poland by Germany. For four long years a succession of actual wars and constant crises have shaken the entire world and have threatened in each case to bring on the gigantic conflict which is today unhappily a fact.
>
> It is right that I should recall to your minds the consistent and at time successful efforts of your Government in these crises to throw the full weight of the United States into the cause of peace. In spite of spreading wars I think that we have every right and every reason to maintain as a national policy the fundamental moralities, the teachings of religion (and) the continuation of efforts to restore peace -- (for) because some day, though the time may be distant, we can be of even greater help to a crippled humanity.
>
> It is right, too, to point out that the unfortunate events of these recent years have, without question, been based on the use of force (or) and the threat of force. And it seems to me clear, even at the outbreak of this great war, that the influence of America should be consistent in seeking for humanity a final peace which will eliminate, as far as it is possible to do so, the continued use of force between nations...

> You must master at the outset a simple but
> unalterable fact in modern foreign relations
> between nations. When peace has been broken
> anywhere, the peace of all countries everywhere
> is in danger.
>
> It is easy for you and for me to shrug our
> shoulders and to say that conflicts taking place
> thousands of miles from the continental United
> States, and, indeed, thousands of miles from the
> whole American Hemisphere, do not seriously
> affect the Americas -- and that all the United
> States has to do is to ignore them and go about
> (our) its own business. Passionately though we
> may desire detachment, we are forced to realize
> that every word that comes through the air, every
> ship that sails the sea, every battle that is fought
> does affect the American future.[11]

Roosevelt ended the chat saying that he hated war, and he assured the American people that every effort would be made to keep the United States out of war. Of course, this was not to be.

In 1939, when Germany invaded Poland, the United States military ranked only eighteenth in the world.[12] According to the National WWII Museum, in 1939, the U.S. Army had a total of about 190,000 active personnel, the Navy 125,000, and the Marines were about 19,000 strong. By 1945, those numbers ballooned to 8.2 million, 3.4 million, and 425,000.[13]

In 1939, the Army Air Corps—the precursor to the U.S. Air Force—had about 1,700 aircraft. By the end of the war, the United States had produced over 300,000 airplanes, twice as many as the Soviets, nearly three times as many as the Germans and the British, and four times as many as the Japanese. In less than five years the American aircraft industry went from forty-first in manufacturing to first.

In 1939, the U.S. produced 18 tanks, by 1944, over 20,000. Total tank production in America during World War II was over 88,000.

The Germans produced about half that number, while the Soviets produced over 100,000. However, Soviet tanks were generally considered significantly inferior to U.S. and German models.

By the end of World War II, the U.S. military was the most powerful the world had ever known. While Europe and many other parts of the world were ravaged by the war, the U.S. mainland was barely touched. The United States military suffered just over 400,000 military deaths in WW II. By contrast, the next most powerful nation exiting the war, the Soviet Union, lost about 8 million troops and nearly 16 million civilians. The total number of American civilians to die within the 48 continental states as the result of enemy action was six—a young woman and five school children, who were killed by a Japanese fire bomb dropped from a balloon over south-central Oregon.

The U.S. was the lone nation to exit the war stronger than when it entered it. After the U.S. victory over Japan, Winston Churchill declared that the triumphant United States stood "at the summit of the world." As author George C. Herring put it, "On V-J Day, the United States had 12.5 million people under arms, more than half of them overseas. Its navy exceeded the combined fleets of all other nations; its air force commanded the skies; it alone possessed atomic weapons. Washington took London's place as the capital of world finance and diplomacy."[14] After WW II, the U.S. and the Soviet Union were the only nations capable of exerting any significant influence beyond their own borders. This influence would be enhanced by the possession of the most powerful weapons the world has ever known.

# CHAPTER 24

# A Super Power is Born, Part 3: America Enters the Nuclear Age

Nothing speaks to the military power and might of the United States as does our nuclear arsenal. Perhaps no other event in American history so cemented the U.S. as a superpower than did the creation of atomic weapons. If the Germans or the Soviets had been the first to develop such a weapon, the world today would almost certainly look and feel quite different.

Born in 1865, John Hendrix lived in the Bear Creek Valley area of northeastern Tennessee. Around the turn of the twentieth century, Hendrix suffered tragic loss. Ethel, his youngest child, died of diphtheria when she was just two years old. John's wife Julia Ann took their remaining three children and headed to Arkansas to be closer to her family. She and the children never returned. In the depths of his despair, John turned to God. He prayed for God to speak to him. According to many who spoke to Hendrix firsthand, God did speak.

Around 1900 Hendrix's prayers led him into the woods where he fasted and prayed for 40 days and nights. In 2013, *The Washington Post* reported, as the "Prophet of Oak Ridge" prayed, he "gazed up at the sky and heard a voice like a clap of thunder."[1] According to multiple accounts, Hendrix declared,

> In the woods, as I lay on the ground and looked
> up into the sky, there came to me a voice as loud
> and as sharp as thunder. The voice told me to

sleep with my head on the ground for 40 nights and I would be shown visions of what the future holds for this land...And I tell you, Bear Creek Valley someday will be filled with great buildings and factories, and they will help toward winning the greatest war that ever will be. And there will be a city on Black Oak Ridge and the center of authority will be on a spot middle-way between Sevier Tadlock's farm and Joe Pyatt's Place. A railroad spur will branch off the main L&N line, run down toward Robertsville and then branch off and turn toward Scarborough. Big engines will dig big ditches, and thousands of people will be running to and fro. They will be building things, and there will be great noise and confusion and the earth will shake. I've seen it. It's coming.[2]

Hendrix was right.

On October 11, 1939, President Roosevelt received a letter written by Hungarian-American physicist Leo Szilard. The letter was signed by Albert Einstein. Written about one month prior to the German invasion of Poland and in consultation with fellow Hungarian physicists, Edward Teller and Eugene Wigner (Einstein, Szilard, Teller, Wigner were all Jews), the letter warned that Germany might be developing atomic bombs and encouraged the United States to begin its own nuclear program. The letter reads:

Some recent work by E. Fermi and L. Szilard, which has been communicated to me in manuscript, leads me to expect that the element uranium may be turned into a new and important source of energy in the immediate future. Certain aspects of the situation which has arisen seem to call for watchfulness and, if necessary, quick action on the part of the Administration. I believe therefore that it is my duty to bring to your attention the following facts and recommendations:

In the course of the last four months it has been made probable—through the work of Joliot in France as well as Fermi and Szilard in America - that it may become possible to set up a nuclear chain reaction in a large mass of uranium, by which vast amounts of power and large quantities of new radium-like elements would be generated. Now it appears almost certain that this could be achieved in the immediate future.

This new phenomenon would also lead to the construction of bombs, and it is conceivable - though much less certain - that extremely powerful bombs of a new type may thus be constructed. A single bomb of this type, carried by boat and exploded in a port, might very well destroy the whole port together with some of the surrounding territory. However, such bombs might very well prove to be too heavy for transportation by air.

The United States has only very poor ores of uranium in moderate quantities. There is some good ore in Canada and the former Czechoslovakia, while the most important source of uranium is Belgian Congo.

In view of the situation you may think it desirable to have more permanent contact maintained between the Administration and the group of physicists working on chain reactions in America. One possible way of achieving this might be for you to entrust with this task a person who has your confidence and who could perhaps serve in an inofficial capacity. His task might comprise the following:

a) to approach Government Departments, keep them informed of the further development, and put forward recommendations for Government action, giving particular attention to the problem of securing a supply of uranium ore for the United States;

b) to speed up the experimental work, which is at present being carried on within the limits of the budgets of University laboratories, by providing funds, if such funds be required, through his contacts with private persons who are willing to make contributions for this cause, and perhaps also by obtaining the co-operation of industrial laboratories which have the necessary equipment.

I understand that Germany has actually stopped the sale of uranium from the Czechoslovakian mines which she has taken over. That she should have taken such early action might perhaps be understood on the ground that the son of the German Under-Secretary of State, von Weizsäcker, is attached to the Kaiser-Wilhelm-Institut in Berlin where some of the American work on uranium is now being repeated.[3]

Szilard conceived the idea of a nuclear chain reaction in 1933. In 1939, Szilard and Enrico Fermi looked for and discovered neutron multiplication in uranium, which proved that a nuclear chain reaction was possible. Later, with Enrico Fermi, Szilard patented the idea of a nuclear reactor.

Fermi, an Italian physicist, is known as the "architect of the nuclear age," and the "father of the atomic bomb." In 1938, Fermi won the Nobel Prize in Physics for his work on induced radioactivity by neutron bombardment. After collecting his prize in Stockholm, Fermi did not return to his home in Italy. Because his wife was Jewish, and fearing for her safety in Nazi-allied Rome, Fermi took his family to New York where they sought and received permanent residency. Einstein, who also fled Nazi persecution, settled in the United States as well.

In response to the Szilard/Einstein letter, Roosevelt asked the director of the National Bureau of Standards, Lyman James Briggs, a distinguished engineer and physicist, to organize the Briggs Advisory Committee on Uranium. This committee authorized and funded neutron experiments conducted by Fermi and Szilard.

On June 27, 1940, the National Defense Research Committee (NDRC), headed by the esteemed Vannevar Bush, was formed. In addition to his time at MIT, Bush served as the president of the Carnegie Institution of Washington (also the Carnegie Institution for Science), and the chairman of the National Advisory Committee for Aeronautics (the predecessor of NASA). He was a renowned engineer and science administrator. As previously noted, Bush also led the Office of Scientific Research and Development (OSRD).

The OSRD was the agency that coordinated scientific research for military purposes during World War II. At Bush's insistence, by an Executive Order from President Roosevelt, on June 28, 1941, the OSRD was created. On matters of military scientific research, the OSRD superseded the NDRC. Bush reported directly, and only, to Roosevelt.

For security reasons, on July 1, 1941, the Briggs Advisory Committee on Uranium became the S-1 Uranium Committee and came under the direction of Bush at OSRD. Soon after the Japanese attack on Pearl Harbor, the S-1 Committee was dedicated to the development of an atomic bomb.

In order to create a bomb, research was done on two types of fissile material (material capable of sustaining a nuclear fission chain reaction)—enriched uranium and plutonium.

On August 13, 1942, under the leadership of Major General Leslie Groves of the U.S. Army Corps of Engineers, in a race to beat the Nazis to a nuclear weapon, the Manhattan Project was officially born. The Manhattan Project was a massive undertaking unlike anything in U.S. history. It involved over 130,000 people—most of whom were in the dark about what was really happening—and cost about $2 billion (about $26 billion in 2015 dollars).

Because of its sparse population, access to electricity, the number of nearby roads and railroads, and true to John Hendrix's prophecy about four decades earlier, in 1942, the federal government of the United States commandeered 60,000 acres of rural farmland in the northeast corner of Tennessee. Nearly 4,000 residents were given two to three weeks to vacate their homes or else be removed by force.

What later became Oak Ridge, Tennessee was then known only as Clinton Engineering Works, or more clandestinely, "Site X." Oak Ridge, along with Los Alamos, New Mexico (Site Y), and Hanford, Washington (Site W), was one of three secret U.S. cities—not appearing on any maps—chosen by Manhattan Project director Gen. Groves for the specific purpose of building an atomic bomb.

Tens of thousands of Americans (most were in Oak Ridge) of a wide variety of backgrounds, education, and expertise worked to help America lead the world into the nuclear age. Most workers had little knowledge of what they were actually working toward. Best estimates reveal that only about five percent of the workers knew what was happening at their individual worksites, with only three percent being aware of the full operation.[4]

Led by Enrico Fermi, on November 2, 1942, construction of the world's first nuclear reactor, the Chicago Pile-1, began. The pile went critical about a month later, on December 2.

**An Illustration of Chicago Pile-1**

Less than one year later, on November 4, 1943, the X-10 graphite reactor at Oak Ridge went critical. X-10 produced the first reactor-bred quantities of plutonium supplied to the Los Alamos laboratory and heavily influenced atomic bomb design.

General Groves chose Robert Oppenheimer to lead the Manhattan Project's weapon's laboratory. Groves and Oppenheimer chose Los Alamos, New Mexico, as the site on which the atomic bomb would be built. On July 16, 1945, in central New Mexico, the world's first detonation of a nuclear weapon took place.

The test, designated "Trinity" by Oppenheimer, was of an implosion-type plutonium device, nicknamed "The Gadget," of the same design as the "Fat Man" bomb that would be detonated over Nagasaki, Japan, a few weeks later. The test resulted in an explosion that was the equivalent of about 20,000 tons of TNT.

On August 6, 1945 the United States became the world's first, and remains the only nation, to use an atomic weapon against another country. At about 8:15 a.m. local time, the bomb dubbed "Little Boy" was dropped on Hiroshima, Japan. The bomb contained about 141 pounds of fissionable uranium-235 from Oakridge, Tennessee. It detonated at an altitude of about 1,900 feet. Approximately 70,000 Japanese died from the blast and the ensuing firestorm. About 50,000 of these were civilians. Over 90 percent of tens of thousands of buildings were destroyed. Three days later, "Fat Man" exploded over Nagasaki. Again, about 70,000 Japanese were killed. Less than a week later, on August 15, 1945, Japan surrendered.

**Photograph of a model of the Little Boy atomic bomb. (Declassified in 1960, this was the first photograph released by the U.S. Govt.)**

**The Mushroom cloud after Fat Man was dropped on Nagasaki.**

The most powerful and terrible weapon in the history of humanity ended the largest, bloodiest, and most destructive war in the history of humanity. After the atomic bomb fell on Hiroshima, U.S. President Harry Truman declared,

> Both science and industry worked under the direction of the United States Army, which achieved a unique success in managing so diverse a problem in the advancement of knowledge in an amazingly short time. It is doubtful if such another combination could be got together in the world. What has been done is the greatest achievement of organized science in history. It was done under pressure and without failure.[5]

Interestingly, many of the scientists who were most involved in the creation of the atomic bomb—Einstein, Szilard, Teller, Wigner, and Oppenheimer, along with Fermi's wife—were all Jewish. Ironically, fleeing Nazi persecution, Einstein, Szilard, Teller, and Fermi all left Europe and helped the U.S. beat the Nazis in the race to a nuclear weapon. Thus, the atomic age and victory for the Allies in World War II came about in no small way through the efforts of God's chosen people.

With the science to build nuclear weapons and the technology to build rockets, both the United States and the Soviet Union embarked on a long and dangerous Cold War. By 1950, the U.S. had an arsenal of nearly 300 nuclear weapons. The rest of the world's nuclear weapons were in the hands of the Soviet Union, which had five. By 1960, the U.S. had well over 18,000 nuclear arms. The Soviets had just over 1,600. By the 1980s, the Soviets had caught and surpassed the U.S. in terms of its total nuclear arsenal. In 1980, the Soviet lead was about 30,000 to 23,000. By 1990, the gap had widened, with the Soviets possessing about 37,000 nuclear weapons to the U.S.'s approximately 11,000. The 1990s brought the fall of the Soviet Union and the official end to the Cold War. Also, a string of several arms reduction treaties between the U.S. and the Soviets began in the early 1990s. Today, both nations possess around 8,000 nuclear warheads.

In addition to its overwhelming nuclear arsenal,[6] according to Global Fire Power's "Power Index,"[7] the United States today stands alone in the world with regard to convention weapons. The following chart comparing the U.S. with the world's next two strongest militaries illustrates this:

| | United States | Russia | China |
|---|---|---|---|
| Tanks | 8,848 | 15,398 | 9,150 |
| Armored Fighting Vehicles | 41,062 | 31,298 | 4,788 |
| Attack Helicopters | 6,196 | 1,120 | 908 |
| Total Aircraft | 13,892 | 3,429 | 2,860 |
| Aircraft Carriers | 19 | 1 | 1 |
| Destroyers | 62 | 12 | 25 |
| Submarines | 72 | 55 | 67 |
| Nuclear Warheads | 7,650 | 8,420 | 240 |

Note the advantage in aircraft and aircraft carriers. Combine this with the human, technological, and natural resource advantage, which Global Fire Power also includes in its Power Index, and our fighting force is the envy of the world. Furthermore, since the early 1960s—well before any other nation—the United States military has been developing and using unmanned aerial vehicles (UAVs or drones) in warfare. Today (2016) the United States is by far the world leader in drone use and drone technology.[8]

The power and might of the U.S. military isn't merely a matter of national pride, nor is it (nor has it been) an opportunity to bully the rest of the world. On the contrary, the strength of the United States military has enabled us to be one of the greatest tools for truth, justice, and liberty in the history of humanity. More than any other single human factor, the might of the United States military brought an end to World Wars I and II. The determination of America's Cold War warriors brought an end to the Soviet Union and slowed the spread of communism.

For decades now, in skirmishes small and large the world over, the U.S. military has been a force for good, keeping much evil at bay. Of course, we haven't been perfect in the use of our military might. The character and courage of the American military is generally a reflection of the character and courage of its leadership, which, in turn, is generally a reflection of the character and courage of our nation at large. In other words, it's important to remember that in order to make good and proper use of the strongest military in the history of humanity, America herself must remain a virtuous people.

# CHAPTER 25

# The Era of Big Government and Institutionalized Immorality Begins

When I pray with my wife and my four children, I sometimes make it a point to thank God for allowing us to live our lives in the greatest nation the world has ever known. The United States of America not only has the largest economy and most powerful military in the world, but America leads the world in nearly every metric imaginable. Whether our economy, our military, or education and technology, medicine and healthcare, the production of food, and so on, the United States leads the world.

The United States of America has been one of the greatest instruments for good the world has ever known. With our military might, we have been an unequaled force for freedom and liberty around the world. We have liberated millions and defended millions more. America is the most generous nation the world has ever known.[1] Americans account for nearly half of all the charitable giving in the world. The vast majority of these contributions is private, not government, funds. Whether wars or hurricanes, floods or famines, earthquakes or tsunamis, with our abundant human, natural, and technological resources, time and again Americans have come to the aid of their world neighbors. According to Mark Tooley, "America accepts more immigrants, about a million legally every year, than any other nation and, by some measures, than all other nations combined. America permanently resettles more refugees than any other nation."[2] Most importantly, the U.S. sends out more Christian missionaries than any other nation, nearly tripling the second place nation Brazil.[3]

However, in the last few decades the United States has seen more than its fair share of disturbing trends.

An old adage, sometimes wrongly attributed to Tocqueville, often referenced (at least the final sentence) by politicians of the last several decades (among them Dwight Eisenhower, Ronald Reagan, and Bill Clinton) declares that,

> I sought for the greatness and genius of America in her commodious harbors and her ample rivers—and it was not there . . . in her fertile fields and boundless forests and it was not there . . . in her rich mines and her vast world commerce—and it was not there . . . in her democratic Congress and her matchless Constitution—and it was not there. Not until I went into the churches of America and heard her pulpits flame with righteousness did I understand the secret of her genius and power. America is great because she is good, and if America ever ceases to be good, she will cease to be great.

Jedidiah Morse, noted American geographer, pastor, theologian, and the father of Samuel Morse, the inventor of Morse Code, in an-election day sermon on April 25, 1799 warned Americans,

> The foundations which support the interest of Christianity, are also necessary to support a free and equal government like our own. In all those countries where there is little or no religion, or a very gross and corrupt one, as in Mahometan [Islamic] and Pagan countries, there you will find, with scarcely a single exception, arbitrary and tyrannical governments, gross ignorance and wickedness, and deplorable wretchedness among

the people. To the kindly influence of Christianity we owe that degree of civil freedom, and political and social happiness which mankind now enjoy. In proportion as the genuine effects of Christianity are diminished in any nation, either through unbelief, or the corruption of its doctrines, or the neglect of its institutions; in the same proportion will the people of that nation recede from the blessings of genuine freedom, and approximate the miseries of complete despotism. I hold this to be a truth confirmed by experience. If so, it follows, that all efforts made to destroy the foundations of our holy religion, ultimately tend to the subversion also of our political freedom and happiness. Whenever the pillars of Christianity shall be overthrown, our present republican forms of government, and all the blessings which flow from them, must fall with them.[4]

In other words, it's the pillars of Christianity that support the life, liberty, and pursuit of happiness that we all enjoy in America, and the quickest and surest way to turn the United States of America into a nation unrecognizable to those who lived only a few generations ago is to remove these pillars. Tragically, many people in the U.S. are working hard at doing just this.

As I've pointed out before,[5] and as this book illustrates, America isn't a Christian nation simply because most of our citizens are Christians. Nor is it because most of our political, industrial, scientific, military, and faith leaders are or have been Christians, though, historically, this is the case on both counts. As Supreme Court Justice David Brewer (1837-1910) wrote in his book *The United States: A Christian Nation*, "This republic is classified among the Christian nations of the world. It was so formally declared by the Supreme Court of the United States. But in what sense can it be called a Christian nation?"[6] Answering his own question, Justice Brewer declared that America is "most justly called a Christian nation" because Christianity "has so largely shaped and molded it."[7]

Likewise, in the middle of the nineteenth century, noted author and professor of constitutional law Edward Mansfield concluded:

> In every country, the morals of a people –
> whatever they may be – take their form and spirit
> from their religion. For example, the marriage of
> brothers and sisters was permitted among the
> Egyptians because such had been the precedent
> set by their gods, Isis and Osiris. So, too, the
> classic nations celebrated the drunken rites of
> Bacchus. Thus, too, the Turk has become lazy
> and inert because dependent upon Fate, as taught
> by the Koran. And when in recent times there
> arose a nation [i.e., France] whose philosophers
> [e.g. Voltaire, Rousseau, Diderot, Helvetius, etc.]
> discovered there was no God and no religion, the
> nation was thrown into that dismal case in which
> there was no law and no morals. . . . In the
> United States, Christianity is the original,
> spontaneous, and national religion.[8]

Historian and author David Barton adds that, "A Christian nation as demonstrated by the American experience is a nation founded upon Christian and Biblical principles, whose values, society, and institutions have largely been shaped by those principles...Christianity is the religion that shaped America and made her what she is today."[9] Thus, if one wants to remake America, one must undo and remove those Christian influences.

As Satan targets Christianity in America, I believe that two pillars in particular have suffered the brunt of the attacks: the family and the Word of God.

Other than the church itself, no institution in human history is as important as is the family. The family, consisting, of course, of a mother and a father, rooted in Christ, is the foundation of a moral and civil society. God began all of human history through the union of one man and one woman. Marriage is the oldest institution in the history of humanity—older than God's covenant with the nation of Israel, older than The Law, older than the church. Marriage is one of the earliest truths revealed by God. Other than our relationship with our Creator, the most important relationship in the universe is the relationship between a husband and a wife.

This is why the family is such a target. At the foundation of any great nation or culture is a strong and healthy (i.e., a biblical) view of marriage. Strong and healthy marriages lead to strong and healthy families. Strong and healthy families lead to strong and healthy communities. Strong and healthy communities lead to strong and healthy churches, schools, businesses, governments, and so on. Each of these institutions lies at the heart of a great nation.

For decades the family in America has been under relentless assault. The sad consequences are staggering. Today in America, over 40 percent of American children are born to unwed mothers. In the mid-1960s, only about six percent of U.S. children were born out-of-wedlock. In 1930, less than five percent of children were born out-of-wedlock. The chart below shows a revealing timeline of this tragic trend:[10]

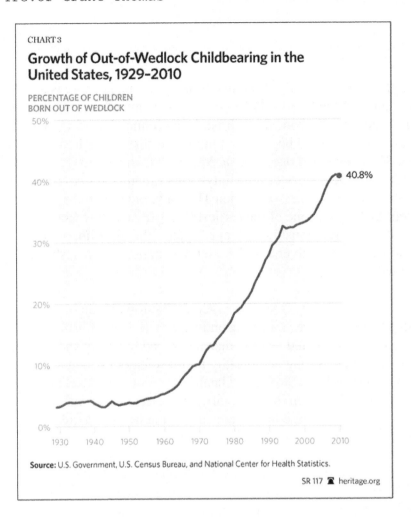

CHART 3

**Growth of Out-of-Wedlock Childbearing in the United States, 1929–2010**

PERCENTAGE OF CHILDREN
BORN OUT OF WEDLOCK

40.8%

**Source:** U.S. Government, U.S. Census Bureau, and National Center for Health Statistics.

SR 117 ☎ heritage.org

Note the sharp rate of increase during and after the 1960s. Sadly, there are several disturbing episodes during the decade of the 1960s that contributed significantly to the breakdown of the family in America. In 1964, U.S. President Lyndon Johnson declared an "unconditional war on poverty in America." Since then, America has spent an astounding $22 trillion on Johnson's war, creating a massive welfare state.[11] Adjusting for inflation, that is equal to about three times the amount spent on every military conflict in American history combined. As a result of this and other big government spending, the United States suffers from historic levels of national debt.[12]

Yet, after all of this time and money, the poverty rate in America remains nearly unchanged. However, spending such a vast sum of money is bound to result in some change on the poor in America. Poverty today looks nothing like it did 60 years ago. According to the *Wall Street Journal* and various federal data,

> [T]he typical American living below the (government-defined) poverty level in 2013 lives in a house or apartment that is in good repair, equipped with air conditioning and cable TV. His home is larger than the home of the average non-poor French, German or English man. He has a car, multiple color TVs and a DVD player. More than half the poor have computers and a third have wide, flat-screen TVs. The overwhelming majority of poor Americans are not undernourished and did not suffer from hunger for even one day of the previous year.[13]

Because of the way the government defines poverty and because the Census doesn't include welfare benefits as income, welfare spending can increase infinitely, and no change in the poverty rate will result. Thus, politicians, almost always liberals, who promise to give away other people's money can use such promises continuously to win elections. Ignoring my proverb that, "It is no act of charity to be generous with someone else's money," such a give-and-take has been happening for decades in America.

As a result of the war on poverty, the attitudes and behaviors of tens of millions of Americans changed. Among other dysfunctional behaviors, the regular recipients of welfare became much less likely to work and get married. To a large extent, as a result of the war on poverty in America, big government has replaced dads. Of course, common sense and sound morality reveal that if people are not encouraged to work, and if people are not encouraged to marry before having children, many are going to take advantage of such opportunities.

As of May 2015, for over four consecutive years, the number of Americans receiving food stamps (transactions are now done with an EBT card) surpassed 45 million.[14] About 20 percent of U.S. children now receive food stamps.[15] Thus nearly one-fifth of our future electorate is being conditioned to the idea that it is government's responsibility to make sure they are fed.

A 2014 report showed that a record 23.1 percent of Americans received benefits from one of three major welfare programs: Temporary Assistance to Needy Families (formerly Aid to Families With Dependent Children), Supplemental Security Income, and the Supplemental Nutrition Assistance Program (food stamps).[16] The report also revealed that a startling 38 percent of U.S. children age five or under were welfare recipients.

As I alluded to in a previous chapter (13), the war on poverty has been particularly devastating to black Americans. An astonishing 72 percent of black children in the U.S. are born to unwed mothers.[17] As a result, over 38 percent of black children in America live in poverty, which is nearly four times the poverty rate among white children.[18]

Aided and abetted by our massive welfare state, Americans across the board are shunning marriage as never before. In December of 2011, Pew Research revealed that according to U.S. Census data, "Barely half of all adults in the United States—a record low—are currently married, and the median age at first marriage has never been higher for brides (26.5 years) and grooms (28.7)... In 1960, 72 percent of all adults ages 18 and older were married; today just 51% are."[19]

Similarly, Pew Research from 2014 revealed that "the share of American adults who have never been married is at an historic high. In 2012, one-in-five adults ages 25 and older (about 42 million people) had never been married... In 1960, only about one-in-ten adults (9%) in that age range had never been married."[20] Sadly, the same Pew research reveals that only about half (53 percent) of never-married adults say that they would like to marry eventually.

Pew also revealed that:

> [N]ever-married women place a high premium
> on finding a spouse with a steady job. However,
> the changes in the labor market have contributed
> to a shrinking pool of available employed young
> men…Labor force participation among men—
> particularly young men—has fallen significantly
> over the past several decades. In 1960, 93% of
> men ages 25 to 34 were in the labor force; by
> 2012 that share had fallen to 82%. And among
> young men who are employed, wages have fallen
> over the past few decades.[21]

No doubt, the massive welfare state that exists in the U.S. has contributed to these declines.

Additional Pew research reveals that, since 1997 the percentage of men ages 18 to 34 who say that having a successful marriage is important to them dropped from 35 percent to 29 percent, while for women in the same age group, the numbers rose from 28 percent to 37 percent. According to family and feminism expert Suzanne Venker, many men have decided never to get married because "women aren't women anymore."[22]

And neither are men "men" anymore. "Ever since the sexual revolution" (another tragic "gift" from the 1960s) adds Venker, "there has been a profound overhaul in the way men and women interact." With its lies about sex, parenting, and gender roles, the modern feminist movement that "birthed" the sexual revolution has been devastating to men and women alike.

Thanks tremendously to the sexual revolution, our society is obsessed with sex. Author and pastor John MacArthur, referring to Saint Augustine, notes that the war that is raging between the City of God, or biblical Christianity, and the City of Man, or the satanic world system, surrounds one single area: sex. MacArthur observes that, "Within the moral realm in our society the conflict is almost exclusively about sex." Abortion, fornication, homosexuality, divorce, and the like, he adds, are all sexual issues. As J.R.R. Tolkien put it nearly three-quarters of a century ago, "The dislocation of sex-instinct is one of the chief symptoms of the Fall. The world has been 'going to the bad' all down the ages... [T]he 'hard spirit of concupiscence [lust]' has walked down every street, and sat leering in every house, since Adam fell."[23]

One of the worst results of the "hard spirit of concupiscence" is that many American men have been deceived into thinking they can have all the sex that they want without any real commitment or negative consequences. Thus, it is little wonder that so many men bought into the modern feminist lies. With the explosion of pornography and the hook-up culture, and with little societal stigma against engaging in such behavior, far too many men have allowed themselves and the roles that they were created to fulfill to be cast aside. Ironically, this has led to a "neutering" of the American male.

Many women have been deceived into thinking that, among other things, they are no different than men and can have careers and children without marriage or devout motherhood. (Certainly not all women with careers are unfit mothers, but being successful at both can be overwhelming.) Thus we end up with women in combat.[24,][25] In addition, many U.S. women are now attempting to be, or, in many situations are being forced to be, the breadwinners of the family, with the vast majority of such breadwinners poor single mothers. For the first time in American history, women outnumber men in the workforce, and more women than men are obtaining college degrees.

Many women today who do marry are doing so much later and are having one child, or at most two, as they attempt to postpone motherhood, or at least balance motherhood with careers. According to the National Center for Health Statistics, in 1970 only one percent of U.S. births were to women 35 and older. Today that rate has increased nearly ten-fold. Such data is especially true for white women. While the marriage rate in the U.S. is much higher for whites than for other ethnic groups, the childbirth rate is devastatingly low, so much so that, according to the U.S. Census Bureau for the calendar year ending 2012, for the first time in U.S. history more whites died than were born.[26]

The breakdown of marriage is having a significant negative impact on the American economy. This fact was highlighted at the 2016 Conservative Political Action Conference (CPAC). As the Christian Post pointed out, economist Larry Kudlow, speaking on a CPAC panel called "State of the Family in America: How Do We Measure Success?" concluded that "much of the reduction of economic growth in America is being caused by an increase in poverty resulting from a reversal in the traditional child-rearing paradigm."[27]

Kudlow himself concluded, "We are doing it backwards. We are having the kid first and don't even bother with the marriage, don't even bother with the job, don't even bother with the education." He later asked, "Where [did] this [come] from? I don't know. We lost track of the very traditional American value and that is the culture of marriage and child rearing. We must not lose that."

It's a bit amazing to me that a speaker at CPAC, especially someone with Mr. Kudlow's credentials, can't put his finger on why "We are doing it backwards" when it comes to child birth and marriage. I'll answer his "Where did this come from?" question in the next chapter.

Of course, Americans are not only shunning marriage at a record pace; once married, many Americans are ending their unions. In spite of what you may have heard, the actual divorce rate in America is very difficult to ascertain. Nevertheless, some of the best research puts the number at about 40 percent.[28]

Whether they are born out-of-wedlock or their parents are divorced, children not living in a home with their married biological parents are more likely to exhibit a whole host of behavioral problems. Such children are more likely to get in trouble at school, drop out of school, fight, engage in pre-marital sex, participate in criminal activities, use drugs and alcohol, and commit suicide.[29]

However, children in the worst danger are those in homes with cohabitating couples. As Americans ignore the eternal truth on marriage and go their own way, cohabitation, or "shacking-up" is another disturbing trend taking place at an alarming rate.
According to the 2010 edition of the State of Our Unions report by the National Marriage Project at the University of Virginia and the Center for Marriage and Families at the Institute for American Values, "The number of unmarried couples has increased dramatically over the past five decades. Most younger Americans now spend some time living together outside of marriage, and nonmarital cohabitation precedes most new marriages."[30]

According to the report, between 1960 and 2009, cohabitating couples in the U.S. increased more than fifteen-fold. Also, "About a quarter of unmarried women age 25 to 39 are currently living with a partner, and an additional quarter have lived with a partner at some time in the past. More than 60 percent of first marriages are now preceded by living together, compared to virtually none 50 years ago."[31]

Of course, these trends have tragic results for children in the U.S. According to a recent federal study, the Fourth National Incidence Study of Child Abuse and Neglect, children living with their mother and her boyfriend are about 11 times more likely to be sexually, physically, or emotionally abused than children living with their married biological parents.[32] Likewise, children living with their mother and her boyfriend are six times more likely to be physically, emotionally, or educationally neglected than children living with their married biological parents. In other words, according to W. Bradford Wilcox (referencing the Fourth National Incidence Study of Child Abuse and Neglect), "one of the most dangerous places for a child in America to find himself is in a home that includes an unrelated male boyfriend — especially when that boyfriend is left to care for a child by himself."[33]

The same study also reveals that children who live with their cohabitating biological parents don't fare much better. In these circumstances, children are more than four times more likely to be sexually, physically, or emotionally abused, and they are three times more likely to be physically, emotionally, or educationally neglected than children living with their married biological parents. Again, according to Wilcox, "a child is not much safer when she is living in a home with her parents if her parents' relationship does not enjoy the legal, social and moral status and guidance that marriage confers on relationships."[34]

Also according to the study, not only does cohabitation do little to prepare couples for marriage (which is often the excuse for cohabitating), but "a substantial body of evidence indicates that those who live together before marriage are more likely to break up after marriage."

Divorce, shacking-up, out-of-wedlock births—one would think that America could not descend any further toward the ruin of marriage and the family. However, as anyone in the U.S. who has been conscious for the last 15 to 20 years well knows, the debate surrounding marriage in America has centered on one topic alone: same-sex "marriage."

In 1993, the Supreme Court of Hawaii, one of the most liberal states in the U.S., ruled that denying marriage to same-sex couples violated the Equal Protection Clause of the state Constitution. As a response, the federal government passed the Defense of Marriage Act (DOMA). For federal purposes, DOMA defined marriage as the union of one man and one woman. Furthermore, DOMA allowed states to refuse to recognize same-sex "marriages" granted under the laws of other states. DOMA was sufficient, claimed many, including some conservatives, to protect conservative states from liberal states that were likely to adopt same-sex "marriage."

Additionally, as a response to the Hawaii ruling, through a variety of constitutional amendments, dozens of states across the U.S. began banning legal recognition of same-sex "marriage." Typically this was done through a voter ballot measure. By average margin of nearly 67 percent to 33 percent, U.S. voters across 31 states rejected same-sex "marriage."[35]

However, elections have consequences. The election of the most liberal president in U.S. history helped reverse the vote of tens of millions of Americans. With Barack Obama's presidency came the nomination and subsequent approval of liberal Supreme Court justices Elena Kagan and Sonia Sotomayor. Thus, when it came to marriage, the fears of many Christian conservatives were realized.

In 2013, by a narrow five to four ruling, the U.S. Supreme Court overturned DOMA. In 2015, by another narrow five to four ruling, the U.S. Supreme Court overturned same-sex "marriage" bans across the U.S. Thus, deceived by a foul wickedness, liberal U.S. Justices gave legal protection to a perverse re-definition of marriage throughout the United States. As many of us have warned for over a decade now, if marriage were redefined to include same-sex relationships, Christians and Christian institutions across the U.S. would be targeted.[36]

As most of us now know, as same-sex "marriage" has gained legal protection across the U.S., many American Christians who have refused to acquiesce to such perversion have suffered the wrath of the law, with several violators facing tens of thousands of dollars in fines. Such results are even less surprising when we consider the words of law professor Doug Kmiec from 2005.

At the Becket Conference held in December of 2005, Kmiec warned, "Were federal equal protection or substantive due process to be construed to require states to license same-sex marriage, those who have profound moral or religious objection to the social affirmation of homosexual conduct would be argued to be the out-liers of civil society."[37] Therefore, he argued that Christians could be targeted for legal penalties and disadvantages. He added that, "This is hardly a far-fetched (idea), as apparently one of the main aspirations of the homosexual movement is retaliation against the defenders of traditional marriage."[38]

And there you have it. Ultimately, this debate isn't about marriage or "discrimination." (As I've noted often before, *every* position in the marriage debate "discriminates.")[39] This is an attempt, using the power of the American legal system, to force moral legitimization of homosexual behavior upon the American people, and it is about revenge upon all those—past and present—who have stood and continue to stand in the way of such "progress."

Prior to any legal recognition of same-sex "marriage," homosexuals in some parts of the U.S. were allowed to adopt children. Homosexual adoption is now legal across virtually all of America. Thus, tens of thousands of U.S. children are now not only growing up in homes without a mother or father, but are also growing up with homosexuality lived out before their very eyes.

As if we needed science to reveal what common sense and sound morality have always known, several recent studies have shown the ill effects suffered by children raised in same-sex households.[40,][41] Among other things, children from same-sex households are more likely to suffer from depression, need mental health therapy, identify as homosexual, contract sexually transmitted diseases, be sexually molested, drink to get drunk, and use marijuana. Well over 100,000 children in the U.S. live in households headed by a same-sex couple.[42] (All of this is in addition to the grave dangers that come from living a homosexual lifestyle.)[43]

At least these children are alive. Undoubtedly the greatest tragedy of the 1960s sexual revolution is the legal recognition of abortion across the U.S. With the Supreme Court of the United States again ignoring sound science and morality and doing what was "right in its own eyes," well over 50 million American children have been slaughtered in their mothers' wombs.[44] America has turned what should be one of the safest places for a child into a killing field.

For millennia human beings have sought to shed the tenets of our Creator and go our own way. This is especially true when it comes to our sexuality. Much of the history of ancient Israel, as described by the Old Testament, included the struggle of the Jewish people with idolatry, false gods, and sexual immorality. In their wicked worship of the heathen gods Baal, Ashtoreth, or Molech (or Molek), the Israelites engaged in lewd sexual acts with temple prostitutes and even sacrificed their infant children in the fiery arms of a false god. In lieu of sacrificing unwanted children at the altar of a heathen god, we now sacrifice them in the hygienic atmosphere of a clinic. Falling prey to the dehumanizing lies and propaganda of modern liberalism, generations of Americans have been deceived into believing that a child in the womb is not a human life worth protecting. Abortion apologists have gone so far as to say that the term "baby" doesn't apply until birth.[45] Of course, this definition flies in the face of nearly everything we now know about prenatal science. Life in the womb for a child is as well documented as anything in science. With ultrasound and Doppler machines, as well as other technology, one can monitor the life of a baby in the womb from very near the beginning until birth.

Moments after conception (hardly a serious biologist in the world would argue that life does not begin at conception), the resulting single cell contains all 46 chromosomes necessary to grow into an adult human being. Within 48 hours of conception, the mother's body starts producing a hormone to let her know that she is pregnant. In the beginning of the third week, the baby's heart begins to beat with a blood type that is often different from its mother's.

During week five, eyes, legs, and hands have begun to develop. By week six, brain waves are detectable. In week eight, it has every organ in place, bones begin to replace cartilage, and the baby can begin to hear. By week 12, the baby is nearing the end of the first trimester. She has all the necessary parts to experience pain, including her nerves, spinal cord, and thalamus. She can grasp objects placed in her hand and has fingerprints, a skeletal structure, and circulation.

By week 15, she has an adult's taste buds. At week 20, the earliest stage at which the ghastly procedure of partial-birth abortion was performed, the child can recognize her mother's voice. She is within one or two weeks of the stage where babies can routinely be saved outside the womb.

Yet, in spite of all that science clearly reveals here, and in spite of their claims as "champions of science," for decades now, modern liberals have denied or ignored the science of the human womb. In the name of money—abortion is a billion dollar-plus industry—and sexual "freedom," liberals have placed their wallets and their libidos above science and morality.

For far too many Americans, "the right to choose" now trumps the "right to life, liberty, and the pursuit of happiness." As Mother Teresa taught us,

> Roe v. Wade has deformed a great nation. The so-called right to abortion has pitted mothers against their children and women against men. It has sown violence and discord at the heart of the most intimate human relationships. It has aggravated the derogation of the father's role in an increasingly fatherless society. It has portrayed the greatest of gifts—a child—as a competitor, an intrusion, and an inconvenience. It has nominally accorded mothers unfettered domination over the independent lives of their physically dependent sons and daughters.
>
> And, in granting this unconscionable power, it has exposed many women to unjust and selfish demands from their husbands or other sexual partners.
>
> Human rights are not a privilege conferred by government. They are every human being's entitlement by virtue of his humanity. The right to life does not depend, and must not be declared to be contingent, on the pleasure of anyone else, not even a parent or a sovereign...
>
> I have no new teaching for America. I seek only to recall you to faithfulness to what you once taught the world. Your nation was founded on the proposition—very old as a moral precept, but startling and innovative as a political insight— that human life is a gift of immeasurable worth, and that it deserves, always and everywhere, to be treated with the utmost dignity and respect.[46]

Along with valuing human life, one of those "old moral precepts" upon which this great nation was founded is the idea of the family. Families founded America. The family is deeply imbedded in the fabric of America. Abortion "deforms" America because it tears at the family, and not only abortion, but also rampant divorce, promiscuity, pornography, fornication, homosexuality, a perverse redefinition of marriage, the welfare state, and the like, "deform" our nation as well.

Many of those involved in these radical movements have not been shy about stating their destructive goals for the biblical family model. In 1973, Gloria Steinem, one of the most recognizable names and faces of the sexual revolution, said, "We have to abolish and reform the institution of marriage...By the year 2000 we will, I hope, raise our children to believe in human potential, not God...We must understand what we are attempting is a revolution, not a public relations movement."

In 2011, Hollywood "scholar" Cameron Diaz gave an excellent illustration of the secular/godless worldview on marriage and the family: "I do [think marriage is dead]. I think we have to make our own rules. I don't think we should live our lives in relationships based off old traditions that don't suit our world any longer."[47]

Recall the words of George Bourne (chapter 10), author of the 1816 book, *The Book and Slavery Irreconcilable*. Bourne considered slavery a grave sin and questioned whether those who owned slaves should be considered Christians. He wrote, "Every man who holds Slaves and who pretends to be a Christian or a Republican, is either an incurable Idiot who cannot distinguish good from evil, or an obdurate sinner who resolutely defies every social, moral, and divine requisition.... Every ramification of the doctrine, *that one rational creature can become the property of another*, is totally repugnant to the rule of equity, the rights of nature, and the existence of civil society."

The same argument that Bourne made regarding slavery can easily be made regarding abortion, homosexuality, and a perverse redefinition of marriage. For example, substitute "holds Slaves" with "supports abortion," and then substitute *"that one rational creature can become the property of another"* with *"that a child in the womb is a mere 'choice.'"* And like slavery, abortion, homosexuality, promiscuity, and a perverse redefinition of marriage are "totally repugnant to the rule of equity, the rights of nature, and the existence of civil society." As was the case with slavery, Americans today must choose if they are going to be on the side of truth or if we are going to "make our own rules."

If we continue to make our own rules, not only will children in the womb continue to die, but we will also witness further erosion of marriage and the death of the family itself. If in the United States of America, the family dies, that will herald the end of our republic.

# CHAPTER 26

# The War on God and His Word

Of course, those "old traditions" to which Miss Cameron Diaz was referring are traditions rooted in biblical truths. If one wants to destroy the family, redefine marriage, promote promiscuity, and put a secular government in charge of charity, one needs to redefine truth.

In 1961, after Soviet cosmonaut Yuri Gagarin became the first human in outer space, *Life* magazine asked, "What is our national space objective: Survival, knowledge, or prestige? [Then there] is the question of the role of science in the organized life of mankind.

> For the Soviets, this question does not exist. They answered it long ago by making science their god. Despite the wholly unscientific character of their political dogmas, they look to science as the chief tool and ultimate vindication of their system. It is a science-oriented system. Thus there is an eerie element of truth in Khrushchev's wild boast that Gagarin's flight "contains a new triumph of Lenin's ideas, a confirmation of the correctness of Marxist-Leninist teaching." Gagarin, too, gave the credit to "our own Communist party," the vanguard on the "great road to penetrating the secrets of nature."[1]

It's as if the writers at *Life* were glowingly saying "See what can result when you make science your god?" Shortly thereafter, in

1962 and 1963, two landmark cases decided by the U.S. Supreme Court helped science supplant God in the public school classrooms of America. In 1962, in Engel v. Vitale, the court ruled that a prayer approved by the New York Board of Regents for use in New York public schools violated the First Amendment because it represented establishment of religion. Similarly, in 1963, in Abington School District v. Schempp, the court decided against Bible readings in public schools.

It is no mere coincidence that, around the same time that many Americans found the sexual morals taught by Christianity to be coercive, constraining, and outdated, like-minded people thought it was also time to kick God out of the schools. Thus in just over 300 years—from the Old Deluder Satan Act of 1647, which required education as a means of better understanding God and His Word, until the early 1960s—Christians had gone from the pioneers of education in America to the outcasts. Theodore Roosevelt warned us, "To educate a man in mind and not in morals is to educate a menace to society."[2] Sadly, it seems that America today is overrun with such menaces.

The decline of American public education began within the science curriculum. Around the middle of the nineteenth century, "old-earth" opinions from the European scientific community began to corrupt views of geology in American textbooks. Though the Bible was still important in American education, some U.S. educators began to cast a suspicious eye toward certain parts of Scripture. Parts of the Bible meant to be taken literally were now seen as allegory.

During this same period, Charles Darwin published his infamous *On the Origin of Species*. The biggest impact of Darwin's book was that it gave those eager to push an anti-biblical worldview an opportunity to do so. Many in the scientific community took advantage of this opportunity, and Darwin's evolutionary theory on the origin of all life gained in popularity. Few things in the modern era are more enthusiastically embraced by those running from God and His Word than is Darwinian evolution (D.E.).

Completely contradicting the account of Creation revealed in the book of Genesis, D.E. teaches that all life—plant, animal, human—billions of years ago sprang from the same single-celled source, strictly as a product of nature and natural processes (billions of years of death and struggle).[3] Thus, as a liberal writer at Salon recently put it, "Darwin…explained the evolution of life in a way that doesn't require the hand of God." His piece is gleefully entitled "God is on the Ropes," and he writes about the "brilliant new science"—isn't it always—that expands on Darwin's work and will finally liberate us from **any** idea that God was involved in creating life.[4]

Many people, including those who call themselves Christians and/or conservatives, would like to ignore this tenet of D.E. Thus we now have the nonsense that is "theistic evolution." This is nothing more than the sad attempt to reconcile God's Word with what is perceived as the "settled science"—isn't it always—on the beginning of life, that has misled the likes of even the Pope.

Though many Christians today are eager to compromise with D.E., the rabid atheist and Darwinist Richard Dawkins understands the fallacy of such efforts. When asked recently what was the particular point at which he was able to conclude that God doesn't exist, Dawkins replied that "by far" the most significant event for him was "understanding evolution." He went on to say that he thought the evangelical Christians have it "sort-of" right when they see (Darwinian) evolution as "the enemy," adding that there "really is a deep incompatibility between evolution and Christianity." The "sophisticated theologians" who are "quite happy to live with evolution" are, as Dawkins puts it, "deluded."[5] How sad that it takes an atheist to point out the truth in this debate!

In his infamous book, *The God Delusion*, Dawkins mocks and criticizes the account in the book of Genesis of The Flood. However, he correctly points out that many theologians today, in an attempt to reconcile the biblical record with evolution, "don't take the book of Genesis literally anymore." He continues, "[T]hat is my whole point! We pick and choose which bits of scripture to believe, which bits to write off as symbols or allegories."[6] In other words, if you can't trust the Bible on one topic, why should you trust it on any topic?

As more and more Americans ignore the Word of God, we now find ourselves with a nation in which a significant majority of the people enthusiastically engage in immoral behavior. Also, porn performers and prostitutes seek legal legitimacy and "moral" acceptance,[7, 8] while transvestites grace the covers of our "distinguished" news magazines.[9] And to answer Larry Kudlow's question in the last chapter, ignoring God's eternal truths on marriage and the family is why "we do it backwards" when it comes to children and marriage.

Ready to push the envelope of immorality even further, in 2014, *Time Magazine* joyfully declared, "Nearly a year after the Supreme Court legalized same-sex marriage, another social movement is poised to challenge deeply held cultural beliefs."[10] *Time* conducted a very sympathetic interview with Laverne Cox, a man who is living his life as a woman. Of course, in this "mixed up, muddled up, shook up world," this is something we are supposed to celebrate.

As schools begin to accommodate the transgendered, as states pass laws giving students the "right" to use whichever bathroom or locker room they feel like, as athletic departments seriously debate banning the use of gender pronouns,[11] how long before the gender-confused are before the Supreme Court demanding their "rights"?

The 2015 Gallup survey on "moral issues"[12] is Exhibit A in the case of the collapse of the moral foundation of America that we have witnessed the last few decades. Whether sex outside of marriage, out-of-wedlock births, divorce, gambling, or embryonic stem cell research, Gallup found that at least 60 percent (over 70 percent on some issues) of Americans find such behaviors unconditionally "morally acceptable." (The option of "depends on the situation" was given in each question.) Gallup found the U.S. evenly split (45 percent to 45 percent) on the moral acceptability of killing children in the womb.

Widely abandoning virtually any notion of absolute truth, America today is a nation where far too many call "evil good and good evil." Things that Americans once overwhelmingly considered immoral, so much so that many such things were also illegal, have become popular to the point that not only are they now legal, but it is also easy to find churches in the U.S. giving their blessing to these sinful behaviors.

Too many of us have forgotten that "America is great because she is good," and many have ignored the warning that, "if America ever ceases to be good, she will cease to be great." Generations of Americans have ignored Jedidiah Morse's instruction that, "The foundations which support the interest of Christianity are also necessary to support a free and equal government like our own."

Thinking themselves free, tens of millions of Americans have instead become slaves to sin. Through a wide array of media, Americans are told again and again that they need to be "true to themselves" and take what is theirs. Christians, secularists, atheists, liberals, conservatives, and libertarians alike have all fallen prey to this selfish, pride-centered view of the person.

Recently, as a parade of topless women plagued Times Square in New York City,[13] New York's political leaders were at a loss. On the bare-breasted bimbos, New York City Mayor, Bill de Blasio— a full-fledged supporter of the homosexual agenda, pro-abortionist, big government-loving, and otherwise all-around superb member of the liberal elite—said, "It's wrong, it's wrong."[14]

As these hedonistic hussies seek payment to be photographed by willing Times Square patrons, according to CBS News, New York Governor Andrew Cuomo—another unapologetic liberal—"has said he believes the women posing for the photos are breaking the law and are undermining efforts to keep the tourist area family friendly." Of course, neither de Blasio nor Cuomo offer any moral standard upon which they base their conclusions.

As the topless women took their act to Austin, Texas, one political observer asked the protestors to "explain reasons why women should be topless." The number one reason given: "It frees oneself from guilt and sin."[15]

This reasoning sounds a lot like the pro-abortion Satanists recently documented at National Review. As the author David French notes, "The Satanists adhere to such edifying statements of principle as 'Satan represents indulgence instead of abstinence!' and 'Satan represents all of the so-called sins, as they all lead to physical, mental, or emotional gratification!'"[16]

As Mr. French also points out, though most pro-abortionists are not Satanists (nor favor the "right" to parade around topless in public), "prominent Satanist involvement in the abortion debate does have a clarifying effect." Of course, this "clarifying effect" is also present with those who clamor for their "right" to be topless in public.

As French concludes,

> A person who is willing to kill another person for the sake of preserving [her] own prosperity or emotional health is declaring that [her] life is supreme — [her] existence is at the center of all things. This is the core of Satanist theology. So when Satanists declare their creeds, they strike uncomfortably close to the rotten core of the abortion-rights regime.[17]

Writing for Patheos, author and philosopher Michael Novak makes note of this "theology of self" when he writes of a two-decades-old study on abortion that he only recently encountered. "Two main findings of the study startled me," Novak writes, "but they are also fairly obvious once one sees them from the point of view of the young women in the study...To such women, having an unplanned child represents a threat so great to modern women that it is perceived as the equivalent to a 'death of self.'"[18] Recently, 45-year-old actress and radical liberal Sarah Silverman perfectly illustrated such views when she admitted, "I ache for children, but I love my life more."[19]

Such a selfish theology is not exclusive to Satanists. Even the U.S. Supreme Court has embraced this theology. Nearly a quarter of a century ago, ruling in favor of the "right" to kill children in the womb (Planned Parenthood v. Casey), Justice Anthony Kennedy wrote, "At the heart of liberty is the right to define one's own concept of existence, of meaning, of the universe, and of the mystery of human life."[20] (Thus, no one should have been surprised at his vote in favor of same-sex "marriage.")

In fact, the desire to make oneself "the center of all things," or, as it is stated in Genesis chapter 3, to make oneself to "be like God" is almost as old as humanity itself. C.S. Lewis called it "The Great Sin." The Great Sin, the utmost evil, Lewis wrote, is pride. "Unchastity, anger, greed, drunkenness, and all that, are mere fleabites in comparison. It was through Pride that the devil became the devil. Pride leads to every other vice. It is the complete anti-God state of mind."[21] It was an appeal to the pride of Adam and Eve which introduced sin into God's perfect creation. "The Christians are right," Lewis continued, "it is Pride which has been the chief cause of misery in every nation and every family since the world began." The only cure for the disease of pride, as the life and words of Jesus reveal, is the "death of self," and a rebirth as a new creature.

Of course, this is not easy. As Lewis also notes,

> The terrible thing, the almost impossible thing, is to hand over your whole self – all your wishes and precautions – to Christ. But it is far easier than what we are all trying to do instead. For what we are trying to do is to remain what we call "ourselves", to keep personal happiness as our great aim in life, and yet at the same time be "good." We are all trying to let our mind and heart go their own way – centered on money or pleasure or ambition – and hoping, in spite of this to behave honestly and chastely and humbly. And that is exactly what Christ warned us you could not do. As He said, a thistle cannot

produce figs. If I am a field that contains nothing
but grass-seed, I cannot produce wheat. Cutting
the grass may keep it short: but I shall still
produce grass and no wheat. If I want to produce
wheat, the change must go deeper than the
surface. I must be ploughed up and re-sown.[22]

There is only one way to "free oneself from guilt and sin." We
cannot find this freedom in the redefining of sin, in the election of
one politician over another, in the ruling of a judge, or in
uninhibited acts of hedonism. There is but one way to such
freedom, and that is the Way of the Cross.

As our culture continues its descent into more and greater
immorality, perhaps the best question to ask *is* "How long?" How
long until families led by fathers and mothers are the minority?
How long until it is no longer legal to speak or write the truth, as
revealed by God, on sexual issues? How long before America
wakes up? How long before we are past the point of no return in
this moral collapse? How long before we become as those
described in the Psalms? "So I gave them over to the stubbornness
of their heart, to walk in their own devices." (Psalm 81:12) The
great Charles Spurgeon provides the perfect insight here:

No punishment is more just or more severe than
this. If men will not be checked, but madly take
the bit between their teeth and refuse obedience,
who shall wonder if the reins are thrown upon
their necks, and they are let alone to work out
their own destruction. It were better to be given
up to lions than to our hearts' lusts.

"[T]o walk in their own devices."—There was
no doubt as to what course they would take,
for man is everywhere willful and loves his own
way,—that way being at all times in direct
opposition to God's way. Men deserted of
restraining grace, sin with deliberation; they
consult, and debate, and consider, and then elect

338

evil rather than good, with malice aforethought
and in cool blood. It is a remarkable obduracy
(stubbornly persistent in wrongdoing) of
rebellion when men not only run into sin through
passion, but calmly "walk in their own counsels'
of iniquity."[23]

Going our "own way," instead of in the way of a nation whose
laws are rooted in "the eternal immutable laws of good and evil"
laid down by God, we have succumbed to the principal virtue of
the modern liberalism: tolerance.

Far too many Americans have become blind to the fact that some
things should not be tolerated, and further still, deserve no debate.
C.S. Lewis alluded to this as he rather bluntly declared, "An open
mind, in questions that are not ultimate, is useful. But an open
mind about the ultimate foundations either of Theoretical or of
Practical Reason is idiocy."[24] More plainly put, one would have to
be an idiot not to recognize that certain things are settled for all
time.

Such a conclusion is in direct contradiction to the modern
American idea of tolerance. As the United Nations' Declaration of
Principles on Tolerance instructs, "Tolerance ... involves the
rejection of dogmatism and absolutism."[25] Of course, such a
declaration reveals how the definition of tolerance has changed.
Today tolerance no longer simply means "to recognize and respect
others' beliefs and practices without sharing them." Today's
tolerance is little more than a self-refuting system of thought that
attempts to impose liberal values onto any culture unable or
unwilling to recognize the fallacy.

The United Nations' description of tolerance above illustrates well
such fallacy, as the statement that, "Tolerance ... involves the
rejection of dogmatism and absolutism" is itself a dogmatic and
absolute statement. Today's liberalism is full of such nonsense.

On "tolerance," G.K. Chesterton, who greatly influenced the life
and writings of C.S. Lewis, noted that "Tolerance is a virtue of a

man without convictions." What better describes those opposed to the absolute truths revealed by Christianity than men and women "without convictions"? When a person lacks convictions, he aligns himself with whatever worldview provides the most benefits in this world—or at least allows him to have the most "fun."

What we are really dealing with here is competing views of truth. Those peddling "tolerance" generally reject the notion of absolute truth. As noted apologist William Lane Craig stated when writing about the Christian perspective on homosexuality, "Today so many people think of right and wrong, not as matters of *fact*, but as matters of *taste*."[26] And if taste determines truth, then we're all at the mercy of whoever's in charge, because, ultimately we're all intolerant. It's simply a matter of who's right.

Lamenting the rampant sexual immorality in our culture, in 2014 Al Mohler noted that, "We are in the midst of a massive revolution in morality."[27] Dr. Mohler referred directly to a "crossroads" and alluded to an unavoidable showdown that is looming within the evangelical church in America. However, I believe this is the case for our nation in general.

# CHAPTER 27

# A Return to "Wisdom and Godliness"

As Screwtape cautioned Wormwood, just as warfare with bullets and bombs renders one of the best weapons of Satan ("contented worldliness") useless, the mounting moral conflicts in America are pushing many of us out of a contented and willful ignorance and complacence into a place that the enemy of all mankind really doesn't want us to go; a place where we are forced to confront the social, political, and spiritual consequences of our beliefs and behaviors; a place where we also must examine why we believe what we believe, and determine if what we believe is really the truth.

This is why I say...let's have it out. Let's passionately debate the morality and the justness of all the moral issues that weigh so heavily upon our culture, and let us not forget, as the brilliant Russell Kirk, author of the seminal *The Conservative Mind,* declared in his Six Canons of Conservatism: "Political problems, at bottom, are religious and moral problems."[1] Let us each loudly and clearly proclaim our moral and religious standards before the American people, the courts, and most importantly, the Creator and see where we stand. This is certainly not to imply that, at least when it comes to the American people and the courts, such a confrontation will produce results that many of us will like. However, as Christ warned the Church at Laodicea, let us not be "lukewarm!"

William Penn, the founder of Pennsylvania said, "Those who will not be governed by God will be ruled by tyrants." If America is to stem her descent into a spiritual, moral, and tyrannical winter, then Christians across the country must do their best to ignite fires of faith in their families, churches, communities, schools, places of work, and so on, and be the light we are called to be. We do not need Christians who see compromise as the way forward. Neither do we need Christian monasteries or compounds where biblical values and truths are hoarded and hidden from our nation.

What we need are communities full of faithful families led by fathers and mothers who want to work hard, raise children, believe God's Word, and pass on their biblical values to the next generation and each succeeding generation. As Psalm 78 implores the rebellious nation of Israel: fathers teach your children, so that they will in turn teach their children—so it should be with every nation that wants to walk in the truth.

Such communities need to be "cities on a hill," welcoming all those who want to join, so that the American people can clearly contrast the ways of those who are "lovers of themselves, lovers of money, boastful, proud, abusive, disobedient to their parents, ungrateful, unholy, without love, unforgiving, slanderous, without self-control, brutal, not lovers of the good, treacherous, rash, conceited, lovers of pleasure rather than lovers of God" (2 Timothy 3:2-4) with those who seek to live the "godly life in Christ Jesus." Thus Americans can clearly choose whether to be part of, as Augustine put it, the City of God or the City of Man.

Perhaps more than ever before in the history of our great nation, we now need people who will gaze unwaveringly at their "fiery furnace" and boldly declare: We do not need to defend ourselves against any other human being in these matters. If we face fines, or imprisonment; lose our jobs, our possessions, our positions, or even our lives, the God we serve is able to provide for us, and He will deliver us from any immoral hand. But even if He does not, we want those who stand against the truth to know that we will never bow down to their perverse idols.

Perhaps more than ever before in the history of our great nation, the pulpits of American churches need to "flame with righteousness." As we stand strong against the immorality that so many—whether through our legal code, the media, or lukewarm churches—seek to legitimize, who knows but that the end result could be—as it was with Nebuchadnezzar and a later Babylonian king Darius—a recognition of the truth and subsequent repentant words and actions.

By almost any standard, the United States of America is the greatest nation the world has ever known. We have been a powerful force for good unlike any other nation in the history of humanity. The only reason for our greatness and goodness is that we are a nation built upon the "pillars of Christianity" preached by Jedidiah Morse and countless others throughout our history. In other words, only Christians could have founded a nation like the United States of America. Tellingly, people of other faiths have never come close to building a nation like America.

With the pillars of Christianity intact, with our unique constitutional republican form of government, with an abundance of human and natural resources, and with more Christians than any other single nation on earth, the United States has a great opportunity to remain a powerful instrument for truth, justice, and righteousness. However, if we continue to abandon the faith of our founders and go our own way, we will reap destruction.

In many ways, America today is like Israel when Moses stood before her and declared,

> See, I set before you today life and prosperity, death and destruction. For I command you today to love the Lord your God, to walk in his ways, and to keep his commands, decrees and laws; then you will live and increase, and the Lord your God will bless you in the land you are entering to possess.

> But if your heart turns away and you are not obedient, and if you are drawn away to bow down to other gods and worship them, I declare to you this day that you will certainly be destroyed. (Deut. 28:15-18a , NIV 1984)

Until the end of all days, may the United States of America remain "One Nation Under God," and let there come increased devotion to be a nation filled with faith and hope, life and love, truth and justice, prosperity and peace.

# CONNECT
# WITH
# TREVOR GRANT THOMAS

## VISIT TREVOR'S WEBSITE:
TrevorGrantThomas.com

## EMAIL TREVOR:
TThomas@TrevorGrantThomas.com

## FIND TREVOR ON SOCIAL MEDIA:
Like Trevor Grant Thomas on Facebook

# End Notes

## Chapter 1: The Discovery

1.  Roberto Rusconi and Christopher Columbus, *The Book of Prophecies* (University of California Press, 1997), p. 67
2.  Salvador De Madariaga, *Christopher Columbus: Being the Life of the Very Magnificent Lord Don Cristóbal Colón* (New York: Macmillan, 1940), p. 16
3.  Steve Byas, "Why the Left Hates Columbus," The New American, 2015, http://www.thenewamerican.com/culture/history/item/2174 2-why-the-left-hates-columbus
4.  Salvador De Madariaga, *Christopher Columbus: Being the Life of the Very Magnificent Lord Don Cristóbal Colón* (New York: Macmillan, 1940), p. 17
5.  Ibid, p. 18-19
6.  James R. McGovern, *The World of Columbus* (Mercer University Press, 1992), p. 37
7.  Peter Marshall and David Manuel, *The Light and the Glory* (Revell, 1977), p. 17
8.  Kevin A. Miller, "Why Did Columbus Sail?," Christianity Today, 1992, http://www.christianitytoday.com/history/issues/issue-35/why-did-columbus-sail.html
9.  Peter Marshall and David Manuel, *The Light and the Glory* (Revell, 1977), p. 33
10. Ibid, p. 17
11. Ibid, p. 43
12. Ibid, p. 53
13. William J. Federer, *America's God and Country Encyclopedia of Quotations*, (Amerisearch, 2000), p. 119

## Chapter 2: Laying the Foundation: The Faithful Friars, Dominicans, and Jesuits

1. Leonard Woolsey Bacon, *A History of American Christianity* (New York: Scribner's Sons, 1898), p. 3
2. Ibid, p. 3, 5
3. Lippy, Charles H., Robert Choquette, and Stafford Poole, *Christianity Comes to the Americas, 1492-1776*, (New York: Paragon House, 1992), p. 19
4. James Muldoon, "Papal Responsibility for the Infidel: Another Look at Alexander VI's Inter Caetera," *Catholic Historical Review*, 64, n. 2 (April 1978): 183
5. Lippy, Charles H., Robert Choquette, and Stafford Poole, *Christianity Comes to the Americas, 1492-1776*, (New York: Paragon House, 1992), p. 84
6. Ibid, p. 84
7. Ibid, p. 26
8. Robert Ricard, *The Spiritual Conquest of Mexico* (University of California Press, 1966), p. 4
9. Lippy, Charles H., Robert Choquette, and Stafford Poole, *Christianity Comes to the Americas, 1492-1776* (New York: Paragon House, 1992), p. 43
10. Ibid, p. 43
11. Leonard Woolsey Bacon, *A History of American Christianity*, (New York: Scribner's Sons, 1898), p. 9

12. Professor Thomas O'Gorman, *The Roman Catholic Church in the United States* (New York: Scribner's Sons, 1898), p. 112

13. Leonard Woolsey Bacon, *A History of American Christianity* (New York: Scribner's Sons, 1898), p. 19
14. Peter Marshall and David Manuel, *The Light and the Glory* (Revell, 1977), p. 74
15. Leonard Woolsey Bacon, *A History of American Christianity*, (New York: Scribner's Sons, 1898), p. 23

## Chapter 3: The English Migration, Part 1: A Fool's Errand

1. Peter Marshall and David Manuel, *The Light and the Glory* (Revell, 1977), p. 82
2. King James I, "The First Charter of Virginia," Yale Law School, 1606, http://avalon.law.yale.edu/17th_century/va01.asp
3. Peter Marshall and David Manuel, *The Light and the Glory* (Revell, 1977), p. 84
4. Ibid, p. 93
5. Ibid, p. 93
6. Lorri Glover, "Sea Venture," Encyclopedia Virginia, http://www.encyclopediavirginia.org/Sea_Venture
7. William Strachey, "A True Reportory," http://fas-history.rutgers.edu/clemens/Jamestown/Strachey.html
8. Ken Curtis, "Christianity in Jamestown," Christianity.com, http://www.christianity.com/church/church-history/timeline/1601-1700/christianity-in-jamestown-11630060.html
9. Emily Jones Salmon and John Salmon, "Tobacco in Colonial Virginia," Encyclopedia Virginia, http://www.encyclopediavirginia.org/Tobacco_in_Colonial_Virginia
10. Ibid
11. National Black Robe Regiment, "History of the Black Robe Regiment," http://nationalblackroberegiment.com/history-of-the-black-robe-regiment/

## Chapter 4: The English Migration, Part 2: The Pilgrims and the Puritans

1. David Roach, "Pilgrims & Baptists: the little known connection," Baptist Press, November 26, 2014, http://www.bpnews.net/43822/pilgrims-and-baptists-the-little-known-connection
2. John Robinson, "John Robinson's Farewell Letter to the Pilgrims," The Writings of John Robinson, http://www.revjohnrobinson.com/writings.htm

3. John Robinson, William Allen, John Waddington, The Works of John Robinson: Pastor of the Pilgrim *Fathers, Volume 2*, (Congregational Churches, 1851), p. 304

4. William Bradford, *History of Plymouth Plantation* (Little Brown, 1856), p. 90

5. Peter Marshall and David Manuel, *The Light and the Glory* (Revell, 1977), p. 130

6. Ibid, p. 132

7. Ibid, p. 139

8. Rush Limbaugh, "The Real Story of Thanksgiving," The Rush Limbaugh Show, November 21, 2012, http://www.rushlimbaugh.com/daily/2012/11/21/the_real_story_of_thanksgiving

9. Peter Marshall and David Manuel, *The Light and the Glory* (Revell, 1977), p. 143

10. William J. Federer, *America's God and Country Encyclopedia of Quotations*, (Amerisearch, 2000), p. 66

11. Peter Marshall and David Manuel, *The Light and the Glory* (Revell, 1977), p. 144

12. John Winthrop, "A Model of Christian Charity," The Winthrop Society, http://winthropsociety.com/doc_charity.php

13. Nathaniel Ward, "The Massachusetts Body of Liberties," The Winthrop Society, http://winthropsociety.com/liberties.php

14. Roger Ludlow, "The Fundamental Orders of Connecticut," Connecticut History.org, http://connecticuthistory.org/the-fundamental-orders-of-connecticut/

15. David Barton, "What is the Black Robed Regiment?," Virginia Christian Alliance, http://www.vachristian.org/Our-Nation-Under-God/What-is-the-Black-Robed-Regiment.html

16. Alexis De Tocqueville, *Democracy in America* (Penguin Group, Vol.1), p. 46

17. Ibid, p. 43

18. Ibid, p. 46

19. Ibid, p. 47

20. Ibid, p. 48

## Chapter 5: The Foundation of Education in America

1. Notable Alumni, Boston Latin School, http://www.bls.org/apps/pages/index.jsp?uREC_ID=203830&type=d&pREC_ID=404406
2. Richard Gummere, *The American Colonial Mind and the Classical Tradition* (Harvard University Press, 1963), p. 57
3. Jeff Wallace, *In God We Trusted* (CrossBooks, 2014), p. 330-331
4. Martin Cothran and Cheryl Lowe, "The Classical Education of the Puritans," Memoria Press, http://www.memoriapress.com/articles/classical-education-puritans
5. Stephen McDowell, *Restoring America's Christian Education* (Providence Foundation, 2000), p. 8
6. Ibid, p. 7
7. Ibid, p. 7
8. Georgia Purdam, "Harvard: No Longer 'Truth for Christ and the Church,'" Answers in Genesis, https://answersingenesis.org/blogs/georgia-purdom/2011/10/11/harvard-no-longer-truth-for-christ-and-the-church/
9. Everett Emerson, *Puritanism in America, 1620-1750* (Boston: Twayne, 1977), p. 104
10. Ibid, p. 105
11. Perry Miller and Thomas Herbert Johnson, *The Puritans: A Sourcebook of Their Writings* (Courier Corporation, 2001), p. 721
12. Herbert Baxter Adams, *The College of William and Mary: a Contribution to the History of Higher Education* (U.S. Government Printing Office, 1887), p. 18
13. Ibid, p. 17
14. College of William & Mary, https://www.wm.edu/offices/deanofstudents/services/studentconduct/studenthandbook/history_of_the_college/index.php

15. Dan Graves, "Yale Founded to Fight Liberalism," Christianity.com, http://www.christianity.com/church/church-history/timeline/1701-1800/yale-founded-to-fight-liberalism-11630185.html

16. "Regulations at Yale College," Constitution Society, http://www.constitution.org/primarysources/yale.html

17. William C. Ringenberg, Mark Noll, *The Christian College: A History of Protestant Higher Education in America* (Grand Rapids, MI: Eerdmans, 1984), p. 38

18. William Bland Whitley, "Samuel Davies (1723-1761)," Encyclopedia Virginia, http://www.encyclopediavirginia.org/Davies_Samuel_1723-1761

19. C. Richard Wells, "A Noble Treason," John Witherspoon College, http://www.johnwitherspooncollege.org/page/president.aspx

20. Alexander Leitch, *A Princeton Companion* (Princeton University Press, 2015), p. 526

21. Columbia University, "A Brief History of Columbia," http://www.columbia.edu/content/history.html

22. Phil Webster, *1776 Faith* (Xulon Press, 2009), p. 226

23. Alvin J. Schmidt, *Under the Influence: How Christianity Transformed Civilization* (Zondervan, 2001), p. 190

24. Sam Blumenfeld, "Colonial Education: Superior to Today's Public Schools," The New American, http://www.thenewamerican.com/reviews/opinion/item/10758-colonial-education-superior-to-todays-public-schools

25. William J. Federer, *America's God and Country Encyclopedia of Quotations*, (Amerisearch, 2000), p. 433

## Chapter 6: Revival Lights a Fire

1. Robert W. Brockway, *A Wonderful Work of God: Puritanism and the Great Awakening* (Bethlehem, PA: Lehigh UP, 2003), p. 44

2. Ibid, p. 44

3. Institute for the Study of American Evangelicals, "Jonathan Edwards," Wheaton College, http://www.wheaton.edu/isae/hall-of-biography/jonathan-edwards

4. Edward M. Panosian, "Jonathan Edwards: America's Theologian-Preacher." *Faith of Our Fathers: Scenes from American Church History* (edited by Mark Sidwell, 33-39, Greenville, SC: BJU Press, 1991), http://greatawakeningdocumentary.com/items/show/31

5. Robert Philip, *The Life and Times of...George Whitfield, M.A.* (1838), p. 3

6. Robert W. Brockway, *A Wonderful Work of God: Puritanism and the Great Awakening* (Bethlehem, PA: Lehigh UP, 2003), p. 67

7. *From Columbus to Colonial America: 1492 to 1763*, Britannica Educational Publishing (2011), p. 57

8. David Barton, National Black Robe Regiment, "History of the Black Robe Regiment," http://nationalblackroberegiment.com/history-of-the-black-robe-regiment/

9. Jonathan Clark, "The American Revolution: A War of Religion?," History Today, Volume 39 Issue 12, December, 1989, http://www.historytoday.com/jonathan-clark/american-revolution-war-religion

10. Jonathan Mayhew, "A Discourse Concerning Unlimited Submission and Non-Resistance to the Higher Powers," Law and Liberty Foundation, 1999, http://lawandliberty.org/mayhew.htm

11. Daniel C. Palm, *On Faith and Free Government* (Rowman & Littlefield, 1997), p. 87

12. Alice M. Baldwin, *The New England Clergy and the American Revolution* (New York: Frederick Ungar, 1958), p. 90

13. Jerome Dean Mahaffey, *Preaching Politics* (Baylor University Press, 2007), p. 199

14. John Witherspoon, "The Dominion of Providence over the Passions of Men," Constitution Society,

http://www.constitution.org/primarysources/witherspoon.ht
ml

15. "John Witherspoon," The Witherspoon Institute,
http://winst.org/about/john-witherspoon/

16. Noah Webster, *Letters of Noah Webster*, Harry R. Warfel,
editor (New York: Library Publishers, 1953), p. 455, letter
to David McClure, October 25, 1836

17. David Barton, National Black Robe Regiment, "History of
the Black Robe Regiment,"
http://nationalblackroberegiment.com/history-of-the-black-
robe-regiment/

18. Peter Marshall and David Manuel, *The Light and the Glory*
(Revell, 1977), p. 251

## Chapter 7: Let Freedom Ring, Part 1: Colonial Rebellion Builds

1. Samuel Adams, "The Rights of the Colonists," *The Report
of the Committee of Correspondence to the Boston Town
Meeting,* Nov. 20, 1772, Hanover Historical Texts Project,
https://history.hanover.edu/texts/adamss.html

2. William J. Federer, *America's God and Country
Encyclopedia of Quotations*, (Amerisearch, 2000), p. 590

3. Peter Marshall and David Manuel, *The Light and the Glory*
(Revell, 1977), p. 267

4. William J. Federer, *America's God and Country
Encyclopedia of Quotations*, (Amerisearch, 2000), p. 426

5. Peter Marshall and David Manuel, *The Light and the Glory*
(Revell, 1977), p. 269

6. Ibid, p. 306

7. Ibid, p. 306

8. John Adams (as reported by Daniel Webster), "Confidence
in Our Independence," Current Literature - A Magazine of
Contemporary Record, 1895,
https://books.google.com/books?id=AbUGAQAAIAAJ&p
g=PA1#v=onepage&q&f=false

9. Henry Mills Alden, Lee Foster Hartman, Thomas Bucklin
Wells, Harper's Magazine Vol. 67 p. 211, Harper's

Magazine Foundation (1883),
https://books.google.com/books?id=-4UCAAAAIAAJ&pg=PA211#v=onepage&q&f=false

10. Frank Moore, *American Eloquence : a Collection of Speeches and Addresses* (D. Appleton and Company, 1858), p. 324,
https://books.google.com/books?id=pSBGpEvktT8C&pg=PA324#v=onepage&q&f=false

11. First Great Seal Committee, 1776, Great Seal.com,
http://greatseal.com/committees/firstcomm/

12. Ibid

13. Eric Rosenberg, "Why Americans Love Moses," Real Clear Religion.com,
http://www.realclearreligion.org/articles/2015/04/03/why_americans_love_moses.html

# Chapter 8: Let Freedom Ring, Part 2: Revolution!

1. C.S. Lewis, *The Screwtape Letters* (HarperCollins, 2001), p. 26

2. William Johnson, *George Washington, the Christian* (1919), p. 24

3. Ibid, p. 25-26

4. William J. Federer, *America's God and Country Encyclopedia of Quotations*, (Amerisearch, 2000), p. 636-637

5. John C. Fitzpatrick (editor), *The Writings of George Washington* (Washington: Government Printing Office, 1931)

6. *Memorial of Thomas Potts Junior, Who Settled in Pennsylvania* (University Press, 1874), p. 222,
https://books.google.com/books?id=UScAAAAAQAAJ&pg=PA222#v=onepage&q&f=false

7. Ibid, p. 223

8. William J. Federer, *America's God and Country Encyclopedia of Quotations*, (Amerisearch, 2000), p. 644

9. George Washington, David Maydole Matteson, *The writings of George Washington for the original manuscript sources, 1745-1799* (U.S. Govt. Print. Off., 1778), p. 343

10. William J. Federer, *America's God and Country Encyclopedia of Quotations*, (Amerisearch, 2000), p. 645

11. George Washington, "Washington's Inaugural Address of 1789," National Archives and Records Administration, http://www.archives.gov/exhibits/american_originals/inaug_txt.html

12. Robert A. Nowlan, *The American Presidents, Washington to Tyler* (McFarland, 2012), p. 59, https://books.google.com/books?id=MlNWU1e9ppUC&pg=PA59#v=onepage&q&f=false

13. J. Jay Myers, "George Washington: Defeated at the Battle of Long Island," American History Magazine, June, 2001, http://www.historynet.com/george-washington-defeated-at-the-battle-of-long-island.htm

14. Ibid

15. Ibid

16. Henry Phelps Johnston, *Memoir of Colonel Benjamin Tallmadge* (Gilliss Press, 1904), p. 12-13, https://archive.org/details/memoirofcolonelb027409mbp

17. Mary Stockwell, "Battle of Long Island," George Washington's Mount Vernon, http://www.mountvernon.org/digital-encyclopedia/article/battle-of-long-island/

18. W. Cleon Skousen, *The Making of America* (National Center for Constitutional Studies, 2007), p. 104

## Chapter 9: Let Freedom Ring, Part 3: Building the Constitution

1. Arthur L. Friedberg, Ira S. Friedberg, *Paper Money of the United States* (Coin & Currency Institute, 2010), p. 12, https://books.google.com/books?id=eMFWoWl2UYkC&pg=PA12#v=onepage&q&f=false

2. Ben Baak, "The Economics of the Revolutionary War," EH.net, http://eh.net/encyclopedia/the-economics-of-the-american-revolutionary-war/

3. George Washington, "Washington's Letter to Col. Nicola" (May 22, 1782), Freedom Shrine, http://www.freedomshrine.com/historic-documents/washington-letter.php

4. Alexander Hamilton, **"The Insufficiency of the Present Confederation to Preserve the Union,"** *The Federalist Papers*, #15, https://www.congress.gov/resources/display/content/The+Federalist+Papers#TheFederalistPapers-15

5. W. Cleon Skousen, *The Making of America* (National Center for Constitutional Studies, 2007), p. 123

6. Marion Mills Miller, *Great Debates in American History: Colonial rights; the revolution; the Constitution* (Current Literature Publishing Company, 1913), p. 365

7. The Founders' Constitution (Volume 2, Article 1, Section 8, Clause 1, Document 15), The University of Chicago Press, http://press-pubs.uchicago.edu/founders/documents/a1_8_1s15.html

8. George Washington, *The Writings of George Washington* (G. P. Putnam's Sons, 1908), p. 268, 270, https://books.google.com/books?id=LcGylrXPDgUC&pg=PA268#v=onepage&q&f=false

9. W. Cleon Skousen, *The Making of America* (National Center for Constitutional Studies, 2007), p. 137

10. "Franklin's Appeal for Prayer at the Constitutional Convention," Wall Builders, http://www.wallbuilders.com/libissuesarticles.asp?id=98

11. William J. Federer, *America's God and Country Encyclopedia of Quotations*, (Amerisearch, 2000), p. 249

12. Ibid, p. 152

13. "Franklin's Appeal for Prayer at the Constitutional Convention," Wall Builders, http://www.wallbuilders.com/libissuesarticles.asp?id=98

14. William J. Federer, *America's God and Country Encyclopedia of Quotations*, (Amerisearch, 2000), p. 152
15. Earl Taylor, **"Establishing and Preserving Constitutional Government in Ancient Israel and the United States of America," National Center for Constitutional Studies,** http://www.nccs.net/2010-08-establishing-and-preserving-constitutional-government.php
16. Ibid
17. Ibid
18. William J. Federer, *America's God and Country Encyclopedia of Quotations*, (Amerisearch, 2000), p. 18

# Chapter 10: America Confronts the Sin of Slavery, Part 1: A Nation Divided

1. David Barton, "George Washington, Thomas Jefferson Slavery in Virginia," Wall Builders, http://www.wallbuilders.com/libissuesarticles.asp?id=99
2. Thomas Jefferson, "A Rough Draft of the Declaration of Independence," PBS, http://www.pbs.org/wgbh/aia/part2/2h33t.html (For photos of the actual documents, go here: http://www.constitution.org/tj/tj-orddoi.htm)
3. David Barton, "The Founding Fathers and Slavery," Wall Builders, http://www.wallbuilders.com/libissuesarticles.asp?id=122
4. LaRoy Sunderland, *The testimony of God against slavery* (I. Knapp, 1836), p. 153, https://books.google.com/books?id=7n8NAAAAYAAJ&pg=PA153#v=onepage&q&f=false
5. K. Alan Snyder, Alan K. Snyder, *Defining Noah Webster* (Xulon Press, 2002), p. 106
6. Stephen Carter, *God's Name In Vain* (Basic Books, 2009), p. 89, https://books.google.com/books?id=TpETJyq_2wcC&pg=PT89#v=onepage&q&f=false

7. David Barton, "Confronting Civil War Revisionism: Why the South Went to War," Wall Builders, http://www.wallbuilders.com/LIBissuesArticles.asp?id=92

8. Convention of South Carolina, "Address of South Carolina to Slaveholding States," Teaching American History.org, http://teachingamericanhistory.org/library/index.asp?document=433

9. "A Declaration of the Immediate Causes which Induce and Justify the Secession of the State of Mississippi from the Federal Union," The Civil War Home Page, http://www.civil-war.net/pages/mississippi_declaration.asp

10. David Barton, "Confronting Civil War Revisionism: Why the South Went to War," Wall Builders, http://www.wallbuilders.com/LIBissuesArticles.asp?id=92

11. "A Declaration of the Immediate Causes which Induce and Justify the Secession of the State of Mississippi from the Federal Union," The Civil War Home Page, http://www.civil-war.net/pages/mississippi_declaration.asp

12. Orville Victor, *The History, Civil, Political, and Military, of the Southern Rebellion* (New York: James D. Torrey, 1861) Vol. 1, p. 195, "An Ordinance to dissolve the union between the State of Alabama and the other States united under the compact styled 'The Constitution of the United States of America,'"

13. "A Declaration of the Causes which Impel the State of Georgia to Secede from the Federal Union," The Civil War Home Page, http://www.civil-war.net/pages/georgia_declaration.asp

14. "Republican Party Platform of 1856," The American Presidency Project, http://www.presidency.ucsb.edu/ws/index.php?pid=29619

15. "Republican Party Platform of 1860," The American Presidency Project, http://www.presidency.ucsb.edu/ws/index.php?pid=29620

16. "Republican Party Platform of 1864," The American Presidency Project, http://www.presidency.ucsb.edu/ws/index.php?pid=29621

(All previous party platforms are here:
http://www.presidency.ucsb.edu/platforms.php)

17. C.C. Goen, *Broken Churches, Broken Nation: Denominational Schisms and the Coming of the American Civil War* (Mercer University Press, 1985), p. 179

18. Dinesh D'Souza, "How Christians Ended Slavery," Townhall.com, http://townhall.com/columnists/dineshdsouza/2008/01/14/how_christians_ended_slavery

19. "Evangelical Fervor and the Crisis of the Civil War: A Conversation with Historian David Goldfield," Al Mohler.com, http://www.albertmohler.com/2011/05/04/tip-temporary-title-4/

20. William Lloyd Garrison, "Declaration of Sentiments of the American Anti-Slavery Convention," http://utc.iath.virginia.edu/abolitn/abeswlgct.html

21. Mark A. Noll, *The Civil War as a Theological Crisis* (Chapel Hill, NC: U of North Carolina, 2006), p. 31

22. Ibid

23. Ibid, p. 45

24. Ibid, P. 40

25. Ibid, p. 40

26. Molly Oshatz, *Slavery and Sin: The Fight Against Slavery and the Rise of Liberal Protestantism* (Oxford University Press, USA, 2012), p. 40, https://books.google.com/books?id=vVqfW0SXpRUC&pg=PA40#v=onepage&q&f=false

27. Mark A. Noll, *The Civil War as a Theological Crisis* (Chapel Hill, NC: U of North Carolina, 2006), p. 41

# Chapter 11: America Confronts the Sin of Slavery, Part 2: Dueling Sermons

1. "The Return of the Spirit: The Second Great Awakening," Christian History Institute, https://www.christianhistoryinstitute.org/magazine/article/return-of-the-spirit-second-great-awakening/

2. Thomas Paine, *The Age of Reason*, p. 7
   http://www.amazon.com/Age-Reason-Writing-Thomas-Paine/dp/1603863400#reader_1603863400

3. Diane Severance, "The Second Great Awakening," Christianity.com, http://www.christianity.com/church/church-history/timeline/1701-1800/the-2nd-great-awakening-11630336.html

4. "In the Wake of the Second Great Awakening," Christianity Today, http://www.christianitytoday.com/history/issues/issue-23/in-wake-of-second-great-awakening.html

5. Ibid

6. Gilbert Hobbs Barnes, *The Anti-Slavery Impulse: 1830-1844* (Harcourt, Brace & World, 1933), p. viii

7. Ibid, p. 107

8. David B. Chesebrough, *God Ordained This War: Sermons on the Sectional Crisis, 1830-1865* (Columbia, SC: U of South Carolina, 1991), p. 26

9. Dan Graves, "Harriet Beecher Stowe, Abolitionist," Christianity.com, http://www.christianity.com/church/church-history/timeline/1801-1900/harriet-beecher-stowe-abolitionist-11630363.html

10. Mark A. Noll, *The Civil War as a Theological Crisis* (Chapel Hill, NC: U of North Carolina, 2006), p. 44

11. Nancy Koester, *Harriet Beecher Stowe: A Spiritual Life* (Wm. B. Eerdmans Publishing, 2014), p. 241

12. David B. Chesebrough, *God Ordained This War: Sermons on the Sectional Crisis, 1830-1865* (Columbia, SC: U of South Carolina, 1991), p. 19

13. Ibid, p. 20

14. Ibid, p. 20

15. Ibid, p. 22

16. Randall M. Miller, Harry S. Stout, Charles Reagan Wilson, *Religion and the American Civil War* (Oxford University Press, 1998), p. 6

17. David B. Chesebrough, *God Ordained This War: Sermons on the Sectional Crisis, 1830-1865* (Columbia, SC: U of South Carolina, 1991), p. 70-71
18. Ibid, p. 72
19. Ibid, p. 73
20. Ibid, p. 143
21. Donald G. Mathews, *Religion in the Old South.* (Chicago: University of Chicago Press, 1977), p. 157
22. Anne C. Loveland, *Southern Evangelicals and the Social Order* (Louisiana State University Press, 1980), p. 192
23. Thomas Kidd, "The 'Regulated Freedom' of James Henley Thornwell, Antebellum Southern Presbyterian," Patheos, http://www.patheos.com/blogs/anxiousbench/2012/12/the-regulated-freedom-of-james-henley-thornwell-antebellum-southern-presbyterian/
24. Frederick A. Ross, *Slavery Ordained of God* (J.B. Lippincott & Company, 1857), p. 6
25. Robert Lewis Dabney, "The Golden Rule and Slavery," The Confederate Reprint Company, http://confederatereprint.com/golden_rule.php
26. Robert R. Mathisen, *The Routledge Sourcebook of Religion and the American Civil War* (Routledge, 2014), p. 26

## Chapter 12: America Confronts the Sin of Slavery, Part 3: War and the *Divine Will*

1. Mark A. Noll, *The Civil War as a Theological Crisis* (Chapel Hill, NC: U of North Carolina, 2006), p. 50
2. David B. Chesebrough, *God Ordained This War: Sermons on the Sectional Crisis, 1830-1865* (Columbia, SC: U of South Carolina, 1991), p. 323
3. G.D. Carrow, *The Divine Right of the American Government* (Bryston's Caloric Power Printing Rooms, Philadelphia, 1861), p. 3
4. Ibid, p. 4
5. Ibid, p. 9
6. Joel W. Tucker, *God's Providence in War* (Academic Affairs Library, UNC-CH

University of North Carolina at Chapel Hill, 1999), http://docsouth.unc.edu/imls/tucker1/tucker.html
7. Ibid
8. Ibid
9. Michael P. Johnson, "Lincoln's Emancipation Proclamation: The End of Slavery in America," Journal of the Abraham Lincoln Association, http://quod.lib.umich.edu/j/jala/2629860.0026.206/--lincoln-s-emancipation-proclamation-the-end-of-slavery?rgn=main;view=fulltext
10. David B. Chesebrough, *God Ordained This War: Sermons on the Sectional Crisis, 1830-1865* (Columbia, SC: U of South Carolina, 1991), p. 85
11. Brady Dennis, "Willie Lincoln's death: A private agony for a president facing a nation of pain" (October, 2011), *The Washington Post*, https://www.washingtonpost.com/lifestyle/style/willie-lincolns-death-a-private-agony-for-a-president-facing-a-nation-of-pain/2011/09/29/gIQAv7Z7SL_story.html
12. Phineas Gurley, "Funeral Sermon by Dr. Gurley" (February 24, 1862), Abraham Lincoln Online, http://www.abrahamlincolnonline.org/lincoln/education/williedeath.htm
13. Ron C. White, PBS Interview, http://www.pbs.org/godinamerica/interviews/ronald-white.html
14. William E. Barton, *The Soul of Abraham Lincoln* (George H. Doran Company, 1920), p. 280
15. William Wolf, *The Religion of Abraham Lincoln* (Seabury Press, 1963), p. 115
16. "God in America (PBS)," *People and Ideas: Abraham Lincoln*, http://www.pbs.org/godinamerica/people/abraham-lincoln.html
17. Gideon Welles, *Diary of Gideon Welles* (Houghton Mifflin, 1911), Vol. 1, p. 143

18. William J. Federer, *America's God and Country Encyclopedia of Quotations*, (Amerisearch, 2000), p. 380

19. Abraham Lincoln, "Second Annual Message," The American Presidency Project, http://www.presidency.ucsb.edu/ws/?pid=29503

20. Abraham Lincoln, "Proclamation Appointing a National Fast Day," Abraham Lincoln Online, http://www.abrahamlincolnonline.org/lincoln/speeches/fast.htm

21. Christian History Institute, "Christianity and the Civil War: Did You Know?" (Issue 33, 1992), https://www.christianhistoryinstitute.org/magazine/article/christianity-and-civil-war-did-you-know/

22. C.S. Lewis, *The Screwtape Letters* (HarperCollins, 2001), p. 26

23. Abraham Lincoln, "Letter to Eliza Gurney," Abraham Lincoln Online, http://www.abrahamlincolnonline.org/lincoln/speeches/gurney.htm

24. D.J. Tice, "Lincoln's Second Inaugural Address: Finer words were rarely spoken," Star Tribune (March 16, 2015), http://www.startribune.com/lincoln-s-second-inaugural-address-finer-words-were-rarely-spoken/294458091/

25. Abraham Lincoln, "Second Inaugural Address," Wikisource, https://en.wikisource.org/wiki/Abraham_Lincoln's_Second_Inaugural_Address

26. Mark A. Noll, *The Civil War as a Theological Crisis* (Chapel Hill, NC: U of North Carolina, 2006), p. 79

27. Ralph Waldo Emerson, *The Works of Ralph Waldo Emerson, vol. 11 (Miscellanies)* [1909], p. 313-314

28. Ibid, p. 314

## Chapter 13: A New Slavery in America?

1. Susan A. Cohen, "Abortion and Women of Color: The Bigger Picture" (August, 2008), Guttmacher Institute,

https://www.guttmacher.org/about/gpr/2008/08/abortion-and-women-color-bigger-picture

2. Priests for Life,
http://www.priestsforlife.org/africanamerican/howcandreamsurvive.htm

3. Alexander H. Stephens, "Cornerstone Address" (March 21, 1861), Fordham University,
https://legacy.fordham.edu/halsall/mod/1861stephens.asp

4. *"Untermenschen*: The Language of Death," Whose Slave Are You? (www.trevorgrantthomas.com),
http://www.trevorgrantthomas.com/2015/07/untermenschen-language-of-death.html

5. Ibid

6. Jeffrey Lord, "The Democrats' Missing History" (August, 2008), *The Wall Street Journal*,
http://www.wsj.com/articles/SB121856786326834083

7. David B. Chesebrough, *God Ordained This War: Sermons on the Sectional Crisis, 1830-1865* (Columbia, SC: U of South Carolina, 1991), p. 239

8. Walter E. Williams, "The True Black Tragedy: Illegitimacy Rate of Nearly 75%," CNSNews.com,
http://www.cnsnews.com/commentary/walter-e-williams/true-black-tragedy-illegitimacy-rate-nearly-75

9. Robert Rector and Rachel Sheffield, "The War on Poverty After 50 Years" (September, 2014), The Heritage Foundation,
http://www.heritage.org/research/reports/2014/09/the-war-on-poverty-after-50-years

10. Michael Tanner, "War on Poverty at 50 -- despite trillions spent, poverty won" (January, 2014), Fox News,
http://www.foxnews.com/opinion/2014/01/08/war-on-poverty-at-50-despite-trillions-spent-poverty-won.html

11. Drew Desilver, "Who's poor in America? 50 years into the 'War on Poverty,' a data portrait" (January, 2014), Pew Research Center, http://www.pewresearch.org/fact-tank/2014/01/13/whos-poor-in-america-50-years-into-the-war-on-poverty-a-data-portrait/

12. Sabrina Tavernise, "City Neighborhoods Where Life Expectancy is Lowest" (April, 2015), *The New York Times*, http://www.nytimes.com/live/confrontation-in-baltimore/life-expectancy/
13. Generva Pittman, "Black men survive longer in prison than out: study" (July 2011), Reuters, http://www.reuters.com/article/us-prison-blacks-idUSTRE76D71920110714

## Chapter 14: Innovation/Industrial Explosion, Part 1: "Slater the Traitor" and His Textile Mills

1. W. Cleon Skousen, *The Making of America* (National Center for Constitutional Studies, 2007), p. 176
2. George S. White, *Memoir of Samuel Slater: The Father of American Manufactures* (1836), p. 24
3. Ibid, p. 24
4. Ibid, p. 24
5. Ibid, p. 24-27
6. "David Wilkinson Finds Out the Hard Way Why It's Good To Patent Your Inventions" (January, 2014), New England Historical Society, http://www.newenglandhistoricalsociety.com/david-wilkinson/
7. Gary Kulik, Roger N. Parks, Theodore Z. Penn, *The New England Mill Village, 1790-1860* (MIT Press, 1982), p. 149

## Chapter 15: Innovation/Industrial Explosion, Part 2: America and the Gun

1. Gregg Lee Carter, *Guns in American Society: An Encyclopedia of History, Politics, Culture, and the Law, Volume 1* (ABC-CLIO, 2012), p. 922
2. Lee T. Wyatt, III, *The Industrial Revolution* (Westport, CT: Greenwood Press, 2009), p. 110
3. Ian Hogg, *The Story of the Gun* (St. Martin's Press, New York, 1996), p. 12
4. Ibid, p. 12

5. Walter Hammond Nichols, *A Morgan rifleman: A Story of the American Revolution* (Century Co., 1928), p. 124
6. Benjamin A. Gorman, "Discover Eli Whitney," Yale-New Haven Teacher's Institute, http://www.yale.edu/ynhti/curriculum/units/1979/3/79.03.03.x.html
7. Ibid
8. William N. Hosley, *Colt: The Making of an American Legend* (University of Massachusetts Press, 1996), p. 66
9. "The Story of the Gun" (DVD)
10. Zachary Elkins, Tom Ginsburg, James Melton, "U.S. Gun Rights Truly Are American Exceptionalism" (March, 2013), Bloomberg.com, http://www.bloomberg.com/view/articles/2013-03-07/u-s-gun-rights-truly-are-american-exceptionalism

## Chapter 16: Innovation/Industrial Explosion, Part 3: Trains, Tocqueville, and the Telegraph

1. Alexis De Tocqueville, *Democracy in America* (Penguin Group, Vol.1), p. 340
2. Ibid, p. 340
3. Ibid, p. 496-497
4. Ibid, p. 340-341
5. Ibid, p. 342
6. Ibid, p. 342
7. Alexis De Tocqueville, *Democracy in America* (Vol.2), p. 643-644
8. Lee T. Wyatt III, *The Industrial Revolution* (Greenwood, 2009), p. 95
9. Ibid, p. 96
10. **Richard Sylla and Robert E. Wright,** "Early Corporate America: The Largest Industries and Companies before 1860" (September, 2012), The Finance Professional's Post, http://post.nyssa.org/nyssa-news/2012/09/early-corporate-america-the-largest-industries-and-companies-before-1860.html
11. Stanley Buder, *Capitalizing on Change: A Social History of American Business* (Univ. of North Carolina, 2009), p. 111

12. Ibid, p. 107

13. Ibid, p. 112

14. Samuel Willard Crompton, *Alexander Graham Bell and the Telephone* (Infobase Publishing, 2009), p. 9

15. William O. Thompson, *Five Sermons: Delivered to the Students at the University Chapel* (Y.M.C.A., 1914), p. 49

16. Ibid, p. 49-50

17. "The Transatlantic Cable," History Magazine, http://www.history-magazine.com/cable.html

18. "The Great Transatlantic Cable," PBS, http://www.pbs.org/wgbh/amex/cable/filmmore/pt.html

19. Stanley Buder, *Capitalizing on Change: A Social History of American Business* (Univ. of North Carolina, 2009), p. 120

# Chapter 17: Innovation/Industrial Explosion, Part 4: Let There Be Light!

1. Silverberg, Robert. *Light for the World: Edison and the Power Industry* (Van Nostrand, 1967), p. 67

2. Ibid, p. 70

3. Ibid, p. 63

4. Wyatt, Lee T., III. *The Industrial Revolution* (Greenwood, 2009), p. 111

5. Silverberg, Robert. *Light for the World: Edison and the Power Industry* (Van Nostrand, 1967), p. 43

6. Ibid, p. 89

7. Ibid, p. 93

8. Ibid, p. 102

9. Ibid, p. 118

10. Ibid, p. 135

11. Rottenberg, Dan. *In the Kingdom of Coal: An American Family and the Rock That Changed the World* (Routledge, 2003), p. 112

12. Silverberg, Robert. *Light for the World: Edison and the Power Industry* (Van Nostrand, 1967), p. 224

13. Ibid, p. 230

14. Ibid, p. 265

15. Ibid, p. 270

16. WillisCarrier.com, http://www.williscarrier.com/1876-1902.php

17. Robin Roy, *Consumer Product Innovation and Sustainable Design: The Evolution and Impacts of Successful Products* (Routledge, 2015), p. 100

18. Ibid, p. 22-24

## Chapter 18: Innovation/Industrial Explosion, Part 5: Fossil Fuels

1. Rottenberg, Dan. *In the Kingdom of Coal: An American Family and the Rock That Changed the World.* (Routledge, 2003), p. 59

2. Lee T. Wyatt III, *The Industrial Revolution* (Greenwood, 2009), p. 105

3. Rottenberg, Dan. *In the Kingdom of Coal: An American Family and the Rock That Changed the World.* (Routledge, 2003), p. 111

4. Grant Segall, *John D. Rockefeller: Anointed with Oil* (Oxford, 2001), p. 33

5. Ibid, p. 24

6. Ibid, p. 47

7. Ibid, p. 38

8. Ibid, p. 54

9. Ibid, p. 49

10. Bobby Magill, "U.S. Leads Global Oil and Gas Production for Third Year ," Climate Central, http://www.climatecentral.org/news/us-leads-global-oil-and-gas-production-18867

## Chapter 19: Innovation/Industrial Explosion, Part 6: The Engine That Moved America

1. Jean-Pierre Bardou, Jean-Jacques Chanaron, Patrick Fridenson, and James M. Laux, *The Automobile Revolution: The Impact of an Industry* (Univ. of North Carolina, 1982), p. 24

2. Ibid, p. 51

3. Ibid, p. 113
4. T. A. Heppenheimer, *First Flight: The Wright Brothers and the Invention of the Airplane* (John Wiley & Sons, 2003), p. 83
5. Ibid, p. 82
6. Ibid, p. 87
7. Ibid, p. 89
8. Ibid, p. 2
9. Ibid, p. 4-5
10. Ibid, p. 212
11. Ibid, p. 213
12. Ibid, p. 213
13. Ibid, p. 215
14. Ibid, p. 215
15. Ibid, p. 252
16. Ibid, p. 257
17. Ibid, p. 264
18. Ibid, p. 272
19. Ibid, p. 277
20. Glenn E. Bugos, "The History of the Aerospace Industry," Economics History Association (EH.net), https://eh.net/encyclopedia/the-history-of-the-aerospace-industry/
21. Ibid
22. Ibid
23. The Economist, http://www.economist.com/blogs/gulliver/2015/06/worlds-largest-airlines
24. Jeremy Bender, Business Insider (January, 2015), http://www.businessinsider.com/military-aircraft-strength-of-every-country-2015-1

## Chapter 20: Innovation/Industrial Explosion, Part 7: Science Fiction Becomes Science Fact

1. Chris Gainor and Alfred Worden, *To a Distant Day: The Rocket Pioneers* (Univ. of Nebraska, 2008), p. 42
2. Ibid, p. 80

3. Ibid, p. 85
4. Wernher von Braun, "Recollections of Childhood" (1963), Marshall Space Flight Center, http://history.msfc.nasa.gov/vonbraun/recollect-childhood.html
5. Chris Gainor and Alfred Worden, *To a Distant Day: The Rocket Pioneers* (Univ. of Nebraska, 2008), p. 88
6. Ibid, p. 104
7. Paul Dickson, *Sputnik: The Shock of the Century* (Bloomsbury Publishing, 2009), p. 224, https://books.google.com/books?id=ZhgFUyCOhHcC&pg=PA224&lpg#v=onepage&q&f=false
8. Bob Ward, Dr. Space: The Life of Wernher von Braun (Naval Institute Press, 2013), p. 105, https://books.google.com/books?id=pQCEqGZ5KHwC&pg=PT105&lpg#v=onepage&q&f=false
9. John T. Correll, "Airpower and the Cuban Missile Crisis" (August, 2005), Air Force Magazine, http://www.airforcemag.com/MagazineArchive/Pages/2005/August%202005/0805u2.aspx
10. Dan Majors, "From cell phones to computers, technology from NASA's space program continues to touch everyday life" (July, 2009), Pittsburg Post-Gazette, http://www.post-gazette.com/life/lifestyle/2009/07/20/From-cell-phones-to-computers-technology-from-NASA-s-space-program-continues-to-touch-everyday-life/stories/200907200146

## Chapter 21: Innovation/Industrial Explosion, Part 8: The Digital Age

1. Dan Majors, "From cell phones to computers, technology from NASA's space program continues to touch everyday life" (July, 2009), Pittsburg Post-Gazette, http://www.post-gazette.com/life/lifestyle/2009/07/20/From-cell-phones-to-computers-technology-from-NASA-s-space-program-continues-to-touch-everyday-life/stories/200907200146

2. Campbell-Kelly, Martin, and William Aspray, *Computer: A History of the Information Machine* 3rd ed. (Westview, 2014), p. 9

3. Scott McCartney, *ENIAC: The Triumphs and Tragedies of the World's First Computer.* (Walker, 1999), p. 17

4. "The Science vs. Religion Myth," Whose Slave Are You? (www.trevorgrantthomas.com), http://www.trevorgrantthomas.com/2011/10/the-science-vs-religion-myth.html; "A Defense of 'Creationism,'" Whose Slave Are You? (www.trevorgrantthomas.com), http://www.trevorgrantthomas.com/2014/01/a-defense-of-creationism.html

5. Charles Babbage, *The Ninth Bridgewater Treatise* (J. Murray, 1838), p. 65,

6. Charles Babbage, *Passages From the Life of a Philosopher* (Rutgers University Press, 1994), p. 301-302

7. Campbell-Kelly, Martin, and William Aspray, *Computer: A History of the Information Machine* 3rd ed. (Westview, 2014), p. 21

8. Ibid, p. 23

9. *Historical Encyclopedia of Natural and Mathematical Sciences* (Springer Science & Business Media, 2009), p. 4466

10. IBM Archives, http://www-03.ibm.com/ibm/history/reference/faq_0000000011.html

11. Campbell-Kelly, Martin, and William Aspray, *Computer: A History of the Information Machine* 3rd ed. (Westview, 2014), p. 74

12. *ENIAC*, Computer History Museum, http://www.computerhistory.org/revolution/birth-of-the-computer/4/78

13. Eric G. Swedin, David L. Ferro, *Computers: The Life Story of a Technology* (JHU Press, 2007), p. 44, https://books.google.com/books?id=IJXYoPiwvOMC&pg=PA44#v=onepage&q&f=false

14. *UNIVersal Automatic Computer*, http://www.thocp.net/hardware/univac.htm

15. Sharon Gaudin, "The transistor: The most important invention of the 20th century?" (December, 2007), Computer World, http://www.computerworld.com/article/2538123/computer-processors/the-transistor--the-most-important-invention-of-the-20th-century-.html

16. "First IC-based computer developed for U.S. Air Force," Texas Instruments, http://www.ti.com/corp/docs/company/history/timeline/defense/1960/docs/61-first_ic.htm

17. Steve J. Dick, "Why We Explore," NASA, http://www.nasa.gov/missions/solarsystem/Why_We_04.html

18. Campbell-Kelly, Martin, and William Aspray, *Computer: A History of the Information Machine* 3rd ed. (Westview, 2014), p. 199

19. Ibid, p. 210

20. George Gilder, "Computer Industry," Library of Economics and Liberty, http://www.econlib.org/library/Enc1/ComputerIndustry.html

21. "Top Ten Countries with Highest number of PCs," Maps of World, http://www.mapsofworld.com/world-top-ten/world-top-ten-personal-computers-users-map.html

22. Liyan Chen, "The World's Largest Tech Companies: Apple Beats Samsung, Microsoft, Google" (May, 2015), Forbes, http://www.forbes.com/sites/liyanchen/2015/05/11/the-worlds-largest-tech-companies-apple-beats-samsung-microsoft-google/#5c16b300415a

# Chapter 22: A Super Power is Born, Part 1: America's Economic Might—Christianity Creates Capitalism

1. Henry Luce, "The American Century" (1941), LIFE Magazine, http://www.informationclearinghouse.info/article6139.htm

2. Jean Strouse, *Morgan: American Financier* (New York, 1999), p. 412

3. George C. Herring, *From Colony to Superpower: U.S. Foreign Relations since 1776* (Oxford UP, 2008), p. 439

4. Edward F. Denison, *Accounting for United States Economic Growth, 1929-1969* (Brookings Institution, 1974), p. 1

5. Angus Maddison, *Contours of the World Economy, 1–2030 AD* (OUP Oxford, 2007), p. 299

6. "GDP at market prices (current US$)," World Bank Data, http://data.worldbank.org/indicator/NY.GDP.MKTP.CD?order=wbapi_data_value_2014+wbapi_data_value+wbapi_data_value-last&sort=desc

7. Deirdre N. McCloskey, "How the West (and the Rest) Got Rich" (May, 2016), *The Wall Street Journal*, http://www.wsj.com/articles/why-the-west-and-the-rest-got-rich-1463754427

8. Jonathan Adelman, "Why The U.S. Remains The World's Unchallenged Superpower" (November, 2013), Forbes, http://www.forbes.com/sites/realspin/2013/11/24/why-the-u-s-remains-the-worlds-unchallenged-superpower/#19e5986f1fd8

9. Andrew Beattie, "Adam Smith And 'The Wealth Of Nations,'" Investopedia, http://www.investopedia.com/articles/economics/09/adam-smith-wealth-of-nations.asp

10. Endrina Tay, "Wealth of Nations" (July, 2008), The Jefferson Monticello, https://www.monticello.org/site/research-and-collections/wealth-nations

11. W. Cleon Skousen, *The 5000 Year Leap: A Miracle that Changed the World* (C&J Investments, 2011), p. 179

12. Ibid, p. 180

13. William J. Federer, *America's God and Country Encyclopedia of Quotations*, (Amerisearch, 2000), p. 52

14. C.S. Lewis, *The Abolition of Man* (Simon & Schuster, 1996), p. 43

15. David Barton, "Affidavit in Support of the Ten Commandments" (2001), Wall Builders, http://www.wallbuilders.com/libissuesarticles.asp?id=87

16. Bill Fortenberry, "What is the Law of Nature's God?," The Federalist Papers Project, http://www.thefederalistpapers.org/current-events/what-is-the-law-of-natures-god

17. Michael Novak, "How Christianity Created Capitalism" (Vol. 10, Number 3), Acton Institute: Religion & Liberty, http://www.acton.org/pub/religion-liberty/volume-10-number-3/how-christianity-created-capitalism

18. Edmund Burke, *Reflections on the Revolution in France* (J. Dodsley, 1790), p. 9

19. William Doyle, *The Oxford History of the French Revolution* (Oxford University Press, 1990), p. 168

20. Bill Federer, "'Godless Revolution' Led to Religious Revival (July, 2015), World Net Daily, http://mobile.wnd.com/2015/07/godless-revolution-led-to-religious-revival/

## Chapter 23: A Super Power is Born, Part 2: The Birth of the Modern American Military

1. Lyman Miller, "China an Emerging Superpower?," Stanford Journal of International Relations, https://web.stanford.edu/group/sjir/6.1.03_miller.html

2. Ibid

3. Lawrence Lenz, *Power and Policy: America's First Steps to Superpower, 1889-1922* (Algora, 2008), p. 16

4. Ibid, p. 18-19

5. Noel Maurer and Carlos Yu, *The Big Ditch: How America Took, Built, Ran, and Ultimately Gave Away the Panama Canal* (Princeton UP, 2011), p. 187

6. Zimmerman Telegram, National Archives, https://www.archives.gov/education/lessons/zimmermann/

7. John A. Thompson, *Woodrow Wilson* (Routledge, 2015), p. 250,

https://books.google.com/books?id=3k0eCwAAQBAJ&pg=PT250#v=onepage&q&f=false

8. Hans Hoyng, "We Saved the World: WWI and America's Rise as a Superpower" (January, 2014), Spiegel Online International, http://www.spiegel.de/international/world/how-world-war-i-helped-america-rise-to-superpower-status-a-944703-2.html

9. Ibid

10. George C. Herring, *From Colony to Superpower: U.S. Foreign Relations since 1776* (Oxford UP, 2008), p. 439-440

11. Franklin D. Roosevelt, "Fireside Chat, September 3, 1939," The American Presidency Project, http://www.presidency.ucsb.edu/ws/?pid=15801

12. "World War II Overview," The National World War II Museum, http://www.nationalww2museum.org/learn/education/for-students/ww2-history/overview.html

13. "WWII by the Numbers (Charting and Graphing D-Day and WWII Data)," The National World War II Museum, p. 3, http://www.nationalww2museum.org/learn/education/for-teachers/lesson-plans/pdfs/by-the-numbers.pdf

14. George C. Herring, *From Colony to Superpower: U.S. Foreign Relations since 1776* (Oxford UP, 2008), p. 597

## Chapter 24: A Super Power is Born, Part 3: America Enters the Nuclear Age

1. Dan Zak, "The Prophets of Oak Ridge" (April, 2013), *The Washington Post*, http://www.washingtonpost.com/sf/wp-style/2013/09/13/the-prophets-of-oak-ridge/

2. George O. Robinson Jr., *The Oak Ridge: Story; The Saga of a People Who Share in History* (Kingsport Press, 1950), p. 2

3. "Einstein's Letter," The Manhattan Project an interactive history (U.S. Department of Energy),

https://www.osti.gov/opennet/manhattan-project-history/Events/1939-1942/einstein_letter.htm

4. Lindsey A. Freeman, *Longing for the Bomb: Oak Ridge and Atomic Nostalgia* (Univ. of North Carolina, 2015), p. 3

5. Harry S. Truman, "Statement by the President Announcing the Use of the A-Bomb at Hiroshima" (August 6, 1945), Harry S. Truman Library and Museum, http://www.trumanlibrary.org/publicpapers/index.php?pid=100&st=Hiroshima&st1=

6. "Nuclear weapons: Who has what?" (January, 2015), CNN, http://www.cnn.com/interactive/2013/03/world/nuclear-weapon-states/

7. Global Fire Power, http://www.globalfirepower.com/

8. Robert Farley, "The Five Most Deadly Drone Powers in the World" (February, 2015), The National Interest, http://nationalinterest.org/feature/the-five-most-deadly-drone-powers-the-world-12255

# Chapter 25: The Era of Big Government and Rampant Immorality Begins

1. Trevor Thomas, "Sweet Land of Generosity" (July, 2008), Whose Slave Are You? (www.trevorgrantthomas.com), http://www.trevorgrantthomas.com/2008/07/sweet-land-of-generosity.html

2. Mark Tooley, "A Duke Univ. Theologian Attacks America for Being Un-Christian, but Betrays His Own Prejudices" (February, 2016), The Stream, https://stream.org/a-duke-theologian-attacks-america-for-being-un-christian-but-betrays-his-own-prejudices/

3. "The World's Top Missionary-Sending Country Will Surprise You" (July, 2013), Christianity Today, http://www.christianitytoday.com/le/2013/july-online-only/worlds-top-missionary-sending-country-will-surprise-you.html

4. David Miller, "Is America Doomed [Part III]," Apologetics Press, https://www.apologeticspress.org/apcontent.aspx?category=7&article=2587

5. Trevor Thomas, "Is America a Christian Nation?" (July, 2009), Whose Slave Are You? (www.trevorgrantthomas.com), http://www.trevorgrantthomas.com/2009/07/is-america-christian-nation.html

6. David J. Brewer, *The United States a Christian Nation* (Winston, 1905), p. 11

7. Ibid, p. 57

8. Edward Mansfield, *American Education, Its Principle and Elements* (A. S. Barnes & Co., 1851), p. 43.

9. David Barton, "Is America a Christian Nation?" (May, 2016), Wall Builders, http://www.wallbuilders.com/LIBissuesArticles.asp?id=180593

10. Robert Rector, "Marriage: America's Greatest Weapon Against Child Poverty," The Heritage Foundation, http://www.heritage.org/research/reports/2012/09/marriage-americas-greatest-weapon-against-child-poverty

11. Robert Rector, "The War on Poverty: 50 Years of Failure" (September, 2014), *The Washington Times*, http://www.washingtontimes.com/news/2014/sep/19/rector-the-war-on-poverty-50-years-of-failure/

12. Trevor Thomas, "Get'cha Honey for Nothin', Get'cha Chips for Free (I want my, I want my, I want my E-B-T!)" (August, 2015), Whose Slave Are You? (www.trevorgrantthomas.com), http://www.trevorgrantthomas.com/2015/08/getcha-honey-for-nothin-getcha-chips.html

13. Robert Rector, "How the War on Poverty Was Lost" (January, 2014), The Wall Street Journal, http://www.wsj.com/articles/SB10001424052702303345104579282760272285556

14. Ali Meyer, "Food Stamp Beneficiaries Exceed 45 Million for 49 Straight Months" (August, 2015), The Washington Free Beacon, http://freebeacon.com/issues/food-stamp-beneficiaries-exceed-45-million-for-49-straight-months/

15. "One in Five Children Receive Food Stamps" (February, 2015), U.S. Census Bureau,

http://www.census.gov/newsroom/press-releases/2015/cb15-16.html

16. Rick Moran, "Percentage of Americans on welfare hits record levels" (July, 2014), American Thinker, http://www.americanthinker.com/blog/2014/07/percentage_of_americans_on_welfare_hits_record_levels.html

17. "National Vital Statistics Report" (Births) (August, 2012), U.S. Department of Health and Human Services, http://www.cdc.gov/nchs/data/nvsr/nvsr61/nvsr61_01.pdf

18. Sabrina Tavernise, "Black Children in U.S. Are Much More Likely to Live in Poverty, Study Finds" (July, 2015), *The New York Times*, http://www.nytimes.com/2015/07/15/us/black-children-poverty-pew-research-center.html?_r=1

19. D'Vera Cohn, Jeffrey S. Passel, Wendy Wang, and Gretchen Livingston, "Barely Half of U.S. Adults Are Married – A Record Low" (December, 2011), Pew Research Center, http://www.pewsocialtrends.org/2011/12/14/barely-half-of-u-s-adults-are-married-a-record-low/

20. Wendy Wang and Kim Parker, "Record Share of Americans Have Never Married" (September, 2014), Pew Research Center, http://www.pewsocialtrends.org/2014/09/24/record-share-of-americans-have-never-married/

21. Ibid

22. Suzanne Venker, "The war on men" (November, 2012), Fox News, http://www.foxnews.com/opinion/2012/11/24/war-on-men.html

23. Albert Mohler, "From Father to Son — J.R.R. Tolkien on Sex" (March, 2014), Albert Mohler.com, http://www.albertmohler.com/2014/03/11/from-father-to-son-j-r-r-tolkien-on-sex/

24. The Editors, "The Obama Pentagon's Disastrous Decision on Women in Combat" (December, 2015), National Review,

http://www.nationalreview.com/article/427994/obama-pentagon-women-combat-disastrous-decision

25. Kathleen Parker, "Women in combat will put men at greater risk" (December, 2015), *The Washington Post*, https://www.washingtonpost.com/opinions/women-in-combat-put-men-at-risk/2015/12/11/f0e00768-a04b-11e5-bce4-708fe33e3288_story.html

26. Neil Shah, "More White Americans Dying Than Being Born" (June, 2013), *The Wall Street Journal*, http://www.wsj.com/articles/SB10001424127887324049504578541712247829092

27. Samuel Smith, "It's Not the Economy, It's the Family, CPAC Panelists Say" (March, 2016), The Christian Post, http://www.christianpost.com/news/economy-family-breakdown-cpac-panel-larry-kudlow-158938/

28. Scott Stanley, "What Is the Divorce Rate, Anyway?: Around 42 Percent, One Scholar Believes" (January, 2015), Institute for Family Studies, http://family-studies.org/what-is-the-divorce-rate-anyway-around-42-percent-one-scholar-believes/

29. "Effects of Divorce on Children's Behavior," Marripedia, http://www.marripedia.org/effects.of.divorce.on.children.s.behavior

30. "Social Indicators of Marital Health & Well-Being" (2010), The National Marriage Project (Univ. of Virginia) and Institute for American Values, http://stateofourunions.org/2010/si-cohabitation.php

31. Ibid

32. "Fourth National Incidence Study of Child Abuse and Neglect" (2010), Office of Planning, Research & Evaluation, http://www.acf.hhs.gov/programs/opre/resource/fourth-national-incidence-study-of-child-abuse-and-neglect-nis-4-report-to

33. W. Bradford Wilcox, "Cohabitation and the abuse of America's children" (May, 2011), Deseret News, http://www.deseretnews.com/article/700135164/Cohabitation-and-the-abuse-of-Americas-children.html

34. Ibid

35. Trevor Thomas, "Same-Sex 'Marriage' Meets Defeat Again" (November, 2009), Whose Slave Are You? (www.trevorgrantthomas.com), http://www.trevorgrantthomas.com/2009/11/gay-marriage-meets-defeat-again.html

36. Trevor Thomas, "Marriage Under Fire" (June, 2006), Whose Slave Are You? (www.trevorgrantthomas.com), http://www.trevorgrantthomas.com/2006/06/marriage-under-fire.html

37. Ibid

38. Ibid

39. Trevor Thomas, "The Left's Cries of 'Discrimination' on Marriage Ring Hollow" (April, 2015), Whose Slave Are You? (www.trevorgranntthomas.com), http://www.trevorgrantthomas.com/2015/04/the-lefts-cries-of-discrimination-on.html

40. Mark Regnerus, "How different are the adult children of parents who have same-sex relationships?" (March, 2012), Social Science Research, http://www.markregnerus.com/uploads/4/0/6/5/4065759/regnerus_july_2012_ssr.pdf

41. Napp Nazworth, "Another Gay Parenting Study Finds Children Do Best With Mom and Dad; Will the Supreme Court Care?" (February, 2015), The Christian Post, http://www.christianpost.com/news/another-gay-parenting-study-finds-children-do-best-with-mom-and-dad-will-the-supreme-court-care-133939/

42. "Same-Sex Couple Households" (September, 2011), U.S. Census Bureau, https://www.census.gov/prod/2011pubs/acsbr10-03.pdf

43. Trevor Thomas, "Why Aren't We Being Warned? (Dangers of Homosexuality)," Whose Slave Are You? (www.trevorgrantthomas.com), http://www.trevorgrantthomas.com/p/dangers-of-homosexuality.html

44. Number of Abortions—Abortion Counters, http://www.numberofabortions.com/

45. Jen Gunter, "The Many Manipulations of the Planned Parenthood Attack Videos" (July, 2015), New Republic, https://newrepublic.com/article/122355/many-manipulations-planned-parenthood-attack-videos

46. Mother Teresa, "Mother Teresa's Letter to the US Supreme Court on Roe v. Wade," http://groups.csail.mit.edu/mac/users/rauch/nvp/roe/mothertheresa_roe.html

47. Trevor Thomas, "The Sad Consequences of 'Shacking Up'" (May, 2011), Whose Slave Are You? (www.trevorgrantthomas.com), http://www.trevorgrantthomas.com/2011/05/the-sad-consequences-of-shacking-up.html

## Chapter 26: The War on God and His Word

1. Craig Nelson, *Rocket Men:* The Epic Story of the First Men on the Moon (Penguin, 2009), p. 151, https://books.google.com/books?id=LWMivGgbM7kC&pg=PT151&lpg#v=onepage&q&f=false

2. Roy B. Zuck, *The Speaker's Quote Book* (Kregel Academic, 2009), p. 348

3. Trevor Thomas, "A Defense of 'Creationism'" (January, 2014), Whose Slave Are You? (www.trevorgrantthomas.com), http://www.trevorgrantthomas.com/2014/01/a-defense-of-creationism.html

4. Paul Rosenberg, "God is on the ropes: The brilliant new science that has creationists and the Christian right terrified" (January, 2015), Salon.com, http://www.salon.com/2015/01/03/god_is_on_the_ropes_the_brilliant_new_science_that_has_creationists_and_the_christian_right_terrified/

5. "Theistic evolutionists are deluded" (video), Creation.com, http://creation.com/creation-videos?page=1&fileID=BAbpfn9QgGA

6. Richard Dawkins, *The God Delusion* (Houghton Mifflin Harcourt, 2008), p. 238

7. Patrick Wanis, "How women made porn fashionable" (September, 2012), Fox News, http://www.foxnews.com/opinion/2012/09/15/how-women-made-porn-fashionable.html

8. Nisha Lilia Diu, "Legalise it: a former sex worker's view of prostitution" (April, 2014), *The Telegraph*, http://www.telegraph.co.uk/women/sex/10730298/Sex-work-has-it-become-socially-acceptable.html

9. Katy Steinmetz, "The Transgender Tipping Point" (May, 2014), TIME, http://time.com/135480/transgender-tipping-point/

10. Ibid

11. Rick Moran, "Oberlin considers banning gender pronouns in athletic department" (May, 2014), American Thinker, http://www.americanthinker.com/blog/2014/05/oberlin_considers_banning_gender_pronouns_in_athletic_department.html

12. "Moral Issues," Gallup, http://www.gallup.com/poll/1681/moral-issues.aspx

13. "Mayor De Blasio Vows Crackdown On Topless Women In Times Square" (August, 2015), CBS New York, http://newyork.cbslocal.com/2015/08/18/topless-times-square-women/

14. Ibid

15. Lauren Luxenburg, "'Go Topless Day' Protestors in Austin Explain Why They Think Women Shouldn't Wear Shirts" (August, 2015), Independent Journal, http://opinion.injo.com/2015/08/246790-international-go-topless-day-power-breast/

16. David French, "Meet the New Public Face of Abortion-on-Demand: Satanists" (August, 2015), National Review, http://www.nationalreview.com/article/422999/satanist-abortion-advocates

17. Ibid

18. Michael Novak, "Why They Hate Pro-Lifers So" (August, 2015), Patheos, http://www.patheos.com/blogs/michaelnovak/2015/08/why-they-hate-pro-lifers-so/

19. Nicole Lyn Pesce, "Sarah Silverman says women 'can't have it all' on podcast" (January, 2016), New York Daily News, http://www.nydailynews.com/entertainment/sarah-silverman-women-article-1.2493826

20. "Planned Parenthood of Southeastern Pennsylvania v. Casey" (1992), Cornell University Law School, https://www.law.cornell.edu/supremecourt/text/505/833

21. C.S. Lewis, *Mere Christianity* (Zondervan, 2001), p. 122

22. Ibid, p. 197-198

23. C.H. Spurgeon, *The Treasury of David* (Hendrickson Publishers, 1990), p. 402

24. C.S. Lewis, *The Complete C.S. Lewis Signature Classics* (Zondervan, 2002), p. 481

25. "Declaration of Principles on Tolerance" (Paris, 1995), United Nations Educational, Scientific and Cultural Organization, http://www.un.org/en/events/toleranceday/pdf/tolerance.pdf

26. William Lane Craig, "A Christian Perspective on Homosexuality," A Reasonable Faith, http://www.reasonablefaith.org/a-christian-perspective-on-homosexuality

27. Albert Mohler, "The Henry search for church harmony?" (April, 2014), World Magazine, http://www.worldmag.com/2014/04/the_henry_search_for_church_harmony

## Chapter 27: A Return to Wisdom and Godliness

1. Russell Kirk, *The Conservative Mind* (Regnery Publishing, 2001), p. 8

Made in the USA
Monee, IL
25 October 2022